Letters to My Torturer

A journalist, writer, and translator, Houshang Asadi was a member of both the Writers' Association of Iran and the Iranian Journalists' Syndicate, and the co-founder of the Association of Iranian Film Critics and Script Writers. Prior to the Islamic Revolution he served for many years as Deputy Editor at *Kayhan*, Iran's largest daily newspaper, and was for twelve years the Editor-in-Chief of the country's largest circulation film magazine, *Gozaresh*. He is the author of several novels, plays, and film scripts, and has translated into Persian important works by Gabriel Garcia Marquez, Mario Vargas Llosa, and T.S. Eliot.

In 1974 during the Shah's regime, Asadi was arrested along with other journalists and found himself sharing a tiny prison cell for 9 months with a young clergyman by the name of Ali Khamenei, currently Iran's Supreme Spiritual Leader and the appointed successor to Ayatollah Khomeini. The two formed a close friendship that continued until events took a dramatic turn.

Shortly after the Islamic Revolution of 1979, and following the new government's crackdown on all opposition parties, Asadi was arrested once again. He was kept in solitary confinement for almost 2 years and severely tortured, until he falsely confessed to operating as a spy for the British and Russian governments. His sentence was death by hanging. In the end this was reduced to 15 years imprisonment. After 6 years he was freed and eventually escaped Iran in 2003. He now lives in exile in Paris with his wife, where he co-founded the influential Persian-language news website Rooz Online, on which he serves as a member of the editorial board.

To my wife, without whom this book,
and life, would be incomplete

LETTERS
to my
TORTURER

LOVE, REVOLUTION, AND IMPRISONMENT IN IRAN

HOUSHANG ASADI

ONEWORLD

OXFORD

Letters to My Torturer

First published by Oneworld Publications Ltd 2010

ISBN 978–1–85168–750–3 (Hardcover)
ISBN 978-1-85168-783-1 (Export Paperback)

Cover design by www.leonickolls.co.uk
Printed and bound in America by Edwards Brothers, Inc.

Oneworld Publications Ltd
UK: 185 Banbury Road, Oxford, OX2 7AR, England
USA: 38 Greene Street, 4th Floor, New York, NY 10013, USA

Contents

Preface

I'm talking about torture.

I was a young man longing for freedom, deeply patriotic, and in love with literature. I thought the world could be changed. I supported the Iranian Revolution in the fervent belief that green shoots of freedom would sprout up, no one would go hungry, and dictatorship would be consigned to dusty museums.

But suddenly I found myself in hell. In 1983, arrested in a government crackdown on opposition parties, I was assigned to the care of a man who was employed as my "interrogator". I was helpless prey, caught in the trap of the "brothers". In the Islamic Republic of Iran, "brother" is the generic title of all male believers, and each of the interrogators were therefore called "brother" and an assumed name. My whole existence lay in the hands of one such brother, "Brother Hamid". In defending the "holy" government, Brother Hamid saw himself as God's representative, with absolute control over every aspect of my life. Sleep, medication, food, even going to the toilet, were impossible without his permission. His motivation was hatred based on religious ideology, his tools were a whip and handcuffs. He saw me as a traitor, a spy, the embodiment of corruption and evil. Everything he assumed about me I had to "confess" to, and eventually I did, under the onslaught of brutal whippings, my feet raw and swollen from the lash, strung up from the ceiling of my cell by a rope for days and nights on end, deprived of sleep, of every human dignity, and in torment that my wife was being tortured too.

If I needed anything, I had to bark like a dog. And whenever I barked, Brother Hamid laughed.

Brother Hamid transformed me from a young idealist to the lowest form of life on earth. After 682 days in solitary confinement, subjected to every deprivation, my "confessions" were used, in a show trial lasting just six minutes, to sentence me to fifteen years in prison. In the mass killings that were carried out by the government in the summer of 1988, I came very close to being hanged – called up before another kangaroo court, I was forced to lie. Each prisoner was asked three questions: Are you a Muslim and say your prayers? Do you renounce your past? Do you believe in the Islamic Republic, and who is your point of reference. And I lied to all three questions. I said I hated my past and was devoted to Ayatollah Khomeini, and I was spared the rope. Eventually, after spending six years incarcerated in some of the most infamous jails in the Islamic Republic, I was freed to rejoin the mega-prison that is today's Iran. I escaped in 2003, and am now forced to live in exile.

Then one day, a few years ago, someone emailed me an image. He asked if I knew the man in the photo. I did. It was Brother Hamid, by this time one of Iran's ambassadors. Staring into his eyes, I knew I needed to confront my torturer and the living nightmare that was his legacy to me. I searched through my scattered notes, written intermittently over the years since my release from prison, but they were filled with hatred and I no longer identified with them. I didn't wish to view the world, as my torturer had, in black and white terms. I didn't want to respond to the whip with the sword of my pen. No, now that I was the judge, I hated the idea of taking my revenge on him. Instead, I decided to write letters to him, to convey to him in some small way the intimate cruelty of those days and their aftermath.

Writing this book was a painful struggle. Every dawn as I started work on the manuscript, I would return to Brother Hamid's hell. I would weep and write and the soles of my feet would throb. I even had a heart attack. Every fibre of my being protested, but I forced myself to keep going. I wanted to lay bare the life of a person under torture, and to describe the effect of that torture on the mind and body of a human being. In the process, I had to overcome my inner turmoil and remove every trace of hatred, line by line. I did my best to view the scene impartially and to be true to myself, as there is nothing more frightening to me than a victim of torture becoming a torturer himself. In the end, I began to see something of myself in my torturer, and found myself recognizing him as a human being too, as another person born in the same autocratic culture. And finally I gathered up my letters in this book, which I hope will eventually reach Brother Hamid's hands, sooner or later. Perhaps he will recognise himself in these pages.

During my long years in prison, I realised that thousands of men and women, before me, alongside me, and after me, were tortured to death. I wish the story of torture and imprisonment could end with my story, and that of Brother Hamid. I wish the history of torture, which follows in the footsteps of the inquisitions of the Middle Ages, would end with the Islamic Republic of Iran. But even in recent times, from the valleys of Afghanistan to the prison camp of Guantánamo Bay, prisoners have been interrogated using techniques that, just fifty years earlier, the US military had condemned for eliciting false confessions. And we are all familiar with the sexual degradation and torture of Iraqi prisoners that was captured in chilling photographs, and appeared on our television screens and in newspapers around the world.

As I finished the first draft of this book in 2009, Iran descended into political unrest and chaos once again. And the people who are protesting against Iran's autocracy today are sadly being subjected to the same treatment we were a generation ago, as hundreds of new Brother Hamids keep the torture chambers busy. Young men and women are being tormented using ever more refined techniques of physical and psychological manipulation and the application of pain so that they will "confess" to being spies for the USA and Israel.

In the era when my "Brother Hamid" and his fellow interrogators were torturing political prisoners mercilessly, no one knew about it. It took many years for our stories to leak out and be heard. Today, torture is still being practised in many parts of the world, but the news travels more quickly. In the current political climate, then, *Letters to My Torturer* is more than the account of one man's experience of torture. It is the exploration of an issue that sits heavily on humanity's conscience.

At the height of one of his torture sessions, Brother Hamid asked me: If one day things change and we end up being your captives, what will you do to us? My answer is this: we will demolish all the world's infamous prisons of torture and we will sentence the intelligence officers and interrogators to go to their ruins to plant flowers and sing love songs. And the sham trials, the torture, and all forms of degrading and inhuman treatment that went with them will at last be a thing of the past.

Paris, March 2010
hooasadh@yahoo.fr

Chapter 1

Two Articles of the Constitution

And I see stars. No, that's an old-fashioned way of putting it. Fireworks go off in my head.

You say: "That was the first article of the constitution. Now lift up your blindfold slightly." I do as I'm told. You open your military coat. I see the vague outline of a pistol. "And this is the final article, but before we get to this one there will be lots of other articles along the way ..."

Dear Brother Hamid,
Greetings again, this time after an absence of twenty-five years. At this moment, as I begin to write, exactly a quarter of a century has passed since the night your first slap made me see stars. I don't know what you are up to these days at eleven o'clock at night now that you have become an ambassador. I don't know whether you remember the slap or not. But I go to bed at exactly eleven o'clock and most nights I can still hear the sound of that slap in my ears.

Every night, yes, every night, my day ends at eleven o'clock, my life reaches its limit and I enter a dark tunnel. I find myself in pitch blackness and I never know whether I'll manage to get out of the tunnel or not.

Moshtarek Prison, Tehran, Sunday 6 February 1983

It's exactly eleven o'clock in the evening. I'm lying in the corridor, facing the wall. I've loosened my blindfold and put on my glasses.

Since around eleven o'clock this morning, my life has been reduced to the width and length of the blanket. I've learned a number of rules; the most important ones are about the blindfold. When I'm facing the wall, I'm allowed to pull up the blindfold. The damn thing is very coarse, pulling out my eyeballs. Under all other circumstances, I have to tighten it up again.

A hand touches my shoulder. It makes me jolt against my will. Quickly I grab hold of my glasses. I sit up. I place the glasses inside my shirt pocket. I put on my brown jumper – it was a birthday present. I'm exactly thirty-two years old. No, thirty-two years and one month. I'm at the beginning of the thirty-third year of my life. I adjust the blindfold. A voice shouts my name into my ear. It makes me jump again. The voice says: "Come on." I stand up. I put on my slippers, which I had placed by the side of the blanket. My spirits lift: "They're going to release me. They're going to release me ..." We walk along the corridor and I stumble on something. Someone has come to collect and release me. That someone pulls at my shirtsleeve and announces yet another rule: "Pull up your blindfold just enough so you can see what's underneath your feet."

I do as I'm told. I see everything in a slightly darker shade. I see the ground. I see a pair of military boots and trousers. "It's the Revolutionary Guards Corps. Yes, it's them." My hope grows. The Corps was basically *set up* to defend the revolution. I myself have written a number of complimentary articles about them. We go through the "Under the Eight",[1] which is a triangular courtyard. I recognize this courtyard. I've passed through it many times during earlier detentions. The guard accompanying me says: "Be careful. There's a step."

I can't see the step. I find it with my foot. There are two of them. I don't know yet that for years to come I'll have to watch out for these steps when passing through the courtyard. My companion has a kind voice. My heart lights up. "The Revolutionary Guards must have spent the entire morning defeating the American coup and are now freeing us." My optimism is based on the analysis of Iran's Communist Party,[2] of which I was a member. Like many political analyses, it is rooted in a particular worldview. "The revolutionary democrats are our allies; the government is in their hands. If the Party were ever crushed, it could only be as a result of an American coup."

We hadn't yet reached the other side of the courtyard when my mind finds the question that I must ask the guard: "Excuse me. Is my wife coming?"

My wife was also arrested that morning. I am trying to figure out her situation as well as my own. "God willing, she'll come to pick you up tomorrow morning."

I feel a sweet sensation in the pit of my stomach. "In the morning, in the morning, in the morning. They've freed my wife. She is coming to pick me up tomorrow morning."

We enter another triangular courtyard to the left. I hear the sound of the guard's tramping boots but to me they sound like the drums of freedom. He opens a door. I enter. It's a narrow corridor and turns left.

"Pick up the iron rods and follow me."

I pick up the iron rods. It's cold. We walk up the stairs to the first floor.

"Turn around."

I turn around.

"Remove your blindfold and sit down, facing the wall."

I do as I'm told. A chair is placed in the middle of the room. I sit on it. It's wooden, a pale brown school chair.

I look around me. The room is large. The windows, framed on both sides by iron bars, have been painted over. I position myself on the chair and wait. There is silence.

Then I hear the sound of shuffling feet. The sound is coming from a long way off and is moving in my direction. The door opens. The shuffling sound has entered the room. The door closes and you, Brother Hamid, enter my life for good. You who didn't believe a single word I said.

You must at least acknowledge after twenty-five years, as your picture gradually builds up on my computer monitor, that I did hear the shuffling of your slippers that day. Living abroad, in a foreign country – this fact in itself represents a continuation of your presence in my life – I was simply sitting in front of my computer when the messenger alert pinged and the following message appeared: "Have a look. Have you seen this picture?"

And the picture slowly materialized. I had a feeling deep in my gut that it would be you, and that once again you were about to enter my life, as if you were tired of having spent twenty-five years away from me. I'm sure you'd be happy to know that when your photograph finally emerged in full, my body began to shake. A sharp pain went through my back. The soles of my feet started burning. Surely you remember me?

I used to say: "Hello."

You used to respond: "Fuck you."

You used to make me lie on the bed. Face down. You used to ask me whether I had performed my ablution.[3] You used to say "Remember, not performing it is a punishable offence." You used to say that your name was Hamid, but we all called you "The Torturer". And then you would start: "In the name of the Heavenly Fatimeh …"[4] And you whipped me. First strike. Second strike. The harder you beat my feet,[5] the louder your voice became. After you had tired yourself out, you would switch on the tape machine:

"Karbala, Karbala … We are on our way …"[6]

Twenty-five years later, my scars are still stinging and that night, when I saw your photograph, they caught fire. Praise be to Allah a million times, you've grown fat. Your double chin sticks out above your official embassy uniform. Apparently this photo was taken at a dinner party at the Iranian Embassy in Tajikistan. In it, you are look-ing viciously at someone who's not visible in the photo. And I was shaking. The soles of my feet were on fire.

A new message popped up on my screen.

"Do you know him?"

"Yes."

"Who is he?"

"Brother Hamid, my interrogator."

"Are you sure it's him?"

Yes, I'm sure. I have seen you. I've seen you three times, Brother Hamid. You were very careful to ensure I wouldn't see you. But I did. The first time was when you had taken the prisoner in the cell next to mine outside – the one who was working for you and who had used Morse code to try to get information out of me. You were talking to him and I saw you. On the upper part of all the prison cell doors there were little round openings made of metal that were locked from the outside. By chance, the opening in my cell door had been broken and covered with cardboard. Someone had used a needle to make a little hole and I could see out through that hole.

I saw you through that hole. You had positioned the prisoner against the wall. He was blindfolded. He was talking and you were listening. You used to be slim back then. A guard's uniform and slippers. Those damn slippers. And the second and the third time? Do not rush me, Brother Hamid. We are still at the beginning of the story. A story that turned into a horror film. A film that you directed. I was obliged to write the script for the role that you made me play, and then to act it out.

I am sitting on that brown school chair, facing the wall. The guard orders me to put my blindfold back on. I hear the sound of shuffling feet. The sound stops behind me. A hand is placed on my shoulder. Your voice is authoritarian but young. Much younger than mine.

"We know everything."

Then you step in front of me. I see your military uniform from under the blindfold. From the waist down and slightly obscured. I have described you in detail in my novel *The Cat*.[7] Get the novel and read it. You see, you have even entered literature with me. That was a novel, but this is the truth.

You said: "Spying. Coup d'etat. No beating about the bush. Tell us everything you know."

I adjust myself on the seat. I follow the Party's instruction; I have come to believe it myself: "Firstly, we are not spies ... and then ... I am not going to answer these questions. They are against the constitution."

And I see stars. No, that's an old-fashioned way of putting it. Fireworks go off in my head. You say: "That was the first article of the constitution. Now lift up your blindfold slightly." I do as I'm told. You open your military coat. I see the vague outline of a pistol. "And this is the final article, but before we get to this one there will be lots of other articles along the way ..."

I understand that *your* constitution is different from the Islamic Republic's. As you utter these words you position yourself behind me: "Now get up. Think about it ... until tomorrow morning. Remember, we know everything. Spying. Coup d'etat. Just write about those."

The sound of shuffling feet moves away. The door opens and then closes. Complete silence.

A pigeon is cooing outside the window. I take off my blindfold and put on my glasses. The cream-coloured walls and I have been left alone. I don't know yet that years will pass and the walls and I will be alone. I hear a blowing sound in my head. My cheek is burning. Someone inside me keeps asking questions but is not given any answers.

"There's been a coup? But he was wearing the uniform of the Revolutionary Guards Corps? Could they be working for the Americans? Could it be that the Party's analysis of the situation, its instructions, have been mistaken? Could it be? A coup? Have they staged a coup themselves and are now trying to stick it on us? Me, a spy? This must be the work of the CIA ..."

My ears, which have been learning to do the job of my eyes, are waiting for a voice to come for me and take me away. My heart is naïve, it is still waiting for me to be released.

"By the way, where is my wife right now?"

The silence is complete. That pigeon is cooing again, or maybe it's a different pigeon, one of the many pigeons I become acquainted with during my three-year stay in Moshtarek prison.[8] These pigeons build their nests in one of the most horrifying torture chambers of the world. When spring arrives, they pay no attention to the cries from the torture chambers, or to the men and women who are taken away at dawn to be hanged. They lay eggs. The eggs hatch.

The only sound that breaks the silence is the bird's cooing. For the first time, I stand up cautiously and walk a few steps. I learn to listen out for his voice so that when I hear it approach I can throw myself on to the chair and sit down, facing the wall. As I sit there waiting, in my mind I keep replaying the morning of my arrest.

Early in the morning, the doorbell rang. Three short rings, one long one. I looked out of the window. It was Fereydoun, the man in charge of my Party cell. I opened the door and went down the steps. He was frightened. Pale. He was trembling while we talked.

"The arrests have started. Inform everyone you can," he said, and left. His shoulders were shaking, either out of fright or because he was crying.

I had seen him a few days earlier. When I had rung his bell the usual three times, two short rings and one long one, I was surprised to find that he didn't come down as soon as he heard that special ring. Instead one of his daughters opened the door. She went back inside and it took a long time for him to appear. He called me into the courtyard. We talked next to his parked Toyota. His daughters were watching us from the balcony. I was surprised. He gave me a package and said: "Don't come back here. They're going to arrest us. They are going to kill us. All of us."

And now he had come to my home. I stepped out into the street and watched him as he walked away. He was out of breath walking up the steep road, and that four-wheel-drive car was still parked on the other side of the street, right in front of our house. Later, I realized that from very early on they had been watching our home from inside that car. Did Rahman, the deputy editor-in-chief of *Kayhan*[9] newspaper and one of the leaders of our clandestine Party, know about this? Is that why he didn't come himself? What had happened during this last month? Why didn't he warn us? He had always worried for my wife. I went upstairs. I woke my wife; she slept late and only after taking sleeping pills.

I gave her the news. Waves of worry washed over her face and have never left since. She jumped up, quick as lightning.

"What time is it? Manuchehr Khan might be stranded."

Nooshabeh, my wife was very fond of that calm, kind, likeable man, and even though she was neither interested in politics nor a Party member, she was always ready to help him. The bell rang again. This time it was one of the members of the Party Central Committee. He had assumed that Manuchehr Behzadi, a fellow member of the Central Committee and editor-in-chief of *Mardom*, *The People's Letter*, the Party's official newspaper, would be with us and had come to let him know that the Guards had gone down early that morning to the building where Manuchehr lived. I said: "We have to collect Manuchehr Khan at eight o'clock, so we will let him know what is happening. But you shouldn't go home. Stay somewhere else for a few days."

He left, and I heard later that he had managed to get out of the country. I told my wife that we had better leave the house.

Nooshabeh was rushing to get ready to collect Manuchehr. "Pack up everything we need," she said, "I'll be back very quickly."

I insisted that she stayed so that we could go together, but she was worried about Manuchehr, and left the house in a hurry. First of all, I tore up Party paperwork, and threw it into the toilet. I grabbed a small bag into which I put any books that I thought might appear compromising, and my passport, which had a stamp from my trip to the Soviet Union. I put the bag in the cellar. I went back upstairs. I picked up another small bag. I tried to make sure that my wife's mother, who was living with us, wouldn't notice. I threw in basic necessities. I considered phoning the *Mardom* office, but instead quietly left the house with the bag in my hand and phoned the *Mardom* office from a public phone box nearby. Usually, one of the guys I knew well picked up the phone, but this time an unfamiliar voice answered. I realized from the way he spoke that the authorities had already taken over the office. I put down the phone. I didn't know what to do. For a while I waited at the side of the street for Nooshabeh to get back, but there was no sign of her. I couldn't leave without her. I went back into the house. Since then, I've asked myself a thousand times whether I was stupid to do that.

Whatever the answer, that return changed the course of my life. Or perhaps it moved it in a predetermined direction.

Back home, I paced up and down, waiting for my wife. I remember the time exactly. It was precisely twenty to ten on the morning of 6 February 1983 when they knocked on the door. Whoever they were, they hadn't been able to find the doorbell and had come into the hallway and knocked on the inner door instead. I went down and opened the door. Three people were standing there in civilian clothing. One was holding my photograph, and asked: "Are you Houshang Asadi?"

"Yes."

"Let's go to the third floor."

They knew that we lived on the third floor. Together we went upstairs. My mother-in-law was busy with some housework. They closed the door behind them and one of them said: "We've been ordered to arrest you. Your wife is already under arrest." They showed me a piece of paper with my wife's name, Nooshabeh Amiri, on it.

I was already dressed and ready. A pair of brown velvet trousers and a light brown jumper, a birthday present from my wife. I have kept that jumper ever since. It's too tight for me now and is unfashionable, but it's always hanging among my shirts in the wardrobe. And boots. So I was left with nothing else to do. The last thing I did, which I later realized was a mistake, was to take my wallet out of my trouser pocket and place it on the table. That money would have been very useful where I was going. They threw a quick glance around the room and together we proceeded to the little library that my wife and I were using as our office. The room's window opened on to a building where Shirin Ebadi[10] and her mother lived. Shirin's mother was close friends with my mother-in-law and they used to talk to each other through the window. Next door to their building was some open ground where a wild fig tree had sprouted and subsequently grown to full size. The tree was leafless at that time of year, and I could see the Hillman car that had been parked nearby and several men walking around. They were the officials who had surrounded the building and blocked all the escape routes. One of the men in our flat, who must have been the leader of the arrest team, asked: "Where are the weapons?" I laughed.

"Are you making fun of us?" he asked.

"No. The weapons are there," I replied, and pointed to the penholder on the desk.

He said: "We'll find the weapons. If you want to collect some stuff, do it now so we can leave."

I picked up my wife's pills, as I knew she couldn't sleep without them. My mother-in-law was standing by the door. She blocked their way and asked: "Where are you taking my child?"

The man who had spoken before said: "We're going to ask him one or two questions. He'll be back in a couple of hours."

I said: "Mother, dear, if they turn out to be the boys from the Revolutionary Guards, then I'll return. If they are *putchists*, then I won't be coming back. Tell my wife that I'll die shouting 'Death to America!' "

My mother-in-law burst into tears. I kissed her wet eyes and threw one last glance around my home. We walked down the stairs and left the building. On the street, a couple of Hillmans had been parked in front of the carpark. One of them was full. The men from the second car had got out and were walking about. They put me in the middle of the back seat with someone sitting on either side of me. Apart from the people from the Hillmans the street was deserted. When the car started moving, I saw another Hillman setting off from the bottom of the street and when we reached the end of the street, the fourth Hillman, which had been stationed in a guarding position, also started to move. When we made a turn into the side street, I saw my younger brother drive into our street.

I watched the crowds of people who were getting on with their lives on that wintry morning, looking at the passengers of this Hillman with their tired eyes. This wasn't the first time I had been arrested, but somehow the experience was completely different. We were defenders of the revolution. This arrest must either be at the orders of the clerics in charge, and hence would be over in one or two days because, according to the Party's analysis, the clerics were our allies in the struggle against imperialism. Or the Americans had masterminded a coup, which would mean that I'd be saying "Death to America!" while facing a firing squad alongside all the other staunch supporters of the revolution. These thoughts were going round and round in my head while I was looking at the walls, on which were written the fashionable slogans of the time. The last slogan I saw before we turned into a main street said: "Death to the Dashnaks, the agents of ..."

The leader of the arrest team who was sitting next to the driver, suddenly asked: "Are you familiar with the Dashnaks?"

"Yes," I replied. "Armenian fascists!"

He turned and placed his hand on my head. He said: "Now shut up and lower your head." And he pressed my head down, mustering as much force as he could, and threw a blanket over me. Everything went black.

I could hear his voice: "We do this so the public won't see you. If they knew who you were, they would tear you into pieces ..."

From beneath the blanket, I said: "We are defenders of the revolution. I'm not aware who you people are …"

I heard the sound of their laughter. A hand pressed my head down even harder.

I later found out that all the people who had been arrested that morning were taken to the army base in the centre of Tehran. On 11 February 1979, the day the Islamic revolution took power, I had held a gun and helped guard this important post alongside the people who had captured it. That base had become one of the main centres of the Revolutionary Guards Corps.

We reached our destination very quickly. The car stopped. They pulled the blanket off my head and put a blindfold on me. Someone took the bag with my wife's pills from me, tugged at the edge of my brown jumper, and we walked up two or three steps and entered a courtyard, which I sensed was quite spacious. There was the sound of many people, subdued to a general humming. We passed a significant number of bags and bundles. The guard made me sit against a wall and left. I heard the voice of Rahman Hatefi over the humming. He was speaking loudly, answering questions. He was being asked about a typewriter and he was saying: "I'm a journalist. It's my own typewriter."

I realized that the arrests were extremely widespread. It wasn't long before my name was called. I stood up. Someone grabbed the corner of my jumper and pulled me along. We walked down the same stairs. I wasn't alone. I recognized the voices of a number of the Party's cadres. I was put into a car, a blanket was thrown over my head, and the car set off. I tried to figure out from the car's movement where I was being taken. I suspected our destination was Evin prison but I soon lost all sense of direction. After a short while, the car stopped and I realized we had arrived. So it wasn't Evin, it had to be Moshtarek prison. Ironically, back in 1979, I had been one of the people who had helped to capture this notorious prison. Unlike everyone else, I hadn't been looking for weapons or torture instruments that sunny February day, I was looking for the cells where I had been held prisoner during the Shah's time. I had searched almost the entire prison building, and was very familiar with it.

It took a few minutes for the large main gate to the east of the prison to open. We drove through, and the car stopped on the long, cobbled road. They made us step out, one by one. They took me to a room and pulled the blanket off my head.

I am asked for my name, my nickname, my father's name and the number on my identity card. I'm handed a pair of trousers, a grey vest, and regulation prison slippers. I put them on. They collect my trousers, my shoes, my socks and my jacket. I put my own shirt and jumper back on over the vest. The trousers are baggy and falling down. The slippers are old and about two sizes too big for my feet.

They take me into another room. I take off the blindfold. A chubby man with a bushy beard places a placard around my neck and photographs me a few times. Around fifteen years later, when I went to the Islamic court to ask for permission to leave the county and the judge's assistant brought over my file, I saw one of those pictures again. I was a young man in the photograph, thirty-two years of age with a full head of black hair, a thick moustache, a plump, happy face, and a curious smile on my lips. What was I laughing at?

The same chubby man puts his hand into a large basket and selects another blindfold and hands it to me. It's brown and very coarse. The blindfold completely covers my eyes. I tie it up and the man tightens it. I am blind. The Islamic Republic's greatest invention, its most dangerous weapon, is the blindfold, Brother Hamid. I don't know whether you copied the blindfold from some foreign security service, or whether it's an achievement of the "Glorious Islamic Revolution". Either way, it's the most horrifying instrument of torture. Deprived of vision the prisoner is disarmed. Your other senses strive to replace your lost sight. Your hearing is the first to rush to your rescue.

Your interrogator watches every tiny movement you make. Anything you think shows in a movement somewhere in your body. Even the rhythm of your feet translates into something meaningful. When you're blindfolded, you're unable to see the impact of your lies in the eyes of your interrogator, to catch in his movements something that might be useful or to your advantage.

On this battlefield, where the struggle between life and death is being played out, the blindfold removes all advantage from the prisoner. The interrogator has all the weapons at his disposal. He can see you and he can beat you. The prisoner doesn't even know from which direction the next blow will come. Watching an approaching blow, the body automatically prepares for defence. Blinded, you are defenceless. The blindfolded prisoner is deprived of the ability to sense the moment that is vital in all interrogations, and so takes part in a ghastly, one-sided chess game in which the interrogator controls all the pieces. He scrutinizes the prisoner's slightest movements. He watches the impact of his words and whips, and is well placed to move a fresh piece to break the prisoner. His opponent, of course, blindfolded, doesn't even know which piece he has moved.

Someone grabs at the corner of my jumper. I'm not yet familiar with the meaning of this action. During the Shah's time, in this same prison, the guards would grab hold of our hands to lead us away. The blindfold is tight and I can't see a thing. I, who have never had good hearing, am losing all sense of direction in the darkness. I suddenly fall over and hit the floor. I stand up again with difficulty. My guard says: "Pull up your blindfold just so you can see what's under your feet."

I do as I'm told. We are now walking again and I see what's under my feet – that is, with as much sight as I can conjure up without my glasses. I lift up my head and see the vague contours of the landing. He hands me over to another guard. We enter the Under the Eight. We pass through a metal door and enter the detention centre. I'm expecting them to take me into a cell, but we stop by a blanket that has been thrown onto the floor just a few steps ahead of us.

"Stay on the blanket," the guard barks. "Lift your hand anytime you need something."

Then he walks away. I take off the slippers and stand on the blanket. Then, I sit down. I lift up the blindfold and look at the wall. The cream coloured wall is familiar. I have no doubt that I'm in Moshtarek prison. I want to be sure. I lift my hand. The guard comes.

"What's up?"

"Toilet."

"Stand up."

I stand up. The guard tightens my blindfold, tugs at the corner of my jumper and takes me with him. The toilets in Moshtarek prison are at the end of a corridor. They're a filthy green colour. We arrive and enter.

"Take off your blindfold. When you finish your business, knock on the door."

I take off my blindfold. I put on my glasses. I spot several large rats, which make a run for it. I look at the toilet door, the window and the sink. Yes, I'm seeing Moshtarek prison for the umpteenth time. Three arrests during the Shah's time, once the day the crowds over-ran it during the revolution, and now. I wash my face. I dry it with the corner of my shirt. I put on my glasses.

At that moment, the door opens and I see the guard. He's a boy, very young, with plump red cheeks. I ask: "Where are we?"

He says: "Block 2000, Evin ..."

I laugh: "When did Evin prison move from the outskirts into the centre of Tehran?"

The guard becomes irritated and shouts: "Shut your mouth. Put on your blindfold."

I put on the blindfold and we return to the detention area. I hear the muezzin's voice as we walk back and I see, from beneath my blindfold, that the entire floor of the detention area has been covered with blankets. All the blankets are occupied. I discover later that the arrests had started at four in the morning. It is now afternoon and all the cells and blankets of Moshtarek prison's block 1 are occupied. I sit down and hold my head between my hands. I have to collect my thoughts.

The call to prayer and the prayer finishes. I hear the voice of one of the other prisoners shouting loudly: "We are not spies!"

There's a smell of food and they bring in the first meal. It's very tasty, rice with chicken, served in a plastic container, accompanied by a red plastic spoon and cup. As always, when I'm angry, I start eating fiercely. I sit down, facing the wall. I lift up my blindfold and demolish the food.

There's a sound. I tighten the blindfold. It's the sound of boots. Not the shuffling noise of slippers. The two sounds have not yet developed different meanings for me. Later on, I will always be hoping for the sound of boots. The sound of boots meant something else, it was only the shuffling that meant the torture chamber: the two-door cells with blood-splattered walls and a rope hanging from the ceiling.

"Stand up."

It's the guard.

I stand up. He pulls at the corner of my jumper and takes me away. We walk down the stairs; we turn left. We pass a door. The air is freezing cold. We pass through a triangular courtyard. By the two steps.

"Be careful."

How kind they are. They make sure I don't fall. I, who am still dizzy, with stars circling inside my head and burning cheeks. I, who am still hopeful in my heart of hearts.

"The Party's take on the situation … The Party's analysis of the situation …"

We enter the Under the Eight. The guard in charge takes over. He pulls on the corner of my jumper and leads me away.

"If you need the toilet, go now. There'll be no toilet time until tomorrow morning."

I shake my head to say no. He leaves me beside the blanket and walks out. I take off the slippers. I sit down on the blanket. The tight blindfold is making my eyes ache. I turn towards the wall and pull up the blindfold.

Where's my wife right now? Is she on one of these blankets?

But she's never been a Party member.

When Americans carry out a coup, they arrest everybody.

I recall Chile. Those films. The stadium massacres. Victor Jara.

Everywhere that the coarse blindfold has touched is burning. I rub the area with my hands and close my eyes. I must try to sleep. I make a pile with my jumper and slippers, put my head on the pile and close my eyes. Clinging to a faint hope, and imagining my wife's smile, I remember:

"If they've told the truth and these men belong to the Revolutionary Guards Corps, they'll free us tomorrow. They're our allies in the struggle against imperialism. The Corps … our allies … the revolutionary democrats … release … my wife's smile …"

Something is playing with my earlobe. I twist and turn, half-way between sleep and wakefulness. It feels like my earlobe is being chewed. I jump up. A huge rat is nibbling my ear. Another rat is about to walk over me. I shout out. The rats run away. I hear the guard's voice. A hand hits my shoulder. I'm thrown from dream into reality.

"Tighten your blindfold."

I tighten my blindfold and sit up.

"Stand up. Go to the bathroom. Hurry up if you don't want to miss the prayer time."

It must be morning. I put on my jumper and go to the bathroom. I wash my face and dry it with the corner of my shirt. I take off my glasses. I put on the blindfold and exit. The guard says:

"So, you're not into praying."

I don't answer. We walk towards the blanket. I've just reached the blanket and am about to take off the slippers when someone grabs my jumper and pulls me after him. In the years to come, I will have no choice but to walk back and forth on this path.

A metal barrier. Under the Eight. The second metal barrier. Courtyard. Icy winter. My feet freeze. My heart sinks. Two stairs. All the Brothers are worried about these two stairs: "Be careful."

I'm being careful. A metal door. Left turn. The stairs. Right turn. Door. A large room.

"Go, sit down and wait for your interrogator."

I lift up the blindfold. I've not yet seated myself when I hear the shuffling of slippers. I sit down and put on the blindfold. The door opens. And in you come, you, Brother Hamid: "Ready?"

I say: "Hello."

You answer: "Hello and fuck you. You must have slept well."

You don't wait for my answer.

"I didn't sleep a wink. I spent the whole night reading your file and waiting for you."

You put a pile of paper and a blue biro on the arm of the chair. I've never liked writing with a blue biro.

"You are going to write about everything, from the day you were born. Don't leave out any details. We know everything, but you still have to write it down yourself."

You walk to stand behind me. You place your hand on my shoulder. I have not yet seen you and I'm trying to imagine you. You take your hand away. There's the shuffling sound of slippers. The door opens. The door closes. You have left. I take off my blindfold. Put on my glasses. Once again, there's me and a pile of paper that I have to fill.

"As to who you are, that's obvious. From the day you were born ..."

That was the first and also the last time that you told the truth, Brother Hamid. "Who I am" is clear, as clear as daylight. I was one of the millions of young people who had grown up under a dictatorship. We wanted freedom, but didn't know that we were sacrificing our lives only to replace one dictator with another. Like the rest, I wanted freedom, but there were only two options open to me in the monarchist dictatorship that was the Iran of my youth: Soviet-style Marxism, or religion. Iran shared its long border in the north with Russia, a country that for decades radiated with Tsarist dictatorial ideology. But the 1917 October Revolution changed all that. Like millions of other young people around the world, we were hungry for freedom and justice, and for us that revolution seemed to carry a beautiful message of hope for humanity. A message that reached the farthest corners of the world.

Yet all that we knew about this Marxist-Leninist ideal of human society was that one day a world order would emerge in which there would be no hunger, no one would be homeless, discrimination would be a thing of the past, and human beings would be in charge of their collective destiny. Censorship didn't allow us to know what went on behind the Iron Curtain. We had a road map that we thought would liberate our country, but we actually knew very little about it. We didn't know then that the Union of Soviet Socialist Republics only seemed ideal from a distance.

And the religion that the progressive religious people spoke of was another idealized world filled with beautiful sentiments of equality, brotherhood, freedom and purpose. And all of us – the communist and the religious – believed that the main barrier to our arrival at this Promised Land was imperialism and the governments that promoted it.

So it was that by the late 1970s the Iranians living under the dictatorial regime of the Shah (who was supported by the West) chose to stand alongside those who opposed the West and the key Western powers. We were all victims of this battle, both religious and Marxists. We who didn't have the right to know either what went on in Russia, or the true nature of the Islamic Republic that we were called upon to embrace.

Chapter 2

Iran of Those Days: The Age of Compassion

Dear Brother Hamid. This is my second letter to you. I am sitting down, going through the story of my life. It's a good opportunity to review all the things that I still remember. Who knows, maybe one day I might get trapped in your claws again, with you forcing me to confess that Sonia, who looked so like my childhood sweetheart Angie, had been a Mossad agent, or that the rest of our neighbours were spying for this or that country.

Iran, 1958

"Abgie! Abgie!"[11]

We called her Abgie. It would piss her off and she would chase us around the pool, saying: "I'm Angie, not Abgie!"

The house in Tehran where my father rented a room for us was spacious, like Iran. It had two storeys, and in the courtyard there was a pool filled with goldfish. They would come up to the surface of the water and nudge the overhanging geranium leaves and brush past our bare feet dangling in the water, and then dive deep into the water again for fear of cats. The cold water, which arrived in the middle of the night, was accompanied by the neighbours' excited shouts. It filled up the terrifying, ancient reservoir and spilled into the pool. The edges around the pool were slippery and I didn't understand how the neighbour's daughter, thinner and smaller than me, could slide into the water like a fish on moonlit nights. I'd slide towards the edge of the flat rooftop where we all slept on hot summer nights to watch out for her. Lying on the coolness of the mattress surface, I'd look up at the stars, and wait for her to arrive. First I would smell her. Jasmine, accompanied by the rattling of a chubak[12] branch. I'd smell her scent even when asleep, and would wake up. I'd be careful not wake up Aqa Sayyed, one of our neighbours. Both his wives' mattresses were placed right next to ours. Aqa Sayyed, whom people said went begging in the nearby Armenian fort during the daytime, would wrap himself up in a green shawl, throw on a cloak and go to the minaret when the religious mourning season arrived. They said that every night his wives fought over whom he was going to spend the night with. The victorious wife would display a pair of underpants above her bed, so all the occupants of the house could see that she was the chosen one.

The water surface shimmered with stars. Angie would slide naked into the cool water and become a fish. I would try to figure out her colouring in the moonlight, but she was colourless. Maybe she was the colour of the moon and I had failed to understand it. Maybe she was the colour of the fish, and she merged with them, becoming one with them. The rooftops were jam-packed with sleeping people and the lights were off. I was worried that someone might wake up and see me and notice her. She who was different from everyone else; she whose name was unlike anyone else's name.

When the rooster crowed at daybreak, the young watchman, who used to sit in the corner of the courtyard, would squat by the pool in his underpants and perform the ablution. The water must have smelled of fish. His father, dressed in a baggy suit with his shirt always buttoned-up to his neck, was the first to leave the house. He never raised his head. Next, it would be the guard's turn. And as if following a strict hierarchical order, the poet, who limped on one leg, would make a round of the courtyard before reaching the gate. It was said that he used to be a communist and that after leaving prison, he had taken a job in a cafe to pay for his son to study in America. And Monsieur, well he would leave around midday; he had a liquor store somewhere. Last of all, my father would leave the house, cutting a dash, wearing a tie. He would shout "Ya Allah!" and polish his shoes against the side of the pool.

The men would leave and the women would stay behind in the house. My mother always sat next to Afaq Khanum, her uncle's wife. Together they would wash the dishes beside the well. Once, when one of the neighbourhood women objected to their friendship, because Afaq Khanum was a Baha'i, my mother tied her chador around her waist, and making sure that everyone could hear her, she shouted: "To Jesus his faith, and to Moses his. We are all Iranians – whether Baha'i, Jew or Shaykhi, it doesn't matter."

The two of them giggled and whispered conspiratorially together. They would grab hold of the lapis-coloured quilts, shake them out and throw them over the washing line. I would set off, running into the scented wetness.

The house was big and was like Iran. Every time visitors came to see the poet who lived in one of the neighbouring rooms, he would shout out loud: "This house may not have the grandeur of a palace, but what it does have is purity of heart."

Everybody had become accustomed to Monsieur's sudden appearances in the middle of the afternoon. He never bothered to say "Ya Allah" to warn the household about his intention to step out of his room. So the women would shriek, pull their outer skirts over their heads to hide their faces from him, and make a run for it. And I would notice that the women used thin and colourful fabrics to cover themselves down there.

Come sunset, wooden platforms would be brought out and placed next to the pool. My father would turn up the radio. The presenter would abuse the "Russians". The poet would leave for his room. The presenter's shouting made you feel sick in the pit of your stomach. The canaries would fall silent. The grapevines would shake, releasing bunches of grapes. Everybody would be listening and shaking their heads. My family spent seven years living in this house.

My mother, Fatimeh, was the only daughter of a major landowner in the village of Hesar. She came from the Torbat-e Haidariya region, in the Khorasan province, where apparently a walnut tree at the head of a spring still bears my name. A place located in the realm of dreams, the kind that one is not allowed to see close up in the real world.

Khorasan, which means "where the sun rises", was a province in the east of Iran, now divided into three separate provinces. It was the size of France and bordered three countries: Afghanistan and Turkmenistan, which used to be part of Iran until a hundred years ago, and Pakistan, which, when it was part of India, had been conquered three hundred years ago by Nadir Shah, the last of Iran's world conquerors. My mother's birthplace is located in the southernmost part of Khorasan, the place where the pleasant gardens of Khorasan end and one of the world's largest arid regions begins.

A split had taken place in my maternal grandfather's household. One of his brothers (my mother's uncle) had joined the Baha'i faith, and changed his family name. His eldest son later became a prominent member of the Baha'i community, and was one of the first people to be sent to the gallows by the Islamic Republic after the revolution. I haven't even seen a photograph of my grandfather, but he had a free spirit and a lover's reputation, being something of a Casanova. And so it was that one day, right in the middle of work, he grabbed my grandmother (his wife) by the hand and took her to the threshing floor, covering her with a thin, cotton sheet. My mother, their only daughter, was the result of this passionate tryst. She learned basic literacy from her father, as the village had no school for girls in those days. She loved poetry, and often recited poems that she had memorized. Poetry was her way of reasoning, especially the poetry of Iran's three great poets, Ferdowsi, Khayyam and Hafez.[13]

One summer night, when my grandfather was climbing the wooden stairs to get to the rooftop where he was going to sleep, he suddenly slipped, and fell heavily to the ground. The fall of his large body made the house shake. In Iran's deserts, the air at night is heavenly, in contrast to the daytime when the heat is infernal. A cool breeze blows and the sky is so low and filled with stars that you believe you can reach out and grab one. Even today the people who live on the outskirts of deserts spend the nights sleeping on rooftops. My oldest uncle, who later drowned in the Zayendehrood, one of Iran's three largest rivers, which has now dried up, grabbed his younger brother and sister (my mother) and fled the village that night. In the morning, when the news of my grandfather's death had spread and rumours that he had been poisoned began to make the rounds, bandits came to loot the house, but the children were already on their way to Mashhad, in the centre of Khorasan, on foot and empty-handed. My mother never forgot that terrible night, and would repeatedly tell us about how they entered Mashhad alone and utterly unprotected. The image of the Russian soldiers, who occupied Mashhad at the time, would always remain with her.

Ameneh, my paternal grandmother, had fled to Tehran with her two sons and two daughters from the opposite side of Iran. Iran is like a big sleeping cat lying in the heart of Asia. She is the remnant of the grand and ancient Persian Empire that, 2,500 years ago, ruled almost two thirds of the known world. Azerbaijan, my father's birthplace, is in the northwest; on a map of Iran it is by the cat's ears. Its high peaks are covered with snow, and the valleys that spread out between the mountains look like a mini Switzerland. In this dream-like landscape, my maternal grandfather owned land and water that had been handed down to him by his ancestors. Ameneh Khanum, his first legally wedded spouse, who died many years later in Tehran at the age of 103, recalled her husband carrying a gun over his shoulder, leaving home to help Sattar Khan, one of the heroes of the constitutional revolution of Iran[14] in the first decade of the twentieth century. Sattar Khan was an ordinary man, a horse thief, who ended up saving the revolution. An era of revolution had begun, and my birth coincided with its final years.

When my paternal grandfather, Isa Khan, died fighting Reza Shah's troops, Ameneh took charge of his affairs. She gave both his lawful wives and concubines their share and even provided his mistresses, who had suddenly turned up from left, right and centre, with their share. Since the rest of Isa Khan's possessions had been confiscated by the government, Ameneh hid her children inside sacks of wheat and descended from the high mountains in a carriage bound for Tehran.

Iran was going through a period of turmoil in the year of my birth. The very night of my birth, 13 January 1950, was cold and terrifying. My mother, worried that she may not be able to feed her newly born child, wanted to smother me with a pillow. My father talked her out of it. A few nights later my father, who had become exasperated by my ceaseless crying, lost his temper and threw my swaddled body into the cold pool water. My mother saved me and rushed me to a doctor. I was blue and shivering uncontrollably. The doctor said: "He's finished. Give him some watermelon juice. If that doesn't work, put him in a corner and leave him to die."

My mother and father set off in search of a watermelon in the icy coldness of the winter night. My father eventually broke into a fruit shop and stole one. They dribbled the juice into my mouth and waited for me to die. But death didn't come. Death, who had prepared himself to accompany this about-to-die-child, would only clear the pathway to life at the very last minute. A child whose mother, against her husband's wishes, had picked a name for him from Ferdowsi's epic *Shahnameh*, a classic similar to Homer's *Odyssey*. My father had intended me to become a Muhammad, but my mother's resistance ensured that I became a Houshang. Again and again this child would find himself inhaling the air of death. The reason why this death, which had seemed so certain, had been delayed, would remain unclear.

One day, I asked my mother: "Why did you name me Houshang?"

She laughed and said: "Because you are a smart boy."

She was referring to the meaning of my name. I, who had just become interested in reading and books, replied: "Houshang is the name of the second of the ancient Iranian kings. He discovered fire, and the Iranians are his descendants."

Overwhelmed with joy, my mother started kissing my face, never imagining that years after her death I'd be forced to account for my name in one of Iran's most horrifying prisons.

Unlike my mother, my father was bad-tempered. In the 1920s, he was an active member of the shoemakers' syndicate in Tehran. At home, he followed the established patriarchal traditions of the time. On Friday nights, he recited the Qur'an[15] in a loud voice until the early hours of the morning. During the rest of the week, he read us the catchlines that were printed at the bottom of the newspaper's pages.

The child, weak and on the verge of death from the very beginning of its life, felt a peculiar attraction for these newspaper stories, but didn't like those endless nights of Qur'an recitations. From opposite sides of Iran, both my grandfathers had married multiple wives. Lust for women ran in their veins but in me, their first grandchild, desire had turned into love. And love arrived on moonlit nights, and merged with geranium flowers, and the moonlight and the fish, before disappearing under the water. I'd stop breathing. I'd push myself so far forward that I'd come close to falling off the rooftop. I'd clutch the roof edge until she resurfaced.

Linked to politics from birth, I was almost four years old when I took part in the 28 Mohrdad demonstrations (19 August 1953), the Anglo-American sponsored military coup d'etat against Muhammad

Mossadeq[16] who, as prime minister, had attempted to overthrow the Shah's government. The crowds were walking through our neighbourhood, shouting slogans against Mossadeq. I had somehow ended up joining them, and marched along with them. They shouted abusive slogans and I repeated them. Upon hearing this story from my mother, my father, who had gone out onto the streets to search for me and had returned home empty-handed, hit me on the ear and so gave me my first political slap.

And in primary school, I attended two demonstrations, one for and one against the regime. As with the first demonstration, these also happened without my being fully aware of what I was doing. The first one was on the birthday of Reza Pahlavi, the Shah's eldest son. The class had been dismissed and the kids rushed into the playground to celebrate the birthday of someone who is now on the other side of the same world of exile from where I am writing these lines. The second demonstration was the Teachers' Day protest that ended in violence and the killing of a teacher at the hands of the police. It was already evening when I arrived home from the protest, covered in dust and with my clothes torn. My father was waiting for me by the door. He gave me a hard slap on the head and said: "Go back to wherever you've been. I'll break your legs if you come back."

He slammed the door and left. How was I supposed to know that he had been dismissed that very day? His many love affairs had finally affected his chance of getting into the oil business. That day, the head of the National Iranian Oil Company had walked into his office and found my father right in the middle of making love to a woman. My father's response to the man's objections had been to slap him, and he had been summarily sacked on the spot and sent home. Back home he had discovered my disappearance and had scoured the whole neighbourhood with my tearful mother, searching for me.

The distraught boy, thirsty and starving, was sobbing when the door to the house was quietly opened later that evening. It was her. She beckoned me with her hand. She left the door ajar, and disappeared. I slipped into the courtyard, but the only hiding place I could think of was the water reservoir. It was dark and the old steps were steep and worn. Water was dripping down the walls. The further down you went, the wetter and darker it became. I was touching the wall with my hand and carefully feeling my way down the steps. When I reached the large water-tap, I turned my head and saw the sky above the stairs. It looked like a blue stain. With difficulty I turned on the tap, and placed my head underneath it. I drank my fill. I put my school bag on the floor and sat on it. I was shaking and frightened. Suddenly, everything went dark. The blue stain had disappeared. But then it reappeared, looking like a new moon, and I saw a shadow that was slipping and moving in my direction.

What if it's my father?

I was dying of fear. No. The smell was saying, no. The smell that was wafting down the stairs was saying no. The shadow reached me. Called me. Took my hand in the dark and placed an object into the palm of my hand. A bunch of grapes that still felt hot from the sun. Amid silence and darkness, she pulled off a grape and popped it into my mouth.

"Do you like it?"

"Yes."

"I have one condition. Do not call me Abgie."

"Okay Angie."

At first, the voices came from far away. They circled at the bottom of the mouldy brick steps and then broke into a thousand pieces.

"Aaangie!"

Then, beams of light bounced down the stairs. Suddenly, we found ourselves immersed in a cacophony of sound and movement. A pair of hands grabbed us and dragged us up the stairs. Angie was being dragged ahead of me, and I was frightened for her. They made us stand by the pool, under the light of the lanterns. Everyone seemed to be there. First, they looked us over and checked our clothes. I closed my eyes. A pair of hands suddenly grabbed me and threw me into the pool. It was my father, administering my punishment. I fell deep into the water and cried out. I paddled with my arms and legs, trying to scramble out, but as soon as I left the water and reached the air, a hand would push me back in again.

When the time came for school, I went to Mofeed primary school, which was in a long and dusty road. I still miss the neighbour's pomegranate trees whose branches, heavy with fruit, hung over the wall around the school playground. The headmaster would mercilessly beat us with the torn off branches of those trees, but we loved eating the stolen pomegranates.

In those years, reading became my main passion, and I developed a love of writing. I was never good at maths but excelled at essay writing. I would discuss all essay topics with my mother and she would inject into my mind her pure, rural take on the subject mixed with poetry and famous sayings, and inspired I would rush off to write up my essays. One of these topics was "The value of water". I wrote the essay in the usual way with a rural flavour. This was my fifth year at the primary school and our teacher was Mr Ismaili. He was short with a red face and I have always wished that I could see him again. I don't know why, but he called my name first to go up to the front of the class by the blackboard to read out my essay. When I finished reading it, I expected his usual encouraging words. Instead a big slap on the face threw me off my feet. He shouted:

"Sit down. I'm giving you a zero for this."

In tears I asked why.

He said: "So that next time, you don't get your parents to write your essays for you."

I sat down and, still crying, kept repeating that I had written it all myself. Mr Ismaili came and stood right over my head and said "If you're telling the truth, write it again." And so I did, there and then, very quickly, but I wrote about water in a slightly different way. Mr Ismaili read the essay and gave me another big smack on the face saying, "You've memorized this one too."

I started crying again and said: "I wrote it myself."

He said: "If you're not lying, then write it again … "

This time I wrote the essay in the classical style of Sa'di's *Gulestan*. Although at that stage I didn't really know much about the different prose styles, I had an instinctive feel for them. Mr Ismaili read it. His eyes filled with tears and he asked me to stay behind after school. I did and he came with me to our house. My mother, seeing the red finger marks on my face, became an angry tiger. Mr Ismaili started by apologizing and finished by saying: "Your son will be a great writer."

And that's all I wanted to be. I wanted to become a writer, nothing else. I also wrote poems in those days, in the traditional classical style my mother was so fond of. I had several notebooks filled with these poems, which were thrown into a sack and taken away when my house was ransacked in 2003 by the public prosecutor on the grounds that I was a master spy.

Chapter 3

Kissing the Hand of Khomeini

One day they came to collect Khomeini from the house of a wealthy businessman in the north of Tehran to send him into exile. I, who ended up becoming a prisoner of his regime and was subjected to the worst kinds of torture at the hands of his supporters, set off to his house and kissed his hand, without knowing who he was.

And I am in the process of writing my third letter to you.

Tehran, winter 1983

The sound of shuffling slippers approaches. It's you, Brother Hamid. It has taken me very little time to learn to identify which one of the shuffling sounds is yours. I've put on my blindfold. I see your hand picking up the papers.

"Go for lunch while I read these. You better not have written dirty cunt limericks."

You have a peculiar way of saying "dirty cunt limericks"; it's a new addition to your vocabulary. So far, I have picked up two phrases from you: "useless wimp" and "dirty cunt limericks".

You leave. Immediately after you leave, someone else comes in and takes me away. Stairs. Door. Courtyard. Two stairs. Watch out. Eight. The block. The blanket. No, this time the guard is making me enter one of the lower section blocks that have been separated from the main corridor by a wall. Each part of the lower section consists of three or four cells. He opens the door to a cell and throws me in. Cell

number fifteen, block number two. I turn around. It's a familiar
Moshtarek prison cell, around 2.5 metres long and 1.5 metres wide.
The ceiling is very high, with a bare light bulb hanging from it.
Triple glazed window, barbed wired, and divided in the middle to
make two panels. I put on my glasses and look around. I see the light
and the snow that has settled behind the window and the loudspeaker
on the cell wall opposite. High up. Out of reach.

The door suddenly opens.

"Put on your blindfold. Come on."

I put on the blindfold. We set off. No, he has grabbed my sleeve
and is dragging me behind him. When we emerge from the Eight
into the courtyard, you are already there, standing in the open space
and suddenly hitting me around my head with something heavy. It's
the thick pile of paper. You are saying: "Useless wimp. What are
these dirty limericks? You have one more chance before I crack open
your mouth. Spy!"

There's silence. The sound of shuffling fades. The guard takes me
back. I tell him I need the bathroom. We walk between the blankets.
We go to the toilet. I wash my face. I put on my glasses. A newspaper has been left abandoned in a corner of the room. I pick it up. My
eyes fall on a section of the arrest report:

> Our reporter has discovered that the spies who have been arrested by
> the Revolutionary Guards Corps had links with the KGB espionage
> network. According to this report, a well-known figure by the name
> of Nurrudin Kianuri, who was the First Secretary of the Tudeh
> Party, is among the individuals who have been spying on behalf of
> foreigners.

The newspaper is dated 6 February 1983.

I don't know whether the newspaper has been left there on purpose or by accident. I re-read the report. The guard is knocking on
the door. I throw the paper down. The guard takes me back to the

blanket. A bowl of dried-up food and a piece of stale bread is await-ing me.

I swallow the food with difficulty. My thoughts are scattered in every direction. I keep wondering where my wife is.

Words are entering my mind, as if hitting me. "Useless wimp. Dirty limericks. Spy. I'll crack open your mouth." I still can't work out if there has been an American coup or we have been imprisoned by our own "allies". I sense that someone is watching me. I lift my head. The round opening on the iron door is open and a pair of eyes is staring at me. As soon as I return the gaze, the cardboard opening shuts again. A thud. The door opens. A large scruffy head appears. A weathered, wrinkled face, thick hair. A voice with a strong Turkish accent asks:

"You are eating, right?"

"Yes, Haj Aqa."[17]

"Have you performed your prayers yet?"

I don't respond. I realized that he was going to become my prayer instructor. He was going to teach me how to prostrate myself before God's throne. He was going to tell me about Islamic justice. He was going to explain to me why peeing while standing up is a serious sin. Thud. The door closes again. I am still busy, wolfing down the food with peculiar enthusiasm, when the door opens again. I'm reminded of an earlier imprisonment during the Shah's time when I shared a cell with Ayatollah Khamenei, now Iran's supreme leader and one-time president, and we used to give nicknames to the prison guards. I now give nicknames to the prison guards of his government. This one is going to be "God's father" because he obviously doubts the Muslim credentials of God himself. He asks: "Which one is Houshang?"

"I am."

"Are you Houshang?"

For a moment, I doubt myself. Maybe there is someone else in the cell. I automatically look around me. Then I say: "Yes, that's me."

"Put on your blindfold and follow me."

I put on the blindfold and put my glasses in my shirt pocket.

"Take this."

An object hits my hand. I grab it. It's a stick; the guard is holding the other end. This is to prevent him from touching me and so "polluting" himself. He sets off, taking me along the usual route. He asks me out of the blue: "Why did you call yourself Houshang?"

"I didn't call myself Houshang. My parents named me, Haj Aqa."

"Why didn't you call yourself Muhammad[18] or Ali[19]?"

"I am not the one who's responsible for my name."

"Have you got any qualifications?"

"Yes, Haj Aqa. Journalism."

"Why haven't you studied the Qur'an? Or *The Way of Eloquence?*"[20]

I answer: "I have read it, Haj Aqa. But my professional training is in journalism."

"Did you study in a newspaper office?"

"No Haj Aqa. I went to university."

"Why didn't you go to a mosque?"

My feet have completely frozen during the short walk through the courtyard. Door. Stair. Right turn. Door. That same room.

"Sit down until your interrogator arrives."

I sit down, facing the wall. I remove the blindfold and put on my glasses. I'm used to flossing my teeth after lunch, a long-established habit. My teeth are in desperate need of flossing. My ears are listening out for you. Sounds are coming from a distance. A telephone is ringing somewhere. There's no sound of the pigeon. The sound of shuffling approaches and moments later, I am blindfolded and facing the wall and you, Brother Hamid, are standing behind me. You hit my head with the pile of interrogation papers.

"Gobbled up your food? Lift the blindfold, useless wimp!"

I lift the blindfold. You place the papers in front of me. You have drawn thick red lines under large sections of my report. Or maybe it's the others who drew the lines, your colleagues, who also read my words with fascination and attention.

"Your handwriting is so unintelligible that we couldn't decipher it. And you call yourself educated?"

"My handwriting is bad, has always been bad."

I have not yet begun to address you by name. Later on, I get used to calling you Brother Hamid. By the way, do they still call you Brother Hamid or have you got a new name these days? Are they calling you Your Excellency, the Ambassador? Or Respected Brother Sarmadi? I have no idea.

You ask me questions about each and every word that has been underlined in red and I answer. Then you say: "Pay attention."

You are standing behind me. You must be watching me, I who am seated, blindfolded, and rubbing my feet to warm them up.

"Start with the really important information."

Your breath reeks of onion. I remember the lunch: spinach stew. You suddenly kick the back of my ankle sharply with the tip of your foot. You enjoy this. Slowly, gradually, you are getting yourself warmed up for the beating session to come. The palms of your hands must be twitching. You leave, and I pick up the papers and quickly look over what I have written. I pick up the pen and carry on.

I was attending secondary school. It was 1962, during the summer holidays. We were playing football on the dusty grounds of the neighbourhood when one of the local boys turned up, dressed in a bloodstained cloak, his clothes torn to shreds. He told us that the people downtown had rebelled against the Shah and the police had attacked them. I still vividly remember the boy's account, like the memory of a film. We gathered around him and begged him to give us all the gory details.

He was older than us and we looked up to him, so we all wanted to go with him when he offered to take us to see what was happening. He took us to a house, and we went into a large room, with a spiritual atmosphere. Clerics were leaning against the wall and one was seated in the middle of the room. Other people entered the room and kissed the hand of the one sitting in the middle. We proceeded to do that too. Years later I would realize that the cleric's name was Ayatollah Khomeini, and that he had been exiled shortly after that day.

And now, the same Ayatollah whose hand I had kissed all those years ago had become the leader of the revolution and I, his prisoner, was laboriously writing out my answers in an interrogation conducted by one of his many anonymous soldiers.

This was not my first arrest. My first arrest took place when I refused to stand up when the royal anthem[21] was being played in the cinema. A famous Buñuel film was showing. I was arrested that night but released the following day.

I was twenty-four when I was arrested for the second time. As in many parts of the world, developed and developing, Iran in the 1970s was burning with the fever of freedom struggles, of counterculture and social revolution. Two armed factions, one Marxist and the other Muslim, took to the streets, engaging the Shah's police and secret service in sporadic gun battles.

I had recently left university and gone straight to work at *Kayhan*, then one of Iran's largest circulation newspapers. Along with a small group of university friends, intellectuals, idealists, and many of my colleagues at *Kayhan*, I supported the Marxists with their dreams of social justice.

My call-up papers for national service had come not long after I had started working at the paper, and I carried on working as the weekend night-shift editor-in-chief while doing my military service. As a graduate, I served as a duty officer with the navy in the north of Iran, based in the Caspian Sea. This is a lake, but it is so large they call it a sea. Sea, rain and marshland. When the boats set off on the water, they slipped past the waterlilies before stopping beside the little wooden bars on the beach. The sharp alcohol would burn the throat; fish with garlic would be served on little, brightly decorated plates, and the dreamy night seemed to have no end. I would leave when the fishermen arrived before dawn to start preparing their boats. I was returning home, drunk, when I was arrested in the early hours of the morning and shipped off to the south of Iran. One of my leftist friends had just been arrested and had grassed on everyone else.

The preliminary court hearing, conducted by military judges, sentenced me to six months in prison. A week later, I was summoned from my cell, and taken out to the yard where I found the prisoners' families standing on one side, and the prisoners on the other; they communicated by shouting. There I saw my father, standing and holding a bag of grapes. As soon as I arrived he shouted to me: "I'll see you in Tehran in two weeks."

I tried to question him but that is all he said. He gave the grapes to the prison guard and left. Astonished, I had just returned to my cell when my name was called up again. I went to the prison office. They had arranged a second court hearing for the coming week. I was astounded. Usually, it took two or three months before one was summoned to a second hearing. When I reached the block, the other prisoners were amending our strike declaration. We had arranged to refuse food starting that evening. Our motive was that the night before, one of the prisoners had approached a very young political prisoner with the intention of raping him. After sorting the guy out, the other political prisoners demanded that the offender be removed from their block. The prison officials had refused, giving us the perfect excuse for a hunger strike. Each of us was supposed to say that he had taken the decision by himself and that his decision had nothing to do with the rest so that the police would not be able to treat the situation as a collective strike.

When evening arrived, we did exactly that. We rejected the meal, boiled eggs and potatoes. An hour later, my name was announced over the loudspeaker. I left the cell. I was met by a soldier and a bunch of Under the Eight prison guards. They asked me about the cause of the strike, and I gave them the answer we had agreed. The soldier signalled with his hand and one of the prison guards took my wrist and dragged me off. We left the block through the main door. He opened one of the "oven" cells in the courtyard and threw me in. These solitary cells were built behind the prison oven and were horribly hot. I squirmed in that terrible, hellish heat. I couldn't see any openings in the cell and I had no idea how there could be any air at all in there. I was thinking about my father's words, about the following day, my second hearing. Before long I fell into unconsciousness.

By the time the door opened and they pulled me out half alive, the sun had already set and the strike had ended. A week later, I went back to court. I was handcuffed, squatting next to the wall in the prison courtyard when an officer arrived and stood in front of me. I didn't stand up. We were not supposed to respect government officials. He asked my name, I answered. The officer squatted in front of me and said, in an authoritarian manner: "Asadi, if you dare say a single word in court, I'll fuck your sister."

I froze. Who was he? Why was he saying this? I was thinking about these questions when the soldier who was in charge of accompanying me arrived and called my name. I stood up and walked behind him into the courthouse. As usual, the court went through all the accusations and requested punishment. The defence lawyer, whom I saw there for the first and last time, said similar things but towards the end, he requested that the charge be dropped on the grounds of ignorance and youthfulness. The court's head called me up and asked: "Do you have anything to say?"

I answered: "No."

And sat down. This meant that I was confirming my defence lawyer's words. We left the courthouse. I walked outside and sat down again. A bit later, the same officer turned up. This time I stood up for him. He whispered into my ear: "You acted smart. Give my regards to Mahmud."

Mahmud is my father's name. When I returned to Tehran, I realized that my father, who used to come and visit me, had by chance happened to end up in the same train compartment as a former classmate who, in turn, had taken my father to his home one night. There, my father realized that the man was not only an army officer, but the head of the army's appeals' court. So my father told him about the incident. The following day, the officer studied the file and said: "If your son remains silent in court, I can manage to get him out."

The officer had not yet left when the soldier in charge of accompanying me reappeared. He unlocked the handcuffs and said: "You've been offered an amnesty."

I returned to prison and my fellow prisoners gathered around me joyfully. They sorted me out with a shirt and a pair of trousers. One of them gave me his only pair of jeans. Another one his short-sleeved white shirt. The money for my fare to Tehran was taken from the communal budget.

It was usual for the prisoners to line up in the block's corridor and for the person about to leave to kiss them on their cheeks one by one. Messages for the outside world had already been exchanged. When the door opened, the guys would clap and shout: "Hurray!" I left in that heightened emotional atmosphere. Most of those I left behind were released either prior to the revolution or during it. However, many of them were later rearrested and hanged by the Islamic Republic. Many others have ended up like me, in exile.

I found myself on the streets of Ahvaz just as the sun was setting. I bought a sandwich and went to the cinema. The film *Papillon* was showing. I've always remembered the final scene. Steve McQueen and Dustin Hoffman have to jump into the sea in order to escape Devil's Island where stormy waves perpetually break against the rocks.

The cowardly Dustin Hoffman stays put while Steve McQueen jumps into the sea. The film finishes with McQueen shouting at the prison guards: "Hey you bastards, I'm still here!"

I was feeling a strange emotion, triggered by the coolness of the night air mixed with romantic revolutionary fervour. I saw myself as Steve McQueen, while in fact I was Dustin Hoffman. I was already in the path of a terrifying tidal wave, rolling inexorably towards me and my homeland, but at the time, I had no idea.

Chapter 4

In the Shah's Prison with Mr Khamenei

This is my fourth letter to you. Do you remember that night? You said you were going to return in a second but you left and never came back. Later, I would come to understand that this sort of thing is part and parcel of the craft of interrogation. Prior to this, I had not understood the full meaning of the word "interrogation". During my several arrests in the Shah's time, all I was given was a slap. Compared to the way you hit me, that slap now feels like a gentle caress.

Tehran, autumn 1974

No matter how long I wait, you are not coming back. Silence occupies every corner of the room. The cold is such that even the pigeons have been forced to go into hiding. I stand up and walk towards the door, hesitantly. I knock on the door. First softly, then hard. Harder. Nothing. I wait for a while. I knock on the door again. No use. I hear the sound of footsteps. It's not the sound of slippers. I set off in the direction of the chair and sit down. I put on my blindfold. Someone opens the door: "What are you doing in here?"

"I am waiting for Brother Hamid."

"Come on, stand up. Take your papers with you."

I walk towards the door. The man grabs the sleeve of my jumper.

"Where is your room?"

"Block number two, cell number fifteen."

The light has been turned off in the cell. I realize that it's after eleven o'clock. A bowl of food has been left behind in the middle of the floor. I have two blankets. I put my jumper under my head and fall asleep. I wake up with a jump at the sound of the door opening. It's the guard. He makes me hold one end of a stick and we set off in the usual direction. Now I am seated, desperate for sleep and waiting for you, Brother Hamid. First there is the shuffling sound of slippers, then, you arrive.

"Hello."

"Hello and fuck you."

You pick up the papers. You make a new pile. "Write down the rest while I am away."

I take off the blindfold. I put on my glasses, and start writing.

I had made up my mind to focus my energies on my career and my personal life. I was still doing a double shift as the weekend night-shift editor-in-chief of *Kayhan* while completing my national service, but I was determined to get married, and to become a writer. However, destiny had chosen a different path for me.

Sonia turned up one day, out of the blue. She was tall. Bespectacled. She had a crazy way of doing her hair. Her shirt could-n't handle the pressure of her breasts and a button would often pop open. I would stare at her bra, which was always visible, and I'd see a fleeting smile on her lips. She worked on *Kayhan*'s English-language edition, but kept coming into the main editorial office. She was always looking for someone or something. There was a lot of talk about her. One day, I was eating by myself at the self-service canteen when she turned up, looking happy. She picked up her plate and walked in my direction in full view of my colleagues' heavy stares. She sat down opposite me and said: "I hope I'm not disturbing you."

I forced my eyes to look away from her bra. I didn't say a word.

She toyed with the food on her plate and then abruptly said: "You are travelling to the Emirates. Can I ask you to prepare a report for me?"

I burst out: "Your name is on the list of people banned from entering Arab countries, right?"

She lifted her head: "Does it bother you?"

"Not really, but there are lots of issues to consider ..."

"Do you want to discuss them?"

"Of course, Miss Sonia Zimmermann."

She laughed. I don't know why, but she suddenly reminded me of Angie, who I hadn't seen for many years.

I dived deep into the water. I swam with the fish and came up to the surface of the water. I said "But I don't think I can come to your home."

She said: "But I can come to yours. I know your address. At exactly ten minutes to ten tonight."

It rained that night. I was rushing to get home. I had bought a basketful of food and couldn't get the thought of spending the whole night next to those breasts out of my head. When I reached my front door, I looked at my watch. I turned round, and saw someone coming towards me. I shouted through the dark and the rain: "You're early, Sonia!"

But coming towards me were two men dressed in raincoats. And that was my third arrest.

When we reached Moshtarek Prison, the rain had stopped. They put a jacket over my head. They took away my clothes and gave me the prison uniform. I hadn't finished dressing when I heard a voice: "Is that Asadi?"

Someone must have said yes, because I suddenly received a hard slap on my ear. That was my first and last slap in Savak[22] confinement. Someone shouted loudly: "I'll take the penis of Saint Abbas's horse, double it up, and ram it straight up your mother's cunt."

That phrase was my then interrogator's favourite linguistic fallback. He was much ruder than you, but his hand was less heavy. I was immediately taken to the interrogation room on the third floor, where they removed the jacket. Back then, you were allowed to see the face of your interrogator. The blindfold came into use during your time, Brother Hamid. The interrogator placed a sheet of paper in front of me. Unlike your sheets, that paper had an official heading. It had the Iran Police Department logo at the top, and written on the first page, in coarse and untidy handwriting, was the eternal phrase: "We know everything about you."

And he said: "After the first slap, your heroic friend even told us about the colour of his aunt's panties, so you'd better watch out."

On the way to Moshtarek Prison, the thought that kept going round and round in my head was that Sonia must have grassed on me, and that was why I had been picked up. I had no idea why that would be the case, but it didn't upset me particularly. I had no real relationship with her. Now I realized that one of my work colleagues, who had worried that he was being watched and had recently given me a parcel for safekeeping, must have been the one to grass on me. During interrogations after his arrest, he had given the names of several of his Marxist and communist friends, and as a result we had all been arrested. I wrote down what had happened. I explained that I had reluctantly accepted the package out of politeness, and that it was still in my drawer, unopened. The interrogator read it and said: "This had better not be a lie."

He called for the guard: "Take him to his cell and bring in that hooker."

The guard said: "Put your jacket over your head and follow me."

I did as I was told. The guard took me with him. He opened the door to a cell and threw me in. The door closed behind me. I made myself stand up, removed the jacket from my head and put on my glasses. And I saw a man, extremely thin, bespectacled, with a long black beard. He was seated on a pile of black blankets. I realized that he was a cleric because he was wearing a cloak, which he had made out of his prison uniform. He stood up, he smiled a pleasant smile, he stretched out his hand and introduced himself: "Sayyed Ali Khamenei. Welcome!"

For the first time in my life, I found myself in close contact with a cleric. Up until then, I had only known the Sayyed from back home who had spent his days begging in the nearby Armenian fort and come the mourning season, would go up the minaret and make people cry with his sermons. He was always happy to receive an envelope filled with money from my father and would kiss my father's hand in return. The clerics were about a thousand light years from me. I have no idea at what point in my life the stubborn infidel had taken root in me or which ancestor I had to thank this trait for. I held out my hand and burst out: "I am a leftist. My name is ..."

My cell companion laughed a sweet laugh and invited me to sit beside him on the pile of blankets. Since then I have read the story of his life on the internet, so I know that he is exactly a decade older than me. At the time I was twenty-six and he had just turned thirty-seven years of age.

We divided the blankets between us. Usually, prisoners had no more than two blankets, one to put underneath them and one to go on top. I have no idea why so many blankets had ended up in our cell, but to Khamenei, each one of the blankets represented an unexpected treasure, though we ended up losing them almost immediately. One day, when we went to the bathroom one of the guards took away all the spare blankets.

Khamenei, always cheerful and up for a joke, had given each of the guards a nickname.

Dog Fart Number One.

Dog Fart Number Two.

The guards regarded us as political detainees, meaning we were considered dangerous but respectable. Those old guards have now been replaced by guards who work for the government under my former cellmate Ayatollah Khamenei's leadership – these guards regard us as traitors, spies and polluted untouchables. I keep asking myself: had Khamenei been in this cell, what kind of nickname would he have given these brothers?

He used to perform his ablution in the bathroom, in a very serious, solemn manner. But most of his time, and particularly around sunset, was spent standing by the window. He would recite the Qur'an quietly, he would pray, and then he would weep, sobbing loudly. He would lose himself completely in God. There was something about this type of spirituality that appealed to the heart.

Whenever I felt overwhelmed by misery, he would call to me and say: "Houshang, stand up, let's go for a stroll."

During those daily strolls we walked up and down the tiny cell to the point of exhaustion. Sometimes, the stroll took place along the great Tehran Boulevard, sometimes we set off towards Mashhad. We spent those long, cold hours conversing with each other. I talked about my childhood, my family and my work as a journalist. He mostly spoke about his family.

Khamenei told me about the adventure of meeting and falling in love with his wife. He talked about the day when, seated under a tree beside a stream, he had revealed his intention of marriage to his future wife. A large cloth had been spread on the ground, which was covered with salads and bread. A few years later, in the middle of a summer night in 1981, I was running up the stairs of his house on Iran Street to deliver an important piece of information, when I saw his wife for a second on the landing. She was dashing away, her head uncovered. It was then that I understood the meaning of their love. At the time of our imprisonment he had two sons, one called Mustafa and the other Ahmad. Very quickly, a peculiar affection developed between this naïve leftist youngster and that intelligent, pious man in that tiny cell, and it had political consequences.

Even though many years have passed since those days, and I am now locked in exile while Khamenei remains in our homeland, the successor to Ayatollah Khomeini as Iran's supreme leader, that affection has not yet left my heart. My head accepts what is being said about his role in politics, but my heart rejects the accusations.

My love for and familiarity with literature, and poetry in particular, paved the way for lengthy conversations, and I quickly realized that he had a unique mastery of contemporary literature, especially poetry. Even though I was disappointed that he was not fond of Farrokhzad and Ahmad Shamlou, the two famous, contemporary poets of Iran, I joined him in his passionate love for Mehdi Akhavan Saless and Houshang Ebtehaj, two semi-classical poets. He also disliked Sadeq Hedayat, one of the early proponents of the Iranian novel, and I, who loved Hedayat, tried to persuade him otherwise. He wanted me to recount stories that I had read which were unknown to him, or to recite poems I knew by heart. He himself had memorized many poems.

Sometimes I'd sing the revolutionary songs that I had learned in Ahvaz prison and he would listen to them with pleasure. My fellow prisoners had come up with revolutionary words to Vigen's *Once Again Companion to Drunkards* – Vigen was the founder of modern Iranian pop music – and I would sing the song in my terrible voice and Khamenei would listen. When I sang the original song, which talked about drunkards in a bar, he laughed but asked me to stop singing it.

Occasionally I gave him lessons in journalism, and explained whatever I knew in the shape of a theory. He listened with interest and asked precise questions. One of the things I taught him was: "Do not pay attention to the headlines. Look at the main content, search for those words that are repeated, though in various ways. Read between the lines."

He listened carefully, learning how to interpret newspaper content. He was very attached to smoking. Each prisoner was allocated one cigarette per day. I was a non-smoker so I gave him my share. He would carefully divide the two cigarettes into six sections and light up each section with great pleasure.

Sometimes we exchanged jokes. He liked inoffensive jokes; they made him burst out laughing. One time, Dog Fart Number Two overheard us laughing. He rushed into the cell and slapped us both. But Khamenei didn't like even slightly dirty jokes, sexuality being the frontier that divided innocent jokes from dirty ones.

I also told him the story of my first love: the night on the rooftop when I watched Angie swim with the fish.

Khamenei laughed loudly.

"Stop, what was the girl's religion?"

"What do you mean?"

Khamenei shook his head. He said: "But you are a Muslim. I can see God in your heart. Even when you talk about atheism, your breath smells of God."

When the time arrived for our weekly bath, the guards banged on the cell door with their fists: "Bath time!"

The door opened and fresh shirts and trousers were thrown into the cell. We picked them up, never knowing if they would fit us, and got ourselves ready. That meant standing behind the door and throwing our prison shirt over our heads and leaving the cell as soon as the door opened. The people who shared a cell were not supposed to lose sight of each other. So we placed our hands on each other's shoulders, formed a line, and were led to the bathroom enclosure. We were separated cell by cell. We would stand in front of a black curtain that enclosed the shower area and as soon as the guard shouted go, we would run into the shower. We had two minutes to take off our clothes and get under the shower. There was no shower-head, so the water gushed out as if from a hosepipe. A piece of coarse soap made in Qazvin would be placed in the middle of the shower floor. We were supposed to pick it up and wash ourselves and our underwear with it and as soon as we heard the guard's signal, run out of the shower and get dressed again. Any dawdling would be punished with a whipping on bare flesh or a blast of freezing water straight into one's face.

The two minutes were allocated to solitary confinement cells, but in reality it didn't make any difference whether you were alone or four of you shared a cell. Prisoners were expected to manage whatever time was allocated to them. We were supposed to undress quickly, nip in and out in no time, get dressed and dash back out. There was no time or inclination to look at others.

But the situation was more complicated with my new cellmate. They made us run almost all the way to the showers. We stood in front of the black curtain. We ran when the guards shouted. I undressed quickly, and went under the shower. I picked up the soap and rapidly rubbed my head with it and when I passed it on to Khamenei, I saw that he was showering, dressed in his underpants. Then our time was up. We ran out of the shower; got dressed and returned. When we reached the cell, I saw that my cell companion's trousers were wet. I turned to face the wall so he could undress. But he had no trousers left. Forced by necessity, he wrapped himself up in a blanket. I kept joking, and while drying myself with my prison shirt, I kept repeating: "Hey, I am not looking. Seriously ..."

The following week, the incident was repeated and this time round, we were given even less time. We both returned to our cell, having barely managed to wash ourselves, Khamenei still dripping in his wet underwear. My cellmate insisted that it was a sin for a man to see the private parts of another man. Having showered many times in male-only bathrooms with fellow footballers or prison inmates without thinking twice about it, I used to tease him. I finally joked: "Sir. It's not like it's a special gift, all wrapped up, that one isn't supposed to open. After all, I myself possess a specimen – a superior specimen."

Eventually the predicament was resolved with me promising to turn my back to him as soon as we entered the shower and for us not to look at each other until we were fully dressed. The following time, we did just that but for a second, when I turned to hand him the soap I saw that for the first time Khamenei had taken off his underwear. He quickly covered his private parts with his hand, using the free hand to wash his hair. I didn't know whether to laugh or to carry on washing myself.

When I look back at that scene, which took place several decades ago, I realize that behind what I saw as a joke, a subject of youthful mockery, lay two separate worldviews, two separate cultures. Two separate worlds that an oppressive regime had brought together under the same roof. Apparently, of the two worlds, one was supposed to leave and the other to stay. One world was to return home, the other to be sent into exile. Maybe if someone from my world was in power, many in my cellmate's world would have ended up in exile. I am glad that my world failed to come to power, so that the lovers were not transformed into torturers. I know that until the two worlds find some sort of compromise, my life is not going to change.

A month passed in this manner inside the tiny cell intended for solitary confinement, where the two of us were kept. Khamenei was called up for interrogation once or twice and I too was called up once more. The questions, written in illegible handwriting on a piece of paper, were a repetition of the ones I had been asked on my arrest. They focused on my earlier arrest in Ahvaz, and the way my father had handled the court procedures. And I wrote down the beliefs that I used to hold in those days and mixed them with the scenario dictated to me by Rahman. I wrote: "I have lost interest in politics. I just want to get on with my life."

I was in a constant state of anxiety that they might ask me to cooperate with them. I was prepared to refuse, no matter what the consequences. At that time I still had no idea what it meant to find oneself caught in a trap set by a security agency.

One night, around midnight, the cell door opened and someone was thrown in. He was a slight teenager, with badly beaten feet. We sorted out a corner for him. We kept asking him questions but he wouldn't reply. He just kept crying. We stayed up the whole night and asked the first guard that took us to the bathroom for help. The guard ignored us. We dragged the teenager to the bathroom and brought him back. We kept banging on the cell door, requesting a guard, but nothing happened until the evening. Eventually, a guard turned up and opened the door. Khamenei said: "This boy is dying!"

The guard glanced down at the youngster and said: "So what?" and left. I don't remember how much time passed before they finally came back, to take him away and then return him with bandaged feet. Later, when he started to say a word or two, we found out that his name was Sasan and that he had been a supporter of a guerrilla group called Fedayeen-e Khalq, a Marxist guerrilla organization. He had been beaten severely and had suffered a nervous breakdown. He couldn't speak, couldn't sleep and worst of all, he couldn't eat. We began to try out different ways of getting food into his body. We finally figured out that he reacted to the threat of physical violence, jolting back to himself momentarily and allowing his otherwise perpetually sealed teeth to open a bit. Once we discovered this solution, when the food arrived I would play the role of the interrogator while Khamenei dipped his hand into the bowl, pulling out small pieces of meat. The food was always a piece of meat, always served in a metal bowl filled with water, and we were forced to eat with our hands.

I would threaten Sasan with physical violence and as soon as his mouth opened a bit, Khamenei would pop the meat into his mouth. That is how we kept him alive. I recently traced Sasan, who is now living in exile in Germany.

Another night, the cell door opened around midnight and this time a tall young man was thrown into the cell. He had been arrested in a town near Tehran when he had turned up in the main square carrying a bag of explosives, intending to blow up the Shah's statue. He had already been interrogated on his arrest and had been transferred to Tehran for further questioning. He was convinced he was going to be hanged. When he noticed Khamenei, his manners became very respectful. We soon knew everything about him. His name was Ali Husseini, and years later, while in exile, I was to see a photograph of him with some reformists during the sixth parliamentary elections. The court of the Islamic Republic had summoned him on charges of opposition to the administration. The tall eighteen-year-old that I had met in 1975 had, by 2002, turned into a bald man, who spoke with sorrow about his memories of imprisonment, and about his release following the revolution. He had immediately signed up to fight in the war with Iraq, where he had been captured and spent a few years in an Iraqi prison. Now he was talking of "reform" and of "soft revolution", but that wintry night long ago, he had one answer to every single question I posed: "Revolution means bang, bang!"

And he would hold an imaginary pistol in his hand. We would laugh, Khamenei laughing harder than the rest of us. We were now four people in a solitary confinement cell. There was just enough space to allow us, the two leftists and the two religious people, to squat around the food bowl or to sleep side by side. Today the four of us are on opposing sides, but I sometimes wish I was back in that cold winter of 1975 and we were still together.

First they took Ali away, and then Sasan. Both were given jail sentences and were still in prison when the revolution began and they were freed. Once again, Khamenei and I were left alone together. Just like before, we went for walks around the cell and talked about the past. We spent the long, freezing winter nights shivering under thin blankets. We heard the never-ending sound of crying and moaning from the corridor. Days turned into weeks and we always ended up laughing under the shower, with me repeating my joke: "I can boast a superior specimen."

And we would return to our cell. My cellmate occasionally talked about an Islamic project without mentioning any specific names or plans. I would listen to him and quickly change the topic with a joke. In my intellectually oversimplified world, there was no room for religion.

Three months, more or less, had passed; three months that had more depth than three years. Never again was I to become so attached to someone in such a short time or to become as close to someone else. One day, the door opened and the guard called out my name: "Pick up your blanket and get ready."

This meant that I was being allocated to a different cell. We had often discussed how and where we might meet on our release. We embraced each other and wept. I felt that my cellmate was shaking. I assumed that it was the winter cold that was making him shiver so I took off my jumper and insisted he should take it. He refused. I don't know what made me say: "I think I am going to be released."

He took the jumper and put it on. We embraced each other. I felt the warm tears that were running down his face and his voice, still ringing in my ears, said: "Under an Islamic government, not a single tear would be shed by the innocent."

The guard said: "Come on, get out."

I placed my jacket over my head and walked out. We walked down the corridor and up the stairs. I was telling myself: "I am going to be released."

I saw Khamenei again two years later when Rahman and I made a trip to the east of Iran on a story assignment. Together we went to Khamenei's house. Khamenei was waiting for us in a sparsely decorated room. We hugged and kissed each other on the cheeks and reminisced a little about our time in prison, and I introduced Rahman. The conversation turned to politics and went on for three hours. Rahman and Khamenei debated while I listened to them. Rahman was his usual self, assertive but speaking softly and repeatedly flicking his hair. Khamenei spoke firmly and kept smiling. Tea was served.

When the debate ended, we stood up to say goodbye. Just as we were about to leave Khamenei put his hand on my arm and asked me to stay behind. Once Rahman had left, he asked me: "This friend of yours, who is he?"

I said: "The deputy editor-in-chief of *Kayhan*. He is a close friend."

He pressed my arm and asked again: "I really would like to know who he is."

I repeated my answer. Khamenei laughed and with his arm through mine, he walked me to the door. He said quietly: "He is one of the communists' most important leaders."

We shook hands and bid each other a lengthy farewell. I took Khamenei's phone number. He waved to me and shut the door with a smile. We were walking out of the drive into the main road when Rahman asked me: "This friend of yours, who is he?"

I said: "He's a cleric, of course. We were in prison together."

Rahman said: "He is one of the most important leaders supporting Ayatollah Khomeini."

These two men of politics had summed each other up very astutely.

Chapter 5

Playing "Full or Empty" with Mehdi Karroubi

Greetings, Brother Hamid. As I write, Sheikh Mehdi Karroubi is courageously standing up to the oppressive regime for which you have been both torturer and ambassador. When he ran for the presidency in 2009, you were probably in charge of security for the administration. But you probably weren't even born when we used to play Full or Empty[23] with Mehdi Karroubi[24] in a prison cell during the Shah's regime. This is a very straightforward children's game. Sheikh Mehdi, who, to be fair to him, was a kind man, never managed to learn how to play it. But later, he proved that he was a master of the political games, and now he's leading one of the main opposition parties in the country.

You are now reading my fifth letter, Brother Hamid. That day, when you took me out of the cell and straight into the room downstairs and with absolutely no warning launched into administering a "punishment", gave you such pleasure. And just think how much more pleasure it'll give you later on, in the afterlife, when in return for doing your religious duty you will be rewarded with a thousand houris[25] and dare I say, a thousand male slaves.

I am in the room upstairs at the moment. I am lifting my blindfold and putting on my glasses. My feet are hurting. I look at them; they are only slightly swollen, but they're excruciatingly painful. There are a few spots that have turned red and are throbbing, like a red light that keeps going on and off. Two of the spots are on my calf, one on the medial cuneiform bone of the foot. Even now, on this cold summer morning in Paris, when I recall those days, the three spots begin to throb again. The paper is on the table, and I carry on writing.

Tehran, April 1975

We left the tiny cell where I had been locked up with Khamenei, and walked down the corridor, up the stairs, and through Under the Eight. We went through the door and immediately, another door opened. Cell number nine, block number five. They threw me in. I removed my jacket from my head. A number of people were standing around in a spacious cell, looking at me. We shook hands and sat down. An hour later, we had already become acquainted with each other. To begin with, there were seven of us.

Sheikh Karroubi, now a key figure in the Islamic Republic, had the same personality then that he has now. Sometimes it seems to me that he hasn't changed a bit. Hot tempered and outspoken, but very straightforward and incredibly kind. He had been prescribed a small bottle of milk every day because of his stomach ulcer. Initially, he would insist everyone took a sip of the milk before he gulped it down. "Everyone" even included the leftist inmates.

Karroubi spoke in a very simple way, typical of rural Iran, and said that this was not the real Islam. One had to look to Mr Khomeini in order to understand true Islam. Everyone called him Mr Khomeini in those days; it wasn't until much later that he gained the title of Imam. Karroubi spoke with such passion that his mouth started foaming. He said that Islam was capable of creating the true Plato's Republic. Recently, he has said in interviews that when he was young, he wanted to recreate Plato's Republic. Everyone would be free in that republic. Islamic scholars would debate with representatives of other worldviews. Moshtarek prison would be destroyed and its ruins turned into a park.

The atmosphere in the cell changed with the arrival of a man who was clearly a mole. We avoided all talk of politics. We divided into two groups to play a game called Full or Empty. I was the leader of the Tehran group and Ahmad, "the likeable rascal", to quote his own words, was the leader of the Isfahan group. We would change the team members for each round of the game and no one would go for Karroubi. We had figured out after a few rounds that he was incapable of learning the rules of the game. Together or separately, Ahmad and I had explained them to him many times: "You are not supposed to open the hand that the stone is hidden in until the leader of the rival team touches that hand and says, 'give me the stone'."

Karroubi would nod that he understood. But when he had the stone, if a member of the rival team asked, "Mr Karroubi, do you have the stone?" he would say, "Yes, I do have it," and would immediately open his hand to reveal it. If he didn't have it he would say: "No, they haven't given me the stone."

Initially, this situation made us laugh so loudly that the guards had to register their objection by banging on the door. But soon the situation created a problem, because it kept interrupting the game. Ahmad and I decided not to give Mr Karroubi another chance; we made him *persona non grata* in the game and wouldn't give him the stone. But this created a new problem for now Mr Karroubi would open his hand for the other team and say: "They haven't given me the stone."

And so we were obliged to give him the stone yet again. Each time we spent ages explaining the rules. And he would wave his hand to signal he understood and the game would start. But again, as soon as a member of the rival team asked Mr Karroubi whether he was holding the stone, he would either open his hand or tell the truth, and the game would come to an abrupt end.

On bathing days, they would divide us between two showers. We would do a quick solitary confinement-style wash and return. Sheikh Karroubi did not share Khamenei's sensitivities. He felt comfortable with us.

One time, on returning from the shower, I felt my body itching. I took off my shirt. My armpits were full of tiny creatures. I showed them to Mr Karroubi. He picked one up, squeezed it with his fingers and said: "Lice."

The rest of the men searched through their clothes and it became clear that the clean clothes that had just been handed out were infested with lice. We reported this to the guards in charge of bringing the food; they laughed. They laughed and left.

So it became our business to kill the lice, while sitting in the sunlight that came through the cell window and listening to Iranian pop music. The police station's administrative unit was located just outside our cell and the staff used to listen to the radio; thus the prison inmates, considered a threat to national security, enjoyed music at their leisure, courtesy of the police.

When I was released, I saw Sheikh Mehdi Karroubi and the spiritual fathers of Iran's own fundamentalist Taliban on television. It turned out that the Sheikh had become a master of political games. The Sheikh and the representatives of the Islamic Coalition Party[26] had used their struggle against Marxism as the reason to be granted an amnesty by the Shah, and had consequently been released. The rest of us, who had done so well playing Full or Empty, had less luck in the real political game, and remained in custody. We were collectively released only when the revolution began. Later on, the cell's leftists met up once again in one of the prisoner's homes on Bahar Street, but political intrigues eventually destroyed the friendships that had been forged in the cells, and we scattered in different directions.

One day they came for me out of the blue. I quickly kissed and hugged my cellmates, threw my jacket over my head and left. When I reached the interrogator's office, he immediately stood up behind his desk, picked up a file and passed it to the soldier who had brought me in, saying: "Take him away."

To me, he said: "Go, get some fuck and get on with your life. That Jewish broad is quite a good one, right? Do you know that she's been to Her Majesty's office? We'd better not catch you again."

That was it. I knew that I was going to be released. He asked: "Are you going to go back to *Kayhan*?"

I said: "I have to finish my military service first. The navy is expecting me to give some answers, right?"

He laughed and said: "How much time do you have left?"

"Four months."

He laughed again and said: "You'll spend four months with the navy, but with us, you'll spend the rest of your life."

This pronouncement, with its veiled threats, made me shiver. I thought they were about to try to make me promise to cooperate with them, which I'd already decided to refuse to do. But the interrogator said: "Just tell your commander that you've been in the police station. They know what to do next."

He gestured towards the guard, who took me away. Again, I put my jacket over my head. When we walked down the stairs, I saw a girl, her legs bandaged up to her knees, dragging herself down the stairs step by step. The guard and I entered a room. They asked for my name and brought in my clothes. A few minutes later, I found myself alone on Foroughi Road. It was in the middle of the summer of 1975. The heat was incredible and passers-by were looking at me in a curious way. I thought to myself: "They realize that I have been in political confinement and have just been released."

It made me feel proud. It was only when the searing heat brought me back to my senses that I realized I was still wearing the winter clothes in which I had been arrested and was standing in a thick coat under Tehran's mid-August sun. I took it off and threw it into the gutter.

I am busy writing when the door opens and someone comes in. I hear the clump of boots so I immediately know it's not you, Brother Hamid.

"Put on the blindfold."

His voice is coarse. I put on the blindfold. He comes and grasps my sleeve. He takes me out of the room into the corridor. The papers are left on the seat of the chair.

"Go downstairs. Do you know the way? Wait by the door until your guard comes to sort you out."

"Alright."

I walk down the stairs gingerly, touching the wall with my hand. I stand outside the door. I don't know why, but I think that inside there's a white telephone and someone is talking into it. The guard arrives and hands me the tip of a stick. We walk to the courtyard. It's seriously cold. I hear a voice: "Is that him?"

Someone answers: "Yes, the man himself."

Suddenly, a slap hits my face. First, second, third and fourth. From beneath the blindfold I see the hem of a cloak. His hands are heavier than your hands, Brother Hamid. On the night of the supposed coup, he marks my face with his stamp for good. I have not yet come back to my senses. Someone is grabbing at my sleeve and dragging me along. We go through a number of doors. He pushes me down. I land on a metal bed.

"Take off your socks."

I take off my socks.

"Lie down."

I lay down on my back.

"No. Face down."

I lay on my stomach. My hands and feet are quickly tied up.

"In the name of God, the compassionate, the merciful!"

The whip descends. I yell. I am being whipped for the first time in my life. The lash bites into the soles of my feet. Thwack. Thwack. Thwack. Thwack. I am losing count of the lashes. The door opens with a jolt. The next lash descends. I hear the shuffling sound of slippers. It's you, Brother Hamid. My guardian angel. I hear your voice: "Hey! What are you doing to this poor creature of God?"

You untie my hands. You support me under my arms: "Stand up. Can you walk?"

I feel that my legs have swollen. I think they are covered in blood. "I'm bleeding."

You are laughing, Brother Hamid.

"No, Mr Hero."

You are carrying me out, slowly. We reach Under the Eight.

Face the wall.

I am standing, facing the wall.

Take off your slippers.

I do as I'm told.

Stamp your feet and count up to one thousand.

I have no idea what "stamp your feet" means. You are instructing me, Brother Hamid: "Walk on your feet and count to one thousand."

I set off. I hear your voice and you are talking: "Haj Aqa beat you by mistake. He punished you instead of somebody else. If you don't write properly, that's what's going to happen to you."

I keep walking until you come back and take me away, Brother Hamid. You have grabbed hold of my sleeve and are talking to me very gently and kindly. You whisper into my ear that you know everything. That you don't want to resort to physical punishment. Neither does Haj Aqa. This is my last chance, I should start writing. You are taking me into a wooden room. You ask me in a gentle voice: "Want some tea? Cigarettes?"

"I am not a tea-drinker and I do not smoke."

"How peculiar. You, a man of the pen, and you don't smoke and you don't drink tea!"

You are leaving, Brother Hamid.

Chapter 6

As Always There's a Woman Involved ...

I arranged to meet the British ambassador at the Naderi Cafe,[27] which is located right behind the British Embassy.

In fact, the drama began with a trip to England. And as always, there was a woman involved.

This is my sixth letter to you. You came and took me away, Brother Hamid. I saw the other prisoners, sitting outside the room downstairs. They all had their feet in bandages. Later, I will notice raw whipmarks on the feet of many of them. That morning, I had a toothache. The pain's centre was on the right side where my molars are.

Later on, I got that tooth pulled out. Years later, while writing this book, those same teeth suddenly started to ache, and I had a heart attack and collapsed in the Parisian rain, in front of the British Embassy. Inside the ambulance I was yelling in pain and it was this same tooth that was aching. The French doctors couldn't find a connection between the heart and the tooth. They kept shaking their heads and walking away. Later, when my Iranian dentist treated the tooth it would remind him of the drama of my life and he would come close to crying.

London, end of summer 1977

My tooth is aching right now. It's aching badly. I stand up and move around. I knock on the door a few times. There's no answer. Finally, someone turns up. I say: "My toothache is killing me."

"I'll make enquiries with your interrogator."

Brother Hamid, my interrogator, is not around. Maybe you are around but you are busy. I don't remember how much time passed until you arrived.

"Hello."

"What's up little lion?"

Asad means lion, hence my surname, Asadi, means lion-like. Your tone is one of kindness mixed with mockery. I answer you with my eyes closed: "I am dying of toothache."

Astonished, you ask me: "Tooth? Was it aching when you were abroad, Mr Hero? Aren't the Russians masters at treating dental problems?"

Are you hinting at my trip to the Soviet Union? I pretend I haven't noticed it. I've always had this fear of being marked with the stigma of espionage. I try not to react, but you must have seen my fingers shake.

"Can you walk?"

You make me stand up. You grab hold of my sleeve and pull it. When we reach the stone stairs, you ask gently: "Can you make it up three floors?"

I realize that we are going to the treatment room. It takes me a long time to get myself up the ancient stone stairs on my bandaged feet, but you are patient. You even chat to me. You say, have you read this book, *A Man*? You ask me, "Do you know the author, Oriana Fallaci?"[28]

I shake my head and you inform me that arresting journalists is a common tradition in all intelligence agencies around the world, particularly in the CIA and MI6. I have reproduced your speech in full through the character of the interrogator in my novel *The Cat*.

After changing the bandages on my feet, Heydari, the guard, asks as usual: "Any complaints?"

I say: "My tooth is killing me."

And I hear your voice: "This poor creature of God deserves pity. Why don't you take him to the dentist?"

Heydari hands me a tube of toothpaste: "We've got to find out when the dentist is coming. Until then, put this on your tooth whenever you feel the pain."

You take me out of the room. You tell me to keep standing, facing the wall. It's sunny and cold. I am shivering. You go back into the treatment room and it's a while before you come back out. You grab my sleeve and we return. You are mumbling a poem: "Life is beautiful, indeed, indeed."

How interesting, you have read the famous poem by Siavash Kasrai.[29]

Then you say: "That's what poetry is about. You Tudeh dogs and Savak guys, do you have a single person capable of composing such a poem?"

I exclaim: "That is a famous poem by Siavash Kasrai."

You say: "Yeah, he's in here too. I'll ask him whether you are telling the truth or not."

My heart sinks. I say to myself: "So they have arrested Siavash as well."

It appears that you are carefully monitoring every movement of my lips and hands, and my body language. You say: "No worries. We haven't brought your wife to this secret location …"

And you interrupt yourself. At Under the Eight, you hand me over to the guard: "Go, get some rest."

You hesitate. Then you say, sarcastically: "Listen, little lion, I really don't get it. I mean, you have worked so hard for this revolution."

The guard takes me back to the cell. When the door closes, I feel strangely calm. I feel like sleeping for a thousand hours. I stretch out. Exhaustion overwhelms the pain in my feet and tooth. A flare of hope warms my heart until I fall asleep. I will eventually realize that kindness is the interrogator's most dangerous weapon. When whipping is immediately followed by kindness, the prisoner willingly hands himself over to the latter. Torture is intended to break down physical resistance, but the body's defence mechanism automatically puts up resistance. Kindness, by contrast, completely disarms the victim.

My eyes have not yet closed when the door opens.

"Get up. Treatment."

He's the special officer from the treatment room.

"Put on your blindfold."

He grabs my shirtsleeve and drags me over to the middle of the corridor.

"Put your hand on the shoulder of the man in front."

The line of men starts moving. We enter the courtyard. The line moves to the symphony of slippers shuffling over melting snow and making splashing sounds. We skirt the pool, and enter a space that looks like a lane.

"Get in."

We hear the sound of a sliding door opening. One by one we climb awkwardly into a van. We sit on the floor. We are made to wait a while before the van sets off. I try to figure out where we are heading, but to no avail. All I can hear is traffic noise. Normal life is carrying on outside the van. It isn't long before we reach our destination. The guard takes us out one by one. When I get out, he says: "Take off your blindfold."

I take it off and in the glaring sunlight shining on snow-covered fir trees, I see a large garden with an open-sided pavilion in the middle. The guard takes me to a corner under the fir trees. I put on my glasses. There is a group of us and they have spaced us out so that it is impossible to hold a conversation. I study the others closely but don't recognize any of them. I can now clearly see a beautiful old courtyard. Later, I was told that the house had belonged to Dr Muhammad Mossadeq, and had been turned into the Revolutionary Guards' medical treatment centre following its confiscation. When Brother

Davoud takes away some of the people, it occurs to me that it might be easy to escape from this place. There is no one apart from us in the whole of the large courtyard. The heavy, old door on the far side opens directly onto the road and I can't see any guards. The sense of freedom makes my heart swell. It's been such a short time but I had already forgotten that outside prison there is freedom, life and the sun. I was still blissfully unaware that in the days to come I, a young man of the pen who was in love with the revolution, would be turned into a British spy and a dirty Savak agent, either of which, according to Brother Hamid, is preferable to a Tudeh dog since at least it means one is not a communist.

I'm one of the last in the group that the guard comes to collect. The beautiful old house has been turned into a fully equipped dental surgery. A number of dentists are busy working inside the spacious salon with its tall, stained-glass windows. The guard takes me to one of them. I blurt out a greeting. The young dentist gives me a look of hatred and instead of answering, he commands: "Sit down."

I sit down.

"What's up?"

I show him some broken and pain ridden teeth. He carelessly hits each one: "Which is the most painful?"

I point with my finger to the first molar on the right.

He says: "I'll pull it out."

He is chatting away, while getting the tools ready: "The likes of you should be killed. Instead they bring you here for treatment."

He means me. But how am I supposed to respond?

"Shall I administer anaesthetics to this fuck?"

I am not sure whether he's asking himself or the guard.

Against my own will, I am reminded of the film, *Marathon Man*. Someone inside me is asking: "Is this place really a dental surgery or is this part of the interrogation?"

I automatically look around me. The other dentists are busy, treating other patients. I close my eyes. I open my mouth. I have no option. I have to allow this interrogator/dentist to get on with his task. His hand remains in my mouth for a while. I feel the stinging sensation of the anaesthetic needle. A little hesitation. Then I hear the sound of a drill. Pause. I sense he's pulling out my tooth. He is using force. The root is putting up resistance. Someone is tapping my shoulder. It's the guard's voice: "Get up."

I open my eyes.

The interrogator/dentist says: "I haven't finished."

He pulls at my sleeve.

"Don't keep us waiting!"

I get off the dentist's chair. The guard drags me away. Before we leave the room he orders: "Put your blindfold on."

I put it on. He grabs hold of the hem of my shirt and sets off running, dragging me along. We reach a car. Someone gets out of the car and pushes me in. I regain my balance. I am seated between two people. One of them pushes my head down as the car speeds off.

What's happening? Where are we going?

My mind is racing, frantically trying to work it out. I assume that "Soviet friends" have kidnapped me. The piercing toothache has returned. The anaesthetic has apparently worn off. I can hear the voice of the interrogator/dentist: "Half-finished?"

The car is moving fast and I am groaning. A rough hand keeps my head pushed down, not letting me move an inch. When the car stops I hear the sound of a heavy door opening, I realize that we have returned to Moshtarek prison, the one that the interrogators kept insisting is actually Evin prison. A hand grabs me and drags me out of the car and hands me over to someone else. It's you, Brother Hamid. You have been waiting for me, running out of patience: "Useless wimp, who told you that you could leave?"

I am curling up in pain. You drag me through the wet snow. We enter the room downstairs. You throw me unceremoniously onto the bed and ask: "Which hand?"

Without giving me the chance to make use of my Islamic freedom to choose, you take my right hand and pull it up. Before I know it, I am handcuffed and hanging from the ceiling. And you, Brother Hamid, you leave the room, without a single question or explanation. After the whip, hanging is the most common form of torture, or "moral education", as you call it. This torture comes in two forms. In the first, the hands are pulled up and handcuffed together behind the back. The handcuffs are then connected to a rope that is hanging from the ceiling. The prisoner is hauled up until the tips of his toes almost touch the floor. The second option involves handcuffing the prisoner by his feet and then hanging him up. In this position, the prisoner's head hovers just millimetres above the floor. Either the tip of the head, or the toe, just about touches the floor, which remains tantalizingly out of reach, and the prisoner thinks that he'll be back on his feet as soon as he shares the information he has or the information that his interrogator asks him for.

I find myself in the first position. I am yelling and yelling. The pain from my tooth, the pain from my foot, the pain from my shoulder, they all shoot through my body in waves, spilling into my yelling. My heart is racing. I fall silent with the sound of the door opening. It is you, Brother Hamid: "I have done my ablution and been given the order for your moral instruction. Whenever you feel like talking, just bark: 'woof, woof'. In the name of Heavenly Fatimeh ..."

The lash descends. There is no sign of the recording machine. I jerk every time the whip hits my wounded feet. I recoil in pain and arch back.

"Told you you'd start barking! Spy! Savak shit!"

The lashes keep coming: "Spy! Savak agent!"

These insults hurt more than the lashes.

I yell: "I am not a spy! I am not a Savak agent!"

The lash descends and I break into pieces.

"The more resistance you put up, the more serious your secret, right?"

The lash descends and my body fragments. The pain from the soles of my feet locks with the toothache and burns my heart, which keeps racing. I don't know how much time passes until there is silence. Then you untie me, Brother Hamid. You are out of breath. The pain mixes with the pleasure of the handcuffs being removed. My shoulders have seized up.

"Shake your hands, spy!"

I can't. You, Brother Hamid, take my hands and shake them. I give out a heart-rending yell.

"Now keep walking and shake your hands and collect your thoughts. We know everything. How you became a spy. How you went to Savak."

Brother Hamid walks out and I am left alone. I hobble with difficulty and force myself to shake my hands. My whole body has turned into an uninterrupted mass of pain. A voice is echoing inside me: "Spy. Savak spy."

I feel like crying. The sob is stuck in my throat. I have no voice left for crying. I hear the sound of the door opening. Even if I was wearing a watch, I wouldn't have any idea how much time has passed. Under the blindfold, it's always night and time becomes meaningless. Five minutes might feel like five years or vice versa. My hands are brought together. The handcuffs are locked, accompanied by the sound of death.

"If you feel like talking, you have to bark first: 'woof, woof'."

And I am hanging. I gather up the last bit of energy left in me: "Just kill me and get it over with. I am not a spy or a Savak agent. The spies are those who are doing this to me."

"Woohoo! Listen to the bride's mother, how she's talking! Hey, don't worry about us killing you. We'll sort you out in no time."

You say these words and then leave, Brother Hamid. I have no option but to yell. But I have no energy left to yell. It's as if I have spilled all my life's energy into that one sentence. Like those cancer sufferers who suddenly rediscover their energy just before dying.

They sit up. They hold a lively conversation for a few minutes. And then they die. I am also dying but I'm not aware of it. I am killing myself a little bit more and at your hands, and I am not aware of it. The time is passing or not passing. I have no idea. I am yelling or not yelling. I don't know. I don't know anything. I hear the sound of the door opening. From far away. Very far away. I want to reach my blindfold with my hands and put it on. But my hands are tied up. I hear your voice, Brother Hamid: "You are only pretending to have fainted."

I can't believe it is me who is saying: "Woof, woof."

You are laughing: "What's up?"

"Woof, woof."

"You are late, little lion."

"I am a spy …"

"Well done! Whose spy are you?"

"A Soviet spy …"

You laugh in mockery: "That's obvious. The Tudeh party is entirely composed of Russian spies. But who are you spying for?"

I say it again: "A Soviet spy."

"You are not getting it. A Savak agent cannot be a Soviet spy. Now get to the heart of the matter", you say …

… and you leave.

Yes, Brother Hamid, you have left and I am yelling. I yell for as long as I can breathe. You come in every now and then, lower me to the ground, and force me to move my hands and feet. The blood rushing back into my fingers and toes brings new agonies. You tie me up again and leave. Without a sound. You don't even say a word. All I get is the smell of onions. What perfume, what spirituality you are displaying. Your words are spinning round and round in my head. The pain reaches a climax and floods my brain. Deep inside me a silent struggle is taking place between life and death. Somebody is saying: "Spare me and I'll talk. I can't bear it anymore."

Someone else answers: "No. Never accept his filthy accusations."

Whoever wins this battle between the handcuffs and the bones and flesh, whoever wins this unequal struggle between suffering and soul, is the one who'll decide the prisoner's fate. I remember the comment that the Athens police chief made to Oriana Fallaci during an interview: "Only one in a million can withstand torture."

Everyone would like to be the one. I am vacillating between being the one and the rest. I am hanging from a ceiling in the cellar of Moshtarek prison, my body swinging back and forth. The one who wants to be released is going to find the answer. He is analysing Brother Hamid's words: "You are a spy. But not a Soviet spy ... Therefore you must be a 'Western' spy."

The one who's putting up resistance protests, driven by righteous anger: "No! No! All my life I have hated the CIA and MI6. I despise the West and I hate the thought of spying for anyone ..."

The one who's intent on getting himself released, whispers: "So, it's a lie ... But there's no harm in it for anyone. When you get to court, you'll simply admit that you lied."

The battle carries on, back and forth, at the heart of my inner struggle.

"This kind of confession can get you hanged."

"Never mind. The main issue is not to talk about the Party."

The door opens at that exact moment and you come in. It's as if you have been following on a monitor the inner battle between my two selves. I am still able to identify the shuffling of your feet amid a thousand similar sounds. A thousand years pass until you reach me. The final decision is taken by a part of me that I have only just begun to get in touch with in my frenzied inner battle.

"Brother Hamid ..."

"You have forgotten, little lion. You have forgotten to bark."

The part of me that has won obeys: "Woof, woof ..."

You are laughing and are untying me. You are placing me on the bed. You are removing the handcuffs, taking them off my body. This "handcuff kindness" has a far greater effect than the violence. As a prisoner, you are ready to give your whole being in return for having the handcuffs removed, not to experience the agony of being strung up, not to hear the sound of the metal lock clicking into place.

I blurt out a question: "What am I supposed to say?"

You explode in such anger that you slap me on my ear. The slap is even harder than the one on the first night.

"You are asking me? Try answering it yourself. We know everything. We want you, in your own words, to talk about the espionage!"

"I've already told you that I am a Soviet spy."

"Shut up, useless wimp. This place is full of Soviet spies. They have started singing like nightingales. It only took one slap. Kianuri has already filled four hundred pages."

"You can ask him about me as well."

You laugh out aloud.

"Don't try to teach us our job. Keep your expertise to yourself. Comrade Kia is equally interested in finding out which embassy you have been supplying with information about the Party."

Then you drag me to my feet. You haul me up into the air again, and leave. I am spinning helplessly, and yelling. When I come back to my senses, I find myself back in my cell, with my hands tied behind my back. They've even inserted a line into my arm for some sort of liquid. The door is open. The guard, a shepherd who's sitting in the doorway, looks over at me and says gently: "What have you done for them to treat you like this? Why do you refuse to confess?"

I am feeling a terrible urge to urinate. I am about to explode. I say: "Bathroom …"

He shakes his head with regret: "We are not allowed. Your interrogator has to be present."

He departs, leaving the door open. A sharp pain is moving up and down my legs, shooting up to the roots of my teeth. My shoulders feel like they will break under the strain of the handcuffs and the pressure on my bladder is driving me insane. Bladder pain is different from other types of pain. It's yellow. I feel the urine move up and circulate in my veins in place of my blood. I decide to release myself. Reason tells me that as long as I am dressed, that's just not going to be possible for me. It's a lifelong habit. I brush my back against the floor. I put the foot with the thinner bandage into the other trouser leg and try to pull down my trousers. I am all ears for the door, for the shuffling sound of slippers. With great difficulty, I pull my trousers down a little. I try to relieve myself. It's not working. It's burning but not working. I increase the pressure, the pain moves to my shoulders and my teeth. I apply pressure again. There is no relief. My mind is telling me that it's not possible to relieve myself, lying on the floor like this. The blanket will get wet and it will stink. Ah, human habits. The sickness that is called hygiene. My eyes fall on the food bowl on the floor. Stale noodle soup. So it must be night. Eternity, where are you? I have no idea. I push myself towards the bowl. I place my hips over the bowl, with difficulty. My hands, tied behind my back, cannot bear my weight. I try to focus. I apply pressure and imagine the sound of trickling water. I find myself in the same predicament twenty-five years later, in exile, after a heart operation. Doctors have a curious term for what we might simply call urinary retention – *ischuria*. In my case the result of extensive damage to my nervous system.

And suddenly, it's as if I have been given the universe. It starts dribbling and then flows. No, it has just begun to trickle when the guard rushes in and then I hear your voice: "Useless wimp. God help you ..."

A hand grabs hold of my handcuffs and drags me up. Before I know it, my head is inside the soup mixed with urine. You shove my head back in a few times and then pull it out. Then you drag me along behind you. It must be the guard who is pulling up my trousers in the middle of the corridor. We cross the courtyard. We are not returning to the room downstairs. You are dragging me up the stairs.

I haven't been able to stop myself along the way. When you throw me onto the chair, I realize that I am wet. You stand behind me. You pull up my blindfold. There's something on the arm of the chair. I can't see it. You say: "Glasses."

You unlock my handcuffs. Pain mixes with pleasure. I try to clean my face on my sleeve. I take out my glasses and put them on. I hear your voice: "We know everything. I will return in exactly ten minutes."

And you leave.

I look at the photographs. In 1977, the British government had invited a delegation of Iranian journalists to England. British artists were participating in an international festival, and the government had arranged to brief Iranian journalists in a face-to-face meeting.

One day, we were all invited to a lunch hosted by the British Culture Ministry in a beautiful pavilion. We talked about a wide range of subjects, including the changing political situation in Iran. The lunch was attended by British artists, journalists, staff from the ministry, and Sonia Zimmerman, "from the BBC World Service, Farsi".

She took off her sunglasses, looked around the table, and almost imperceptibly raised one eyebrow at me. I stared at her soft brown eyes, shocked into silence. The last time I had seen her was just before my arrest, three years ago. She stood up before lunch had finished, gave a slight bow to everyone, and left.

After lunch, we all started joking. The Intelligence Service had set this up, right?

Curious about her, I telephoned the Farsi desk of the BBC World Service and asked for her. A voice said: "She's not here. Can I take a message?"

"Yes. Will you please ask her to call me back?"

I gave my hotel number, but I didn't hear from her.

And now, the photographs are here. On the arm of the chair in the interrogation room. The photographs that had been taken with the press guys, which I have kept to this day. I didn't have a picture of the table we all sat round, but you did, Brother Hamid. Where had it come from? Then and now, I have no answer.

There was also a picture of us entering the BBC building. Then a photograph inside Buckingham Palace with our young British guide.

What the pictures were telling me was that I had to confess to something. Just at that moment, the sound of shuffling slippers approached and you arrived, Brother Hamid.

"Right. Have you made up your mind?"

I said: "Yes. Yes."

You said: "Have you forgotten? Woof, woof."

I said: "Woof, woof."

You said: "Don't talk. Write."

You put the sheaf of papers and the biro on the arm of the chair. The paper was spotlessly white, but within a few minutes it had turned into one of the foulest documents in history. My hands were swollen so I couldn't hold the biro properly, with my thumb and two fingers. With difficulty I rearranged the biro, gripping it in my fist, and in an illegible handwriting that sprawled across the pages, I wrote: "I am a spy for the British."

You picked up the paper. No, you lapped it up. You asked: "With whom did you arrange meetings in Tehran?"

My head was spinning with dizziness. What kind of British people could I have arranged a meeting with? I blurted out, against my will: "The British ambassador."

"Where did you meet?"

This one was tougher than the first. I recalled the streets around the British winter residence in the centre of Tehran, and again I blurted out recklessly: "Naderi Cafe."

From behind the chair, you hit my head hard with the pile of papers.

"You are a much more seasoned agent than we had anticipated."

Chapter 7

How I became a Spy
for MI6

I now understand why you were so keen on foreign embassies. When I had my heart attack, I was near the British Embassy in Paris. I was on my way to the embassy to get a visa. I dragged myself forward, passing Madeleine Church, and then collapsed in front of the British Embassy. I couldn't stop myself from laughing. If I'd had my file with me, I could have shown it to the British Embassy staff so they would realize that I had been their "spy" from some time way back before the glorious Islamic revolution. Maybe, knowing that, they wouldn't have made me wait three years for my visa.

And this letter is about how I turned into a spy under the onslaught of your lashes. It's about a group of young journalists pictured laughing in a photograph. And I have been singled out to be the spy.

My seventh letter to you, dear, lovely Brother Hamid, is full of love and heartfelt emotions. Do you remember? The day I became a British spy was wintry and romantic. Even the pigeons were cooing happily. We were on our way back from the treatment room when you started going on about poor Oriana Fallaci once again. This time you were talking about her love for a Greek guerrilla fighter. You didn't even know his name. You had modified the love story of Alexandros Panagoulis and Oriana to suit your own purpose. You said that Oriana had been ordered to fall in love with him by the CIA. You were saying that true love is not like that. It's about purity and kindness from the beginning to the end.

London, early autumn 1977

It's a rare day of love mixed with interrogation. You ask me out of the blue: "Have you ever really fallen in love, Houshang?"

For the first time, you call me by my first name. Up until now I have been "useless wimp" or "little lion". I have just finished writing, "voluntarily", that I am a spy.

Fear is making me shiver in the wintry cold. This question hints at my wife. I am sure that you would like to leave the world of espionage and make enquiries about the people in my life. I prefer to be silent. As if reading my thoughts, you say: "By the way, good news. We have not brought in your wife. If you carry on being reasonable, there will be no need to bring her in. What would happen to her poor mother, right?"

You are telling me between the lines that you already know everything. Then you ask: "Your marriage wasn't an arranged one, was it?"[30]

I answer: "No. My wife rejected me for years but, unfortunately, she said yes a year after the revolution."

"Why unfortunately? Didn't you two love each other?"

"Of course. But I am leaving and she will have to remain all by herself."

"Leaving? Nah, not that quickly. To start with, the cells in here are full of spies and putchists. Do you want me to give you a tour?"

We pass the courtyard. You make me stand in the sun. A telephone is ringing in the distance. I can feel the sounds and warmth of life. You ask me: "Were you in love with someone else before you met your wife? Did you have a relationship with someone else?"

The questions have a sour taste. I am worried that I will also be expected to confess to sexual perversions.

I say: "I had normal friendships with people at university, but not the kind you are referring to. When I was very young, I was in love with my cousin but she got married."

"What about the people at *Kayhan*?"

"Nothing. Only my wife."

We walk up the stairs. Enter the room. You leave and return immediately. You put something on the table.

"Pull up your blindfold."[66]

I pull it up. There is a recording device in front of me.

"Listen to some songs while I am away."

And you leave. I put on my glasses. Astonished, I switch on the recording device. Initially there's radio noise and then the BBC's evening programme is announced and I hear the familiar voice of a woman. Yes. That's Sonia's voice.

And at exactly that moment you enter, as if you have been standing right behind me the whole time. You pick up the tape recorder and take me to the room downstairs. You put me on the bed. An ominous voice rises from the device and I don't know whether this is a mistake or something that has been done intentionally: "Karbala, Karbala ... We are on our way ..."

I am made to bark: "Woof, woof."

I bark. You laugh. You sit down beside me.

"Woof, woof, and fuck you. I want to remind you of a love story. Her brother was one of the Fedayeen[31] guys. He was arrested during a mission and later died under torture. He wasn't the first Jewish communist. Your editor-in-chief, in his capacity as a CIA agent, brought her in to *Kayhan*. The chain's links have yet to be connected. Your friendship became solid very quickly. There were even rumours that you were planning to get married. But then there was a change of plan. She moved to Her Majesty's office and then joined the BBC. And you married someone else."

You were talking about Sonia, Brother Hamid. You hand me a pile of papers.

"By the way, we might be old fashioned, yes, but we are not stupid. No spy would meet with the British ambassador at Naderi Cafe. There are quieter places. We know exactly where you were recruited."

You stand up.

"Let's see whether you can do this by the time I come back."

Once again I hear the ominous voice coming from the recording device. Loud. Coarse. It is replacing the whip. My mind starts working. Well, she is not in Iran anyway, and there is no danger threatening her. And I? Well, I am supposed to be a British spy. The first line of the script is written: "She recruited me for MI6."

When, in my messy handwriting, I confessed to being a British spy, I reassured myself that though I'd told a lie, my suffering would soon be over. I hadn't realized that I'd just walked into a real intelligence trap. It's an old saying in Iran that when the poisonous knife of the interrogator is on the prisoner's throat, the lower the head falls, the deeper the cut.

The first confession is the most important one.

Incidentally, why does one assume that the interrogator has no sensitivity for the arts, no knowledge of literature, and doesn't understand love? Does he hate humanity? Maybe he does and that's because he is made to whip you, to handcuff you, to hang you from the ceiling, and make you eat your own shit, and in so doing he wipes from your brain the meaning of love, flowers, hope – the whole world. Once, during the Shah's time, my interrogator was crying his heart out because his father had just died. He was in the same room where people were being beaten, and forced to repent, or in your words, where you break them and extract information from them. I couldn't believe that an interrogator could have a father. That he could be capable of crying. That he could have a heart. Even now, I have no idea why your talk about the arts and defending the Persian script appears revolutionary to me. But it is true. The interrogator too is a human being, with a heart. He goes to a kebab shop after torturing someone and stuffs himself with kebab and onions. He burps. When he goes home at night, he hugs his children. If he is pious and holy like you, he says "Bismillah"[32] before penetrating his wife.

I am reminded of the book *Death is my Trade*, by Robert Merle, in which the camp guard would hold a glass of red wine in his hand and stand by the window while listening to Mozart. And inhaling the smell of a thousand burning bodies that were being turned into ashes in the ovens of the Holocaust only a few metres away from him. What about you?

The first confession takes away your defence shield. You are standing naked, face to face with your interrogator, whom you can't see. The interrogator in the employment of an atheist authoritarian regime is a bureaucrat. He has no personal issues with you. He is working for an administration that has employed him. He wants information. That's all. Once you give him information, he leaves you in peace.

But the interrogator in the employment of an ideological authoritarian regime is either himself ideological or, even worse, pretends to be ideological. He views you as a personal enemy. Usually he comes from the lower classes of society and sees in you someone who has had every privilege, or he worries that you, rather than he, will take the advantage under the new government. His ideology is intensely coloured by class consciousness. So he tries to break you. To empty you of your self. To prove that his ideology is superior. You are his personal rival, political enemy and ideological nemesis. Sooner or later, he has to break you, be it before your first or your last confession. He takes more pleasure in accusing and defaming you than in killing you. But to the bureaucrat interrogator you are simply an opponent. A human opponent. Saqi,[33] a famous interrogator and torturer during the Shah's time, was pleased when a prisoner put up resistance and proved himself a worthy opponent. He belittled those who gave in and praised individuals who were steadfast.

For the Islamic regime's interrogator, who is a carbon copy of the Stalinist interrogator, the prisoner was not a human being. He was dirtier than a dog. He wouldn't touch the prisoner so as not to pollute himself. He would order you to bark "woof, woof" like a dog and then demand information.

He would keep repeating his deep attachment to religion. That he had performed his ablution. He would not drink water without God's agreement and Sharia permission. Each lash was considered a religious punishment. If he turned out to be wrong, he would have to answer in the world hereafter. He is not ready to risk his fate in the hereafter for worldly fortunes.

He is very patriotic. The likes of you are serving the enemy but he's given up his life to saving his country and to protecting the revolution from being stolen by the impure. In the religious worldview, in which everything seems to be traced back to the lower parts of the body, you are dirty and he is sacrosanct. He is pure and you are contaminated. He relies on spiritual help, you on material stuff. And such peculiarities have made him a hero and you a useless wimp, less than a fart.

And Brother Hamid, you were so showy with your heroism. Several times when you strung me up, you asked me: "Can you take it?"

What answer did I have? I who had no pretence or dream of heroism. Until a month ago, I had seen myself as your ally, because that was the Party's line. We were fighting side by side against American-led global imperialism. The "era" of capitalism was on the wane, and the sun of socialism was shining on the horizon.

I would be silent. And you, with a voice filled with pride, would say: "I can take it for forty-eight hours. The brothers, whose faith is even stronger, can go for longer."

And you were not only a hero but also a true lover. Our kind of love was fake, and was for the sake of lust.

I discovered this on those "days of kindness", which were a thousand times more dangerous than the days of whipping and hanging handcuffed from the ceiling. Those days when you would personally take me to the treatment room. You would make sure the bandages on my feet were replaced with new ones. When the guard/doctor finished his task, you would ask solicitously: "Need anything else, little lion?"

And you would pat me on my back. My endless toothache would not leave me but I was afraid to mention this. The fear of dentists had forever taken root in me. I am still frightened. Even now, when the needle filled with anaesthetic begins to pierce my gum and I close my eyes, I am all ears for the door. I fear someone might enter and take me away. Yes Brother Hamid, I'd rather be, as you say, a spoiled brat or as your guard says, a fart, than be a hero the way you are.

You return very quickly, Brother Hamid. The outline of the plot has pleased you. The doomsday scenario is being prepared. It won't put anyone in danger. It just shows that the British have influence inside the Tudeh Party. Once again you become kind, very gentle.

You make me promises.

You say that I have been a victim of the Tudeh Party. You say that I am no longer filthy and can serve my country. You tell me that the doors of Islamic compassion are open to me. You are not taking me back to my cell. You are personally accompanying me to the shower room. I can stay there as long as I want. You whisper to me that you are going to discuss my case with Mr Khamenei. You tell me that I will now be allowed to receive visitors. But you take me to the room downstairs, where I know that I will have to bark. You put me on the bed. I had assumed that we had finished, but then you say: "Collect your thoughts. This is just the beginning."

Chapter 8

Bakhtiar's *Le Monde*, Khomeini's Sandals of Despotism

There is a photograph of my wife, taken in Nouvelle le Chateau, that is exactly the kind of image Khomeini desired for Iran: a woman wrapped up in black, lost in a sea of men. When my wife returned from an interview with Khomeini in Nouvelle le Chateau, she cried and told me: "The boots of despotism are about to be replaced by the sandals of despotism."

And we journalists in Tehran were arguing with Shahpour Bakhtiar, and digging our own graves in the process.

Tehran and Nouvelle le Chateau, winter 1979

I got married in 1978. The black and white photographs of my wedding are the best evidence of your government's crimes. The majority of the people in the photographs have either been imprisoned, executed, or forced to leave their country. Rahman Hatefi, who never usually appeared in photographs, but is in one from our wedding, is one of them. A year later, our people took part in a revolution, and you stole the revolution from them, Brother Hamid.

It was winter 1979. Tehran was unusually warm and sunny. Crude political slogans were shouted openly on the streets. Iran's last king, hovering in a helicopter above the massed people, cried and asked his companions: "What have I done to deserve this?"

Prior to leaving the country, the Shah had appointed a new prime minister, Shahpour Bakhtiar, the head of The Iran National Front.[34] My wife, who was a political journalist and therefore covered the National Front, was in regular contact with Shahpour Bakhtiar, and informed us that he was intending to invite the people in charge of the press to a meeting.

When his invitation arrived, the Writers and Journalists' Syndicate debated the matter, and the syndicate's leadership agreed to send a delegation to attend the meeting to hear what he had to say. We also agreed that we would only restart the printing presses when the military men had left the newspaper offices and we had been given complete freedom of the press. Hidden behind this very specific and rigid condition was the majority view of Bakhtiar and his position. We saw him to be protecting the Shah's interests and blocking the revolution. A revolution which, ironically, would destroy everybody in that assembly of professional Iranian journalists.

The editors-in-chief of *Kayhan*, *Ayandegan* and *Etalaat*, the three largest Iranian newspapers, as well as representatives of the Writers and Journalists' Syndicate attended the meeting. The majority of them were leftists.

Bakhtiar arrived slightly later than the rest of us, he was measured and slightly angry. He confirmed he had taken up the post of prime minister. He claimed he wanted a free Iran with independent journalists. However, we didn't believe him. I asked: "Which independent newspaper would you like us to follow the example of?"

"*Le Monde.*"

Bakhtiar had studied in France, like the majority of Iranian statesmen who belonged to the first generation of post-constitutional revolution. A heated discussion took place about which category of newspaper *Le Monde* represented. Eventually, the syndicate announced its two conditions and Bakhtiar agreed to both of them and left the meeting.

I followed him and as he was about to enter a side room I blocked his path and introduced myself: "Deputy editor-in-chief of *Kayhan* and a member of the Iranian Writers' Association."

I conveyed to him a message from the Iranian Writers' Association: "If Behazin[35] is not released when you become prime minister, the Writers' Association will be your first opponent."

He said with astonishment: "I know Mr Behazin very well. Why has he been arrested?"

I snapped at him: "You must release him."

He looked me in the eye and left.

The next day, Behazin was released. From the day the military men left the newspaper offices until the morning of 11 February 1979, the day of the revolution's victory, the newspapers were independent in the truest sense of the word. I don't think there has been a time in Iran's history when newspapers have been as free as they were during those thirty-eight days. Bakhtiar lived up to his promise but he didn't take cultural differences into account – we were unable to produce an equivalent to *Le Monde*.

That night I phoned Khamenei and related the incident to him. He was worried that the press might side with Bakhtiar. When he realized what was going on, he said that he himself would support the press's decision. He would tell me his colleagues' thoughts on the matter by morning. Early the next day I woke to Mr Khamenei's phone call. He said his friends agreed with him. Mr Khomeini was also going to make an announcement the following day.

When I arrived at *Kayhan* on the morning of 6 January 1979, a crowd had filled the corridors, spilling over into the editorial rooms. I passed through the throng with difficulty. One member of staff was speaking against the reopening of newspapers. *Kayhan*'s staff and employees were listening to him. For the first time the newspaper's staff and employees were being given the opportunity to decide the paper's future and the process revealed the first differences of opinion in the editorial department. When I reached the editor-in-chief's desk, I saw Rahman, about to walk upstairs to answer questions. As soon as he saw me, he took me to one side and said: "You have arrived just in time."

While I kept half an ear open to what the speaker was saying, I told him about my conversation with Khamenei. He relaxed and said: "Go upstairs."

Rahman always stepped aside when I was there. He was not supposed to be in the middle of the battlefield, so I would act as his defence shield. I quickly stood up on the table. I could see a crowd reaching all the way down the corridor. I made a short announcement: "We are going to press today. The paper could be a red carpet, thrown at Bakhtiar's feet or a bullet, hitting his chest. We want the second option. What do you want?"

The crowd shouted unanimously: "Just that! Exactly that!"

When the voices quietened, I asked: "So you agree with the paper going to press?"

They all shouted: "Yes!"

The crowd dispersed and the editorial desk resumed work after a hiatus of sixty-one days. One of the first reports we printed was the announcement of Ayatollah Khomeini's approval of the resumption of the press. Bakhtiar's government came to power.

A few days later, my wife phoned from Paris. She was crying hard. She had just returned from an interview with the seventy-eight-year-old Khomeini. She was crying and shouting from the other end of the line: "The sandals of despotism are on their way. Do not support these people!"

I tried to calm her. She had had to put on a small headscarf for the interview with the Ayatollah. She had said to him: "It is said that the sandals of despotism are replacing the boots of despotism," and had sensed violence in the Ayatollah's answer. At the end of the interview, the Ayatollah had faced her and wagging his finger in a threatening manner, he had said: "You had better not add or delete a single word."

My wife was crying as she repeated this, and told me: "His eyes are frightening."

I calmed her down with great difficulty. She read out the interview and I wrote it down. That was the Ayatollah's first and last interview with an Iranian journalist.

My wife returned to Iran on the same plane that carried Ayatollah Khomeini home after his fourteen-year exile.[36] She was still not wearing a headscarf at that time, and throughout the flight she could sense the disapproval of the radical clerics around her. Interviewing Ayatollah Khomeini on board the airplane was banned. However, the journalist Peter Jennings managed to get close to Khomeini and asked: "Now that you are returning to Iran after so many years, how do you feel about it?"

To which the aged Ayatollah famously replied: "*Hichi. Hich ehsaasi nadaaram*" – Nothing. I feel nothing.

The Iranian TV broadcast this answer, and the footage remained the first document of a bloody revolution, the leader of which had no feelings for Iran. And now, his unknown soldiers[37] are feeling nothing but hatred for the likes of us.

You are not talking at all. You drag me along, and at the door, you hand me over to the guard. He takes me into my cell and then leaves. The light is on. What time is it? I don't know. I take off my blindfold. My teeth are aching. I am spitting blood. The door is open. The guard comes back in as soon as I sit down. I assume he had left the door open so I can go to the bathroom. I say: "Bathroom."

He says: "Come on."

I put on my blindfold again and set off. The corridor is jam packed with men sleeping on blankets. I wash my face. I try to see a reflection of myself somewhere. I wash my mouth. I enter the toilet. The guard says: "Leave the door open."

The door is open and the guard is not averting his eyes. I am embarrassed. I cannot do my business under somebody's prying eyes.

My toothache is killing me. I wash my hands with the washing-up liquid. I put on my blindfold. I tell the guard, who is taking me back to my cell: "My toothache is killing me."

"Tell your interrogator."

We reach the cell. I can no longer handle the pain. I say: "Tooth …"

"Keep your mind busy. He's about to come back. He's reading your report."

I am in my cell, alone with my pain. The guard closes the door and leaves. I take off the blindfold and am about to sit down when the door opens. The guard says: "Stand up! You have no right to sit down – or to lean. Either stand up or walk."

He closes the door. I think he's joking. I've just dropped to the floor in pain and fatigue when the door opens and a heavily booted leg gives a kick to my side.

"Didn't you hear what I said? You've got to stand up. I am watching!"

He closes the door. I know that he's watching through the tiny holes in the cardboard. He is watching me through the same holes that enabled me to see you, Brother Hamid. I can't stand up. I put my hand, the tips of my fingers, against the wall. I quickly remove them. A moment of contact with something to lean on gives me energy. A famous film comes into my mind. It's war time. Prisoners are causing havoc. The Nazis pick up the film's hero. They take him to a place within shooting range of the watchtower. They have drawn a circle on the ground. The make him stand there. They tell him, "The guard has been ordered to shoot you if you sit down or leave the circle."

That was a scene from a film. It was war. And that guy was a hero. I am not a hero. I have never been a hero. But you were like those guards, worse than them. You were worse than those guards, harsher. And that night, my situation was more or less like that of the film hero. That hero put up resistance until the morning. But I am not a hero. I am a sensitive, slender young guy and I collapse, I don't know when. It's not up to me. I hear the sound of the door. Then I feel the kick. It's less painful than the pain of standing up. It can't even begin to compare with the toothache. The guard leaves and I assume I am done. I think about sleeping. I think I am dying. Again I hear voices. It's two or three people. They are hitting me on my face. A voice says, "He has fainted." Another one is saying, "He's pretending," and a hand hits my face. Hits my teeth. I open my eyes and see two people standing over me. I later find out that they are Dr Heydari and Dr Shalchi. The second one really is a doctor and a Baluch lord. He's the doctor in charge of Moshtarek Prison. Dr Heydari is a member of the Revolutionary Guard. He's being trained by Dr Shalchi and is also Shalchi's bodyguard. One of them, who speaks with an accent (I later discover that it's Shalchi), says in a gentle voice: "What's up?"

"My teeth ... ache ... "

He opens my mouth and touches the broken tooth. My yelling reaches the sky.

Shalchi says: "Put some toothpaste on it for now."

"I don't have any."

"Give them money to buy some for you."

I don't have money. At that moment, I hear the shuffling of slippers. The doctors stand up. They leave. The guard comes, grabs me under my arms and makes me stand up. He puts on my blindfold. I put on the slippers and leave the cell. It's you, Brother Hamid, standing outside the door. You drag me along. How frightening is the cold in the courtyard. You throw me onto a chair. I say: "My tooth ... "

You say: "Shut up! Stop playing tricks, okay?"

And you leave. I take off my blindfold. I put on my glasses. A pile of white paper has been placed on the table.

Chapter 9

Khamenei-Kianuri:
Political Ping-pong

"Which day of March is it, Brother Hamid?"

Only once did I ask you, and you mocked me: "Got an appointment with the British ambassador?"

You must still be looking for me. Apparently I'm a British spy and I have made you shoot blanks. Just how clever are the British? Even now they are delaying my visa, just in case. A year ago, I had a heart attack in front of their embassy. Such kindness they showed me. They quickly made a phone call and got me to the hospital. It didn't occur to them that I might have been trained in pretending to have a heart attack.

Tehran, winter 1979

I have lost track of time and space. I am in the room upstairs, writing with great difficulty because of my seriously swollen hands. Day by day, you are becoming kinder, picking up piles of paper and leaving. You personally accompany me to the treatment room and back. You monitor Brother Heydari at his work. You are like a specialist doctor concerned with the way my foot injuries are being treated. You are my only point of reference; I have no contact with anyone else. You don't even trust the guards with me. What affection you have for me. You accompany me to the showers and the bathroom. You open the door of the room and say, mockingly: "Please come in, little lion."

I enter. I am totally broken now. I sit down on the chair, facing the wall. I wait for you to say: "Take off your blindfold."

I take it off and put on my glasses. You put a photograph in front of me. It's Rahman, stepping out of a taxi in a place covered in snow. Rahman has not been arrested!

But I heard his voice on the day of my arrest. I am stupefied. Years after his death I discover that he had been arrested and released on the same day, after a routine interrogation. They let him go so he could serve as bait.

"Who is this?"

"Rahman Hatefi."

"His alias?"

"Haidar Mehrgan."

You put other photographs of Rahman on the arm of the chair. The photographs show him in front of some doors. On different days, in different clothes. I say: "No, I don't recognize ..."

You hit me hard on the head: "Forgotten to bark?"

You put some more photographs on the arm of the chair. My heart jumps into my throat. I try not to react, so you cannot see my fear. A number of photographs had been taken inside the summer garden, near Tehran, that belonged to Rahman's wife's sister.

"Write about these photographs and write everything you know about the meetings of the 'great comrade' with Khamenei. Everything. We can check the details with both of them. You had better not misplace a word."

You leave. I lean against the chair. My world is spinning. I'm reminded of the seventh plenum. When I realize that it's about the day prior to the plenum, I get stomach cramps. Why was I not there? This annoys me. I had asked Rahman indirectly. He had said that only members of the Central Committee, advisors and top leaders participated in the plenum. I had no idea that this ranking would be to my advantage when the court came to discussing the death penalty for me. I ask myself: "How did they get hold of these pictures? Maybe they had a mole in the garden?"

Be that as it may, all I know are the names of these individuals, I have no addresses. I don't know the man who's with Rahman. I write this down. I don't even know where the garden is, I've only been there three times, once with Rahman and twice during the "danger period".

Less than a month had passed since the revolution when we were all declared counter-revolutionaries and made redundant from *Kayhan*. We were sacked towards the end of March 1979.

It was on one of those early days of redundancy that I sought out Khamenei. I wanted to see my former cellmate again. I still had no idea that he was also a member of the Revolutionary Council.[38] It was evening when I turned into the narrow lane in that old neighbourhood and knocked on the door of a decrepit building at the bottom of the lane. A guard opened the door and asked what I wanted. I said: "Is Mr Khamenei home?"

"His Excellency is not at home. You are?"

I still remember the jolt of astonishment when I heard the term "His Excellency". This was one of the early "Islamic revolution" terms, and had stuck in my mind. I introduced myself. He shut the door and left, returning with Mustafa, Khamenei's oldest son. Back in the cell Khamenei had talked so much about his son that when I met him, I felt like I had known him for years. Mustafa kissed me on my cheeks and said: "Aqa will be back late tonight."

I left, and returned to Khamenei's home at eleven that evening. This time, Mustafa himself opened the door. We walked through the old courtyard, passed the pool, and went up the stairs. On the top floor, there was a simple, sparsely furnished room with five doors and stained-glass windows. The whole room was covered in cushions and carpets and when I entered, I saw that the place was jam-packed with clerics. I started shaking their hands, starting by the door. One by one, they would respectfully rise, either fully or half, and shake my hand. The last one, who sat on a small cushion right next to the host's, was a thin cleric with a Turkman's face. Later, I found out that he was Ayatollah Sane'i.[39] He is now one of the leaders of the reformist movement, and opposed to Khamenei.

I had just sat down when Khamenei arrived home. He was holding a huge pile of folders under his arm. He headed towards me as soon as he caught sight of me. We hugged and kissed each other's cheeks. He handed the files to his son and sat down. A small black and white TV was on, showing a prison film. Khamenei faced the guests and said: "It's better than the prison we were in. Our dear Houshang is a leftist and we were cellmates."

Then dinner was served. Adas polow,[40] rice mixed with lentils, without any meat. At the time, Khamenei was still living a simple life. Khamenei invited me to sit down and eat with them. I picked up a spoon. After we had exchanged a few sentences, he asked me to visit him the next day in the office of the Islamic Republican Party.[41] I stood up to leave, Khamenei also stood up and we shook hands. I went in the direction of the first cleric, Ayatollah Sane'i, to shake hands with him but saw that he was holding his hands together and shaking his head. I realized that clerics do not shake hands with leftists. I turned to the guests, said goodbye and left.

The following evening I went to the office of the Islamic Republican Party. Khamenei was teaching a class. I waited outside the classroom until it finished. All around me were young bearded men, girls who were covered up with black chadors, and busy clerics. They were all new to me. I could see them but I still couldn't fathom what had taken place. To us the Islamic Revolution had been reduced to the Party's definition of it: these were the temporary allies of the working class.

The classroom door opened and Khamenei came out. I lit his pipe. We shook hands and went to his large office. He closed the door and sat down next to me. He asked me what I was up to. I summarized what had happened at *Kayhan*. He thought it over and said:

"We intend to set up a newspaper. The permit is under my name. Come, help the new paper."

I said: "I am a journalist and I am not disinclined to work with you …"

"Come on then."

Khamenei stood up and we set off. We walked through a long corridor and entered a room where some clerics and people dressed in civilian clothing were seated behind a large desk. They all stood up when Khamenei entered. Addressing the gathering, he said: "This is our dear Houshang. I have arranged for him to help us launch our newspaper. Back in prison, he taught me a great deal about newspapers, most importantly, how to read between the lines …"

We said our goodbyes and left the meeting. We went back to Khamenei's room and lunch was brought for us. Again it was rice with lentils but no meat.

While we were eating, Khamenei told me that the paper's name would be *The Islamic Republic* and it was supposed to be the party's mouthpiece. He was considering making me editor-in-chief. I said: "I'll think about it and I'll get back to you in one or two days."

When we were standing by the door to say our goodbyes, Khamenei said: "Take my hand. I'll get you to places you haven't dreamed of."

I gave him *The Enchanted Soul* by Roman Rolland, which we had discussed back in prison, and urged him to read it.

I left. I kept thinking about our conversation and Khamenei's offer all the way home. It was only much later that I understood what it really meant. At the time, I was only thinking of one issue: I'd be forced to live in an environment like that of the Islamic Republican Party. Grow a beard and even perform prayers. I felt like laughing and my heart prepared an answer for Khamenei. A few days later I returned, taking with me Mikhail Sholokhov's famous *Virgin Soil Upturned*. We had talked about it while we were in prison.

Khamenei was in his office this time. We embraced and greeted each other warmly, kissing each other's cheeks and then we sat down. He immediately launched into a discussion of *The Enchanted Soul*. It was clear that he had just finished reading the book. I gave him *The Virgin Soil Upturned* and asked: "When do you get time to read all these books?"

He took a long draw on his pipe and said: "When I'm being driven in my car."

Laughing, he then said: "Have you made up your mind?"

I said: "Yes. You see, I am a leftist. If I worked for your paper, I'd be lying to myself and to you."

I don't think Khamenei had anticipated this kind of answer. He drew on his pipe and stood up. I said: "But I can help you launch your newspaper."

And I did help.[42] *The Islamic Republic* was launched from the old editorial desk of the *Rastakhiz*[43] paper. I taught Khamenei's editorial team what a newspaper actually was, what its structure should be, and how to manage and run a paper. *The Islamic Republic* was finally published with Mir Hussein Mousavi as its editor-in-chief. Later, he rose to become prime minister of the Islamic Republic, but subsequently lost that position when the post was abolished in 1988. Now he is the leader of the Green Movement in Iran, and opposes Khamenei.

Early one morning, in the summer of 1979, Rahman came to my house. He asked me to go out with him, and told me that we were going to meet Comrade Kia.

We had not yet finished saying hello to each other when, with his usual forthright manner, Kianuri got straight to the point: "They have closed down the newspaper *Mardom*. I have heard you are friends with Khamenei. I want you to take the Party's letter to him."

He handed me a letter inside a sealed envelope.

I went to Khamenei's house early the next morning. We kissed each other's cheeks, and asked after one another's wellbeing and then

I handed him the letter. He opened it, and after a quick glance at it, said: "What's happened?"

I told him and he replied: "Bring me some examples of the paper's content."

I conveyed the news to Rahman who prepared a booklet of samples. He also gave me a message from Kianuri – if possible, arrange a date for a meeting.

I took the samples to Khamenei's office. At the time he was a deputy at the Ministry of Defence. I told the office director my name and sat down. A number of army men and clerics were also waiting to see him. The door opened and Khamenei stepped out. He called me into his office as soon as he saw me and closed the door behind us. He phoned his office director and said: "No meetings or calls for now."

He turned to me and said: "I am tired. Let's talk for a bit."

For an hour, we talked about this and that – poetry, recently published books, the situation. When he stood up to get ready for prayers and lunch, he asked: "Have you brought the documents?"

I gave him the booklet. He carelessly flicked through the pages and said: "I'll bring it to Aqa's attention tonight. Call me tomorrow."

I said: "Kianuri would like to meet with you."

He said: "Alone or with you?"

He then laughed, and said: "If it's with you, then it would be fine."

I delivered the message to Rahman. The next evening, I called Khamenei, and he said: "Go ahead and print the paper."

I asked: "Is there no need for an announcement or a letter?"

He replied: "If anyone pesters you, tell them to check with the Imam's office."

The paper resumed publication the next day and no one interfered.

The first meeting between Kianuri and Khamenei was one night that summer. It had been arranged for midnight. I had been ready since eleven in the evening, watching the road through a small window facing the street just in case Kianuri couldn't find the doorbell. The white willow outside the window had not yet died and was filled with noisy birds. At half past eleven a car stopped in the parking lot and Kianuri stepped out. I quickly ran downstairs and asked him in. He said: "It's late and we must set off."

I asked: "Then why did you send the driver away?"

Astonished, he said: "Why? Don't you have a car?"

I said: "Of course, but I don't know how to drive."

He became very angry. He hadn't driven for many years but he now had no choice and he kept complaining as we drove through Tehran's empty streets.

We were seated in the large reception room at exactly twelve o'clock. It didn't take long for Khamenei to appear, pipe in his mouth as usual, folders under his arm, and laughing. He greeted me by kissing my cheeks, but only gave Kianuri his hand.

We had barely sat down when Khamenei said: "Mr Kianuri, we have a very serious complaint against you."

I saw Kianuri go pale and say with a cold smile: "You must have been given incorrect information ..."

Khamenei laughed and said: "No. My complaint is that you have taken our dear Houshang from us!"

Kianuri didn't know whether this was intended as a joke or a serious rebuke and he had not yet responded when Khamenei asked: "When did you return to Iran, Doctor?"

Kianuri replied: "Early May."

Khamenei drew on his pipe and said: "So you returned a few months after the revolution."

Tea was brought in and a discussion began. Kianuri explained the Party's position and kept saying that the Party intended to support the revolution with all force. Khamenei, in turn, kept bringing up questions which made it obvious that he regarded Kianuri's words with suspicion.

Kianuri had brought a bundle of Party publications with him and kept insisting that Mr Khamenei read all of them. Khamenei kept saying: "I have read them. I have read them carefully. But back in prison I learned from Houshang to read between the lines …"

Then he brought up a few examples of content from *Mardom* about Afghanistan and the Soviet Union. He had incredible presence of mind. Kianuri defended the contents. Khamenei said: "Come on, please. You are still acting like a Soviet representative! Look here …"

Kianuri said: "The CIA and Savak tend to say that sort of thing. But why are you saying it?"

Khamenei said: "We know the past and are now observing the present from close up."

Kianuri said: "Either way, the Union of the Soviet Republics was the first government to recognize the Islamic Republic and is your ally in the struggle against the United States."

Khamenei responded: "We absolutely do not trust the Russians. I hope you do something to make us trust you …"

The discussion went on and on along these lines until Khamenei stood up to signal that the meeting was over. Kianuri said: "It would please me if I could see you regularly."

Khamenei answered: "No problem. Arrange the meetings with Houshang."

We said our goodbyes. The two of them shook hands and Khamenei and I kissed each other's cheeks. By the door Khamenei asked: "Haven't you brought a new book with you? I have finished *And Quiet Flows the Don*. Amazing the way he manages to show the plight of the people under the Soviet government."

I had never encountered this interpretation of *And Quiet Flows the Don* before. I said: "I'll bring his later books."

And we left. It was a cold, moonlit night. Kianuri was limping. He was deep in thought. He stood still in the middle of the lane and said to me: "This friend of yours is very dangerous. He's a Maoist Islamist."

I wished I knew what Khamenei had made of the meeting.

After we had driven off, Kianuri said: "I wish you had told us just how much he likes you."

Now, when I remember his sentence, I feel a shiver go down my spine. I tell myself: "It was a good job I didn't tell him. Or else they would have wanted me to infiltrate Khamenei's office and I'd have said yes on the spot." I hate that sort of business nowadays, even if it might have been advantageous for the revolution.

My wife and I were looking for work but couldn't find any. My mother-in-law was paying our living costs. I occasionally visited Khamenei at home. We discussed current affairs, literature and poetry. He read every single book I gave him and talked about them with great pleasure.

Kianuri's next meeting with Khamenei took place that autumn. As usual, I phoned and arranged the meeting date. This time, it was at eleven o'clock in the morning. On the way there Kianuri sat beside the driver, while one of Kianuri's guards and I sat in the back. When we entered Boulevard Street, the driver said: "Comrades, we are being tailed."

Kianuri said: "Don't lose them. We are on our way to Khamenei's home."

When we arrived, Mustafa greeted us and said: "Aqa has sent a message that he'll be late. Come in please."

We waited for Khamenei for over two hours. Unusually, he was tired. He kissed my cheeks and shook Kianuri's hand. As always, he was well-mannered and courteous as he warned us that he didn't have much time.

Kianuri handed Khamenei an envelope that apparently contained documents and began talking about the danger of a military coup on the part of the Shah's supporters. Khamenei listened attentively. He asked jokingly: "Have the Russians or your moles inside the army provided you with this information?"

Kianuri was jolted for a moment and gave his usual response: "The Party's supporters put information inside a box and place it by the door."

Khamenei stood up and said: "How strange ..."

And while shaking hands before leaving, he said: "I will look at these. But it would be better if you made sure this information gets to President Bani Sadr."

Kianuri said: "That has already been done."

Khamenei moved in the direction of the door and said: "Very good."

Kianuri and I walked behind him to the door. Kianuri said: "Give us a date for a longer meeting."

"Alright, Houshang can call to arrange it."

One afternoon, I think it must have been 27 December 1979, I was called to Kianuri's office. Kianuri said: "This is very urgent. You've got to find your friend, no matter what it takes and you must arrange a meeting for tonight."

I phoned Khamenei's home a number of times. Mustafa didn't know when his father would return but guessed he might be at the office of the Islamic Republican Party. I told Kianuri. He called one of his drivers and told him to take me there and back. I found Khamenei there, but he said he had absolutely no time, though when I insisted, he agreed: "Twelve o'clock and only for five minutes."

When we arrived just before midnight that night, Khamenei was home. As soon as we had exchanged greetings, he said: "I am about to go to the Revolutionary Council's extraordinary meeting. I only have five minutes."

In a few sentences, Kianuri quickly told him that the Soviet forces were planning to enter Afghanistan that night. Khamenei, who was standing, sat down as if hit by lightning. The wrinkles on his face deepened. He stood up and left the room without a word. Kianuri and I followed him, Kianuri trying to offer his interpretation of the Soviet forces moving into Afghanistan, and the threat of the USA, while Khamenei wasn't listening at all. His guards were waiting for him in the courtyard and escorted him away. We walked out into a cold wintry night. Everything had frozen, even the moon in the sky. For us it was the beginning of a freeze that would never thaw, and would profoundly change Khamenei's attitude towards us. Later, I found out that the Soviet ambassador to Iran had been in Ayatollah Khomeini's office that night and had officially informed him about the Soviet troops' invasion.

One summer night the following year, our doorbell rang. I looked out of the window. It was Rahman. He came upstairs and said: "You must get this envelope to Khamenei right now."

I looked at my watch; it was nearly four in the morning. I got dressed and Rahman drove me to Khamenei's house. He waited at the entrance to the lane while I went to knock on the door of the house. It didn't take long for a sleepy young guard to open the door. I said I wanted to see Khamenei. He told me to leave and return a few hours later. I insisted that he should wake Mustafa. He shut the door and left. It seemed ages before Mustafa came. He invited me into the inner courtyard. I said: "It's very important that I see Mr Khamenei."

He said: "He got back late and is asleep now."

I said: "Wake him up."

Mustafa went back into the house and very soon reappeared with Khamenei. He was dressed in house clothes, with a cloak hanging over his shoulders. I greeted him and handed him the envelope and said: "I have no idea what's inside but apparently it's very important."

Khamenei opened the envelope right there, by the pool, and read it. I saw that his hands were shaking. He walked over to a phone, signalling me to go away. I left the house.

Rahman said: "Once again they owe us for salvaging the revolution."

Now that I am looking at these historical incidents side by side, it seems plausible that the envelope contained intelligence about the Nojeh Coup[44] and I ask myself: "Why were we doing that sort of thing?"

And I remember Khamenei's words: "Either the Russians or your moles inside the army have provided you with this information."

A year later, early one Friday morning, I knocked on Khamenei's door. He had repeatedly told me: "Friday morning is the worst time. I will be preparing for Friday prayers and won't have time to see you."

I was very insistent and managed to see Khamenei for a few minutes to arrange a meeting. This time Kianuri's bodyguard/driver, picked me up to take me to the meeting place. We stopped to collect Kianuri from his daughter's home on the way. He was limping, and had his right hand in his pocket. I later found out that he had got himself a pistol for self-protection in the early years after the revolution.

Kianuri got in and we set off. The situation had profoundly changed since our first meeting with Khamenei. We knocked and I introduced myself. The guard appeared to expect us. He took us to the room by the door where the less important guests were received. We had just sat down when Khamenei came in and, as usual, greeted me warmly, with kisses on my cheeks. His handshake with Kianuri was very cold and as soon as he sat down, he said: "Get on with it."

Kianuri gave a thorough explanation of the pressures that the Party was under and said that his people had once again been arrested. He listed the Party's services to the Islamic Republican Party and referred to the Nojeh Coup. He talked about the Soviet situation and asked for pressure to be removed from the Party. Khamenei listened patiently and said: "We don't trust the Party. We are aware that you are acting in an organized manner and are extending your influence, and you have influence in places that you are not supposed to."

Kianuri said: "The authorities have information on all our connections."

Khamenei said: "We too are not uninformed. I'm telling you my personal opinion in a friendly manner."

Kianuri said: "Our policy towards the Islamic Republic really is 'unity and criticism'."

Khamenei answered: "On the surface, yes. I read your paper everyday, especially the bits between the lines."

The rest of the meeting was about just this. Kianuri kept insisting that both the Party and the Soviet Union were defenders of the Islamic Republic, and Khamenei regarded everything he said with suspicion. He finally said: "In my view, the newspaper's closure would be to your own advantage. If I were in your shoes, and really wanted to defend the Islamic Republic, I would stop all open and covert activity. What kind of doctorate did you say, you have?"

"Architecture."

"So why not teach at the university?"

Kianuri fell silent and the conversation appeared to have ended. Khamenei stood up and we too stood. As we were about to leave, Khamenei said: "By the way, Mr Kianuri, what's your view on Afzali?[45]"

Kianuri froze for a moment. I had noticed before that he tended to lose composure in times of danger. He collected himself: "Why?"

Khamenei laughed: "Nothing. He talks a lot against the Americans. You must like that."

Kianuri laughed out aloud and said: "Tell him to speak out against the Soviets as well to make you like him."

We laughed and left. Kianuri was deep in thought throughout the return journey. When we stopped to let him out of the car at the Forsat crossing, I noticed that he looked isolated and that his limping was more pronounced. Khamenei never agreed to another meeting with Kianuri.

The Mujahedin's[46] failed attempt on Khamenei's life happened in the summer of 1981. I sent a telegram to the hospital where he was recuperating, but I was unsuccessful in my attempts to visit him until he returned home.

The year 1981 was one of terror and hanging, the opening year of a decade of intense horror and political upheaval. The waves of terror even reached Mohammad-Ali Rajai, the then president of Iran. I went to see Khamenei early one morning in October 1981. Kianuri wanted to see him again. Khamenei had lost the function of one of his hands. He looked tired and pale. We hugged and kissed each other's cheeks and I had just sat down when his son, Mustafa, arrived and whispered something into his ear. Khamenei said: "Let them come upstairs."

A bit later, two middle-aged men came in. It was clear that they had a long-standing acquaintance with Khamenei. They shook hands warmly, sat down and looked at me. Khamenei said: "He's fine."

These two men, whom I didn't know and whose names I still don't know, looked like traditional, religious people. They had come to mediate between the Mujahedin and the government. They said that the Mujahedin were the children of the revolution and should be accepted, that there should be an end to the animosity towards the Mujahedin-e Khalq. Khamenei responded: "The Imam has stated his conditions. They must first hand in their weapons and leave the houses where they organize their activities."

This response led to a discussion that rapidly became heated. I wasn't sure whether the men were expressing their personal views or those of their organization, but they insisted on setting up a meeting without any preconditions, and clearly feared a dangerous future. Khamenei insisted that they lay down their weapons first.

The discussion lasted for an hour. For the first time I saw Khamenei speak about the Mujahedin with anger. In the past, he had regarded them kindly, although he was critical of them. Eventually he stood up and angrily, almost shouted: "They have to lay down their weapons today. Whoever is standing against the revolution must be destroyed."

The discussion was over. The two men stood up. They exchanged a cold handshake and left. I realized that it would be better for me to leave as well. I said: "Mr Kianuri really wants to meet up with you."

He shook his head, saying neither yes or no.

"Telephone me. I'll be here for days on end."

By the time I reached the city centre on the bus, it was nine in the morning. The roads in the centre of the city were blocked. I walked on foot towards Boulevard Street. At the time, the *Mardom* offices were located in a high-rise building near the northern corner of the US Embassy. When I got closer, I saw young men and women wearing red bandanas around their heads. They were running around and shouting:

"Today is the day of blood!"

"The downfall of Khomeini!"

Most of them were armed. I could see a number of Hillman cars following them. Men were aiming pistols out of the car windows, hunting them down, one by one. The north of the street was completely blocked and the sound of sporadic shooting could be heard. I don't know whether the shoot-out was the result of the failure of that early morning meeting or not. I considered how to leave the area. I chose a broad road that led east and entered it. The street was eerily empty. A bit further on I reached a side road and saw that a shoot-out was already under way between the Mujahedin and the Revolutionary Guards. I hurried on down the street. I knew I couldn't go back the way I'd come. A bit further along, when the street narrowed, I saw some young men trying to drag a wounded girl with them as they ran away. Judging by their clothing and their age, they must have been Mujaheds. At the next junction, people in civilian clothing arrived, fully armed and carrying heavy machine-guns. It was like a very dramatic scene from a war film. The people in civilian clothing spread out across the road, completely blocking it. They moved forward, clearing the road step by step. They passed me and carried on down the street. Later, when I recalled that scene, my whole body started to shake. All it needed was for one or two of them to mistake me for the enemy and I would have been finished. Fortunately I managed to reach the main road safely; however, the whole area seemed to be in flames. The sound of shooting continued uninterrupted and the roads were blocked.

My last meeting with Khamenei took place a month later, when he was already well on his way to the Presidential Palace. At that time he was bedridden. He was very ill and talked with difficulty. I realized that we could only talk very briefly and would have to stick to neutral subjects that wouldn't tax him. The door opened suddenly and a chubby young man rushed into the room looking agitated. He went to the side of the bed and whispered something into Khamenei's ear. Then he took a piece of paper out of his pocket and gave it to Khamenei, who read it carefully and gave it back to the young man, urging him not to react. The young man agreed, and left.

Khamenei smiled a lifeless smile and said: "Right, so now you have gobbled up the Fedayeen[47] as well."

I realized that the news of the alliance between the Party and the Organization of Iranian People's Fedayeen must have just been announced. I said: "Would it be so bad if they, too, were defending the revolution?"

He replied: "A structured organization with Russian support that is fully behind us and all those young people ..."

He fell silent briefly and then carried on: "You have turned dangerous, Houshang."

I said: "There are rumours that arrangements have been made to launch a communist massacre."

He was about to fall asleep again and said: "There is no need for us to launch it. Once the people understand that we won't stop them they'll tear you all apart ..."

I laughed and said: "So let's say goodbye for good."

He said: "No, we won't let them tear you apart."

We joked, but this was horror and death. I tried not to lose control of myself. I knew that the answer would be negative but I still asked: "When can you see Mr Kianuri?"

He said: "Things have changed now."

I recalled his angry argument about the Mujahedin. We shook hands and I left. The next meeting might be in hell itself. Khamenei went on to take up the post of president, while I went to prison, and then into exile. Two cellmates, one in exile, the other at home.

I delivered this final message to Kianuri. He went pale and fell silent. He must have seen that the tide had turned.

When I related the incident to Rahman, he flicked his hair and said: "This man Khamenei is very dangerous. He has made up his mind to tear the communists into pieces."

Chapter 10

I used to be Ahmadinejad's Torturer!

Hello Brother Hamid. I am about to write my tenth letter to you. You have taken away the papers relating to Khamenei to read. I am now recalling the happy, difficult days in which the idea of the revolution was still alive and well. We were euphoric that we were marching towards freedom. You were arranging for a Taliban-style government.

Political groups were still active on the streets of Iran in those days. Young boys and girls were selling newspapers at the crossroads. Distributing leaflets. A free Iran could have become a role model for the third world. And you were scrutinizing everyone. The first street operations against women had just begun. The headscarf had already become compulsory. I was preparing the ground for freedom. You were getting the prisons ready. You and the likes of Ahmadinejad stayed in the background in those days.

Tehran, spring 1979

We were unemployed and stuck at home. We had nothing to do other than work for the revolution. We could almost hear the sound of bulldozers ploughing through the entire society. The Party line was that they were sowing the seeds of socialism. We would see the chador-clad women and bearded men around us and thought to ourselves that we were fighting a common struggle *with* them. But they were walking towards the past while we looked to the future. There were times when we wanted to wake them up with the sound of bullets, but instead we tried discussions, books and newspapers. We would write and print, and they would set it on fire, and the nation's existential harvest went up in flames.

We were living in our little paradise while around us a wild inferno was raging, with new fires springing up on every corner. Frustrated by the injustices of Iranian society under the Shah, we were united by our socialist ideals. We were a bunch of enthusiastic people who assumed that the anti-imperialist, anti-oppression revolution would finally uproot imperialism and usher in socialism on the whirlwind of change. It was on one of those spring days that Rahman said: "Sooner or later the Savak list is going to turn up. You must prepare your wife, gently, gradually ..."

Rahman and I both knew that my name would be on that list. During the Shah's regime, it was important for the Tudeh Party, for its own protection, to have someone on the inside to warn them of impending acts of repression against the Party or any of its members by Savak, the Shah's secret police. One of the senior leaders of the Party had therefore asked me to infiltrate Savak so that I could monitor its activities, possibly supply disinformation on the Party, and warn Tudeh officials if Savak seemed to be on their trail. It would take a separate book to explain this fully, but suffice it to say that I had eventually managed to join Savak in an informal capacity, and was able to serve the Tudeh Party in this way, as a sort of double agent, for several years. My wife, however, knew nothing about this.

My first words on this sensitive subject created an arctic wind, making my incredulous wife freeze. She looked at me icily, growing colder by the minute, up until the announcement clarifying my role was published on the front page of *Mardom*.

Rahman, who knew the full story, did not consider it wise to interfere directly. He restricted himself to mentioning it obliquely:

"Someone has got to do the dirty jobs of the revolution. Such people are the true revolutionaries."

My wife looked at him with tearful eyes, but didn't respond. She told him that she would only be convinced when the Party made an official announcement on the subject. One night, she left our bedroom to do something, and I discovered, by chance, a large knife under her mattress. On her return, she said: "I'll kill you with this very knife if the Party fails to confirm your story."

Her delicate hands were trembling and tears ran down her cheeks. I immediately informed Rahman, not because I was afraid of death but because I feared for my wife.

He said: "What's your view?"

I said: "My wife is more important to me than myself, but as always, I leave the decision to you."

And the Party leaders came to their decision. One of them was strongly opposed to full disclosure, arguing that bringing the matter up in the present political climate would destroy my life. However, Rahman was extremely worried about my wife, Nooshabeh. Kianuri sided with Rahman and said: "If we announce the truth of this matter, it will reflect well on the Party."

I was at home at the time, and was unaware of the meeting. The telephone rang and Kianuri told me that he wanted to talk to my wife. I handed her the phone. My wife listened for a few minutes, put down the phone, and smiled.

The next day, 28 May 1979, the news was printed in a few lines in a corner of *Mardom*'s front page:

> The office of the Central Committee of Iran's Tudeh Party is announcing herewith that Houshang Asadi is a member of Iran's Tudeh Party and was instructed by the Party to infiltrate Savak via Tudeh's secret network, and in accomplishing this, he has provided a valuable service.

I took the newspaper to my wife. She read the report and the ice statue immediately thawed and she hugged me. From that moment on she saw it as her duty to look after me very carefully. She feared that people loyal to Savak might target me and tear me to pieces.

Later that day I went to a ceremony in Toopkhaneh Square.[48] A famous photographer, who was busy taking photos there, said to me: "You have exploded a bomb, Mr Asadi." He was right. While that bomb had melted my wife's iciness, its detonation had set in chain a series of events that went on to influence the rest of our lives.

I was walking past Tehran University a few days later when I noticed the *Shouts and Noises* tent. This was a well-known but controversial publication that was opposed to and violently insulted all groups that were not Hezbollah.[49] I went into the tent, and immediately saw a long poem written in large letters on a piece of cardboard. It was about me, the Party and Marxism. I was reading it and laughing to myself when a short, ugly young man appeared from behind the cardboard. He asked: "Is everything alright, brother?"

I said: "Yes. Do you know this guy?"

He said: "Yes, he was my torturer in prison."

And then he gave me a lengthy account of how I had tortured him and how every time I raised the whip, I shouted: "Death to Islam! Long live Lenin!"

I left, astounded and laughing. Years later, after he became the president of Iran, I saw a photograph of him and remembered that day.

Chapter 11

Kabul a Few Days after the Red Army's Arrival

It's a cold winter morning in exile, Brother Hamid. The coldness of exile is not only in the air. It freezes your whole body.

My wife wakes up in the middle of the night. She searches my face with worried eyes and says: "Don't write. You are killing yourself."

The symptoms of my heart condition have returned one by one. Once again I have problems with my breathing. Once again. But I must write.

The muezzin's voice told me that it was sunset when you picked up the pile of writing and took it away. I put down the biro when I heard the shuffling sound of slippers. I put on my blindfold and waited. You were laughing loudly. You hit me on my shoulder: "How are you? Written anything?"

I handed over the sheets on Afghanistan.

You said: "Stay right there 'til I come back."

Kabul, winter 1980

In the summer of 1979, we went on our first post-revolution trip abroad. My wife's mother and sister came with us. We went to Greece. A cruise ship took us to fairytale islands in the beautiful

Mediterranean Sea. We made the acquaintance of an American businessman on the boat and the conversation inevitably turned to Iran. The young man was fiercely anti the revolution and predicted an ominous future for Iran. His jaw dropped in astonishment when he heard my wife and I defend it. When he realized that my wife had studied at Oxford he exclaimed: "But why would you support it, madam? Do you want to wear a headscarf?"

My wife responded: "I would be prepared to wear a sack over my head if it ensured my country was free and independent!"

That winter, the Soviet Army entered Afghanistan, an event that shook the world. The Party took the immediate decision to send a *Mardom* reporter together with some trusted reporters from the other major Iranian newspapers to Afghanistan. Mansour Taraji, the editor-in-chief of *Ettelaat*, the second largest pre-revolution newspaper in Iran, was the only one to accept the Party's invitation. He had been a member of the Tudeh Party as a young man, but became a serious critic of the Party.

We set out for Kabul a few days later. First we went to Delhi to get visas from the Afghan Embassy. There was a long queue outside the embassy, almost entirely made up of foreign reporters. No reporters had entered Afghanistan since the Soviets' arrival, even after the dismissal and assassination of Hafizullah Amin[50] and the coming to power of the Parcham Party government led by Babrak Karmal.[51] None of the journalists ahead of us in the queue was granted a visa.

Eventually, our turn arrived. Self-assured, we introduced ourselves to the ambassador who was an intelligent-looking man. Contrary to our expectations, he didn't make a fuss, he simply glanced at his papers and said: "No."

Throughout the meeting, a tall young man had been listening to our conversation. After we left the room he came after us, and called us back. He immediately embraced me and gave me a warm kiss on my cheek. From the beginning, I'd introduced myself as a Party representative and *Mardom* reporter, while Mansour had stressed that he had nothing whatsoever to do with the Party and had come for purely journalistic reasons on behalf of *Ettelaat*. It turned out that the young man, whose name I have forgotten, was a representative of the Parcham Party and was monitoring the Khalqi ambassador who had not yet been replaced. He told us to wait, entered the ambassador's office and returned a few moments later to call us back in. It was clear that he had been having an argument with the ambassador. The young man took our passports and put them on the ambassador's desk. The ambassador stamped in the visas with a complete lack of enthusiasm. We said our goodbyes.

We had just stepped into the road when the young Afghan came running after us, and insisted on inviting us for dinner. He picked us up that night and we went to his home in a poor part of Delhi. It was a place where lanterns were used to light shops and homes, but was only half an hour away from the luxurious Ashoka Hotel, which was on a par with the best international hotels. The young Afghan's wife was, like her husband, in the Parcham Party leadership. She came in once or twice to bring us food and tea. Throughout the evening, we gathered information about the new situation in Afghanistan, information that was repeated to us time and time again from then on, like a Party announcement: "The Khalqis were agents of the West. The Soviet comrades entered the country at the request of the Party and the people of Afghanistan."

We also talked about the situation in Iran. The young Afghan seemed to be carefully repeating the Parcham Party's views, and whenever the conversation turned to Kianuri or Tabari, he spoke about them with great respect. Like all Parcham members, from ordinary rank and file through to their leadership, he was in love with the Party and worshipped Kianuri and Tabari like idols.

The next day we flew from Delhi to Kabul. Except for us and two other foreign journalists, all the passengers on the plane were Afghan. The foreign journalists, whom we knew from Tehran, happily told us that they had bribed the Afghan consul in Bombay for their visas.

They were delighted to be the first international journalists to enter Kabul.

The plane flew over snow-capped mountains and I felt as though I was flying over Iran. I remembered that until a mere hundred years ago all of this territory *had* belonged to Iran.

Large scarlet banners and Russian tanks were the most eye-catching sights on our arrival in Kabul. We were met at the airport by Assadullah Keshtmand, editor-in-chief of *The Truth of the Sawr Revolution* newspaper, who was also the prime minister's brother, the deputy culture minister, and some other Party leaders.

Again, I introduced myself as a representative of the Party and a reporter for *Mardom*, and Mansour said that he had nothing to do with the Party and that he was a reporter for *Etalaat*. This led them to hug me tightly and to kiss my cheeks and to shake hands with Mansour. We told Keshtmand about the foreign journalists. Inside the old airport hall, porters were picking up our suitcases when the loudspeaker called out the two foreign reporters' names. A few minutes later I saw them being escorted back to the plane, bags in hand, looking puzzled. They were being deported. Even now when I think about that scene, I feel ashamed. I now better understand just how deeply ideology can penetrate a person's existence.

That wintry day, Mansour Taraji and I became the first international journalists to drive along the road to Kabul since the Red Army's arrival a few days earlier. Russian tanks still lined the road on either side. We were escorted to the old Hotel Kabul, which was in the centre of the city and were told that the hotel was totally safe.

That night, Keshtmand Junior came to the hotel to have dinner with us. He had a Kalashnikov hanging over his shoulder. It became clear that the fighting took place at night. A bit later, the sound of shooting could be heard. Keshtmand had not yet finished his meal when he said that he needed to leave. I asked him to take me to the hotel's telephone desk to contact Tehran before he left. On the way, he told me that no matter what job they performed in the daytime, the Party's leadership took up weapons at night and fought against counter-revolutionaries on the streets. That same instant, the sound of shooting became louder and the lights suddenly went out. Keshtmand grabbed me and threw me onto the floor and we lay in that position until the lights came back on. We went to the telephone desk together. Keshtmand introduced me to the young man in charge. Like his fellow Afghan Party members, he gave me a tight embrace and kissed me on my cheeks. I said: "I want to contact Iran."

He fiddled with the telephone and told me: "It's not working. You must wait for an hour."

I gave him the number and said: "Alright, I'll come back in an hour."

Keshtmand was leaving to do his nightly patrol duties but refused to let me accompany him. He said: "It's dangerous, the counter-revolutionaries come out of their holes at night."

We were going in the direction of my hotel room when I heard someone call me: "Comrade! Comrade!"

I turned back. It was the young man from the telephone desk. He beckoned me to come to him and it became clear that he had been looking for an excuse to make me wait until Keshtmand had left. He phoned Iran immediately and I talked to my wife.

When I finished talking, the young Afghan served me tea and started pouring his heart out. He insisted that I convey his words to the Party leadership, in particular to comrades Kianuri and Tabari. He had been part of the Khalq Party faction that had been sidelined, a Maoist as we used to call them then. He said that Hafizullah Amin had not been an agent of the US. He had been a true communist. The Parchamis were representatives of the petite bourgeoisie and because they did not enjoy widespread support, they had called on the support of the Soviet army, which led to the destruction of the Khalq faction.

He was also critical of the Iranian government for being reactionary and religious rather than revolutionary. My views at the time ran counter to his, but I didn't express them.

The following morning we went sightseeing. Two Afghan security officials came along with us. They were young men, dressed in black suits and sporting large sunglasses just like in the movies. We insisted that they should not walk with us because they would make us stand out like a sore thumb. We arranged for them to keep an eye on us from a distance.

All the government offices, telephone kiosks, road signs and pylons had been painted deep red, a colour that was said to have been loved by Hafizullah Amin, who saw in it the victory of the communist revolution.

We walked past a dried-up stream, which they called a river. We passed the King of the Two-Edged Sword mosque, the king being Hazrat Ali, and entered the city's filthy, old bazaar. Bazaars like this could be found only in the remotest, smallest towns in Iran. We would enter shops and say we were Iranians and all doors would be opened to us. Through chit-chat we intended to find out the people's views about the presence of Soviet troops, but we encountered silence. No one would say a word. Almost all the shops had pictures of Googoosh, a famous Iranian pop singer.

A couple of hours later we had our first official meeting. The culture minister, Dr Majid Sarboland, was a tall Afghan with Western airs who put his feet on his desk to show off his finely crafted Italian shoes while we talked.

During our interview, he repeated the official line that had been dictated to him. He talked a bit about Afghan history and literature. We asked him to arrange an interview for us with Babrak Karmal and Mohammad Najibullah[52] and allocate a day for us to visit Pul-e Charkhi prison. He gave us promises for the first and second requests but with regard to the third, he said: "That's up to Comrade Karmal."

There was only one cinema in Kabul, which looked like an old shop, and it was showing an Iranian film. Most of the women on the streets were covered in hijab but there were a few women with bare heads in the area around the half-open Kabul University and near the government offices. Mansour tried to start a conversation in a bank with a girl behind the cashier's desk, but instead of responding, she just laughed.

Keshtmand, Mansour and I had dinner together again that night. During our conversation I noticed that the middle-aged waiter was listening to us and paying close attention to me. I stayed at the table after dinner. The Afghan waiter came over and while clearing the table, he said hello. I returned his greeting. He asked me: "Are you Iranian?"

I said: "Yes."

"Going back to Iran?"

"Yes."

He looked around him and while fiddling with my plate, he placed something underneath it and left. I lifted the plate. I found a small photograph of Ayatollah Khomeini and an announcement from the Afghan Mujahedin that they would fight until the infidels left the Islamic land of Afghanistan. There was a fire simmering underneath the ashes.

The next day, we went to see Mohammad Najibullah. He was an imposing man, very polite. Unlike the culture minister, he walked out to the car to receive us. He answered all our questions and even said things that he shouldn't have, bearing in mind my views at the time. For example, he revealed that a quarter of a million Afghans had been killed in Afghanistan's civil wars and when we returned to Iran, this became the headline for Mansour's article for *Ettelaat*. I felt compelled to interfere and told him that he was revealing Party secrets. He said: "I am talking to comrades."

He made a phone call in our presence, securing permission for the interview with Babrak Karmal and a visit to the Pul-e Charkhi prison. That tall Pashtun, who was so in love with Iran and with the revolution, was later brutally tortured and shot at the hands of the Taliban when Kabul fell. Though he may well have earned his nickname, the "Butcher of Kabul", the thought of his disfigured corpse hanging on public display in Kabul always makes my heart ache. But he too would stand when Kianuri and Tabari's names were mentioned, and like the other Afghan officials we met, he repeated the official line about Hafizullah Amin inviting in the Soviet troops.

The next day a jeep was sent for us by Najibullah, along with an official to accompany us to the prison, and we sped out of the city. We drove past high, snow-covered mountains and followed an ancient, narrow road through the middle of a frozen desert until, after an hour or so, we saw the outlines of the infamous prison in the distance. We finally lurched onto a dusty main road, passed through a medieval-looking gate and came to a stop in front of the prison gates. The young prison director was waiting for us. He gave me a tight embrace, shook Mansour's hand and led us into his office, which was more like a bunker than an office. He hesitated a moment when he noticed the official accompanying us, and when we told him we intended to interview Hafizullah Amin's ministers, he immediately called Najibullah for verification. Until he had received his instructions from Najibullah himself, he refused to believe that anybody could have given permission for such politically sensitive interviews.

We were the first and perhaps the last Iranian journalists to visit Pul-e Charkhi Prison. Mansour was caught up with asking his questions and I left the office and found myself at the end of the sort of corridor I had only seen in films. I walked down the corridor. A worn blanket was hanging in front of a hole that was lower than the height of an average person. When I pushed the blanket aside I could see a crowd of people seated around a lantern, huddled in black blankets.

A small metal window at the far end of the corridor opened onto a dusty, round courtyard. Cats were running about the courtyard. A rat was moving up the wall and there was a dreadful stench of human defecation.

I returned to the office, feeling unwell. Mansour had finished his interview. We asked to see Amin's ministers. A young Parchami officer left the office and returned a few minutes later, followed by the twelve former ministers who were being held on suspicion of being American spies. They entered one by one and sat down. They all wore traditional Afghan clothing, were very young and very clean. They reminded me of the young men in the Party's youth organization.

Dark tea was served in delicate glasses. One by one they picked up the glasses, looking at each other in astonishment until the prison director introduced us. When they heard that the Party had sent me, they became extremely happy and animated. Some of them walked up and kissed me on the cheeks.

We spoke with them for two hours. They had no idea what had happened to them. They said that they had been arrested out of the blue and brought to prison. They had assumed that the Americans had launched a coup. When we told them that the Soviets had arrived and that Babrak Karmal had become president they shouted in astonishment. When they heard that the charge raised against them was that of spying for America, they became seriously agitated. With the intensity of very traditional Afghans, they all protested that they were communists, believed in the Soviet Union, and were enemies of America. The farewell scene was sorrowful, as one by one they kissed me on the cheek, embraced me and told me to deliver their messages to comrades Kianuri and Tabari and tell them that they were not spies.

I had no idea that within three years, the bearer of their heartfelt messages would not only "confess" to spying for the Soviets but also for the British.

Years later, when I visited the famous San Quentin Prison in San Francisco, I realized that prisons represent a nation's emotional state. San Quentin was a thousand times more gruesome than the prisons I had known in Iran. A regimented, iron prison. Violent, heartless and resistant to any influence. In the Afghan prison, with its chains and humidity, the violence had a primitive quality that you expected to be ultimately overcome by humanity.

The final meeting was with Babrak Karmal in Muhammad Zaher Shah's palace. I had seen many of the world's great palaces from the outside. And on the day after the revolution I had been inside the palace of the last Iranian Shah's sister, which was on the outskirts of Tehran. In contrast, Zaher Shah's palace was very unimpressive.

Our car stopped in the courtyard, in the shade of some Russian tanks. The chief of the palace security, who was also one of the young Parchami officers, came to receive us. We walked up the stairs and entered the hall. After we introduced ourselves, the young officer acted just like the rest of them: he embraced me tightly, kissed me on the cheeks and shook Mansour's hand. He asked us to walk upstairs. I asked him: "Why aren't you searching us?"

He said: "How can I search Tudeh comrades? I'd be embarrassed."

I argued: "This is not right. You ought to search everyone."

Mansour said: "But I have nothing to do with Tudeh."

The officer responded: "Yes, but still, you are Iranian, comrade."

Mansour said: "I am not your comrade, man."

Eventually we were given a half-hearted search. Karmal came out to receive us while we were walking up the stairs. He was wearing a grey-coloured suit, looking chic and tidy, like a proper Party leader. The kissing on the cheeks routine was repeated once again. The president of Afghanistan waited until we had entered his office – a large sun-filled hall –before seating himself behind his desk. Mansour conducted his interview. After the interview we drank tea and talked. Babrak Karmal was very hopeful. I told him about the jailed ministers and added that I was going to deliver their message to the comrades in the Party leadership.

He asked: "What is your opinion?"

"In my view," I replied, "they are Khalqis but they are not agents of the West. They are radical communists."

"What should I do?" he asked.

"Release them, quietly," I suggested.

He went into deep thought and then sent a very warm message to the Party leadership. We kissed each other on the cheeks and separated. When I returned to Iran, I heard that Hafizullah Amin's ministers had been quietly released and sent to Moscow.

Three years later, while writing yet another draft of this story as a "confession", I kept putting a swear word next to Karmal's name. But whatever he was, he was a man deserving of respect. When his government fell, he returned to the Soviet Union via the same mountains through which he had come, and in Moscow he drank himself to death in the bitterness of exile.

The following day, we were at Kabul Airport, waiting to board a plane to Moscow. Mansour wanted to interview the Soviet foreign minister Andrei Gromyko and I was not disinclined to visit the Soviet Union myself.

While we were waiting, a man with the appearance of a Turkman approached us. He spoke Farsi fluently but with a strong accent. He said he had been sent by the Soviet comrades to receive us and gave us each an envelope. We asked: "What's this?"

He said: "The cost of your trip."

We both returned the envelopes. Mansour said: "My newspaper has paid for my trip."

And I said: "The Party has paid for me."

Astonished, he took the envelopes, gave us a cold handshake and left. On the way, we kept joking – we nearly ended up being in the pay of the KGB.

The room and I have been left alone. I pull up my blindfold. I put on my glasses. I stand up. I pace. I stare at the cream-coloured walls. I am all ears for the door, for who might be coming. I hear the sound of doors closing. A telephone is ringing in the distance. The windows have frosted over. It is getting cold, slowly, gradually. As if the central heating has been switched off. I pace. I try to keep myself warm. The air is getting colder. I knock on the door. There is no answer. Again I pace. I knock harder. There is no answer. I am out of breath. My teeth are hurting, especially that damn molar. When I walk, I feel a sharp pain in my feet, which are wrapped in thin fabric. The shooting pain in my left shoulder has become unbearable. It's getting colder and colder. I sit on the chair and draw my legs up to my chest, hoping to fall asleep. Pressure on my bladder wakes me up with jolt. I try to open the door. Useless. I think of relieving myself in the corner of the room. I don't know whether there are specific rules about peeing in an interrogation room. It dawns on me that I am hungry. How long has it been since I last ate? I don't know. I am getting colder inch by inch. My whole body is aching. The hunger, my burning bladder, the feel of urine, is driving me mad. I am sleepy. The only solution is to knock on the door. A solution that is no solution. A solution that has no answer. I don't know whether it lasts one night or a thousand. I collapse in a corner.

I see my wife in a nightmare; she is running around Toopkhaneh Square in Tehran shouting: "He's frozen! He's frozen!"

I wake to the sound of voices. Doors are opened and closed. The sound of life returns. I bang on the door. There is no answer. I want to run outside and stand under the sun, but I have been tied to something. I bang harder. I yell. And suddenly something hits the door. I jump up with a start. A voice is saying: "Put on your blindfold."

The order to put on my blindfold is the best news for me. I do it with the last of my energy. The door opens and I hear the sound of boots. Two people grab me and drag me along. They take me down the stairs like a sheep's carcass. They drag me across the courtyard. My instinct says that we are heading in the direction of the room downstairs. My brain has still not yet registered this when my hands are handcuffed. I yell out. They shove a piece of cloth into my mouth. They tie my legs with a rope. The marks of that rope are still on my ankles. They throw me face down on the bed and leave.

I turn and twist and each movement multiplies the pain a thousand times. The pressure of the handcuffs has added to all my other pains. I force myself to breathe through my nose. I am suffocating. Then, I don't know when, I descend into blackness. I open my eyes when they unlock the handcuffs. I hear your voice, which is sounding terribly gentle: "I have been to visit Mr Montazeri.[53] I had such a great desire to see the Aqa that I completely forgot about you, little lion. The brothers brought you here by mistake. Good job I am back."

You help me stand up. You shake my hands, making sure my muscles don't go stiff. Gently you take me to the room upstairs and you say: "Have a rest until they bring you food."

And you leave. I take off the blindfold. They have thrown two blankets next to the heater. Without hesitation, I stretch myself out on one of the blankets. I press myself against the heater. I pull a blanket over myself.

My eyelids immediately begin to droop. The pleasure of sleep has not quite washed over me when a spasm makes me jump. I begin to shiver violently. I am aching from my brain to the tip of my toes. My whole body has dissolved into pain and the molar tooth is going on and off like a red traffic light. My body starts to fit. I try to stand up and collapse in a heap on the floor. I try with all my strength to control the shaking, but I can't. Someone has obviously been watching me from behind the door; he rushes in and grabs my hands, trying to still my thrashing body, but he is not strong enough. He leaves. I lie like that, jerking on the floor. Then I start to yell. I hear a voice: "Shut up, useless wimp."

It's you, Brother Hamid. For a moment, the fear makes me go quiet and I look for my blindfold. You are shouting: "This is just a show. He has been trained in all this."

I can't stay silent. I yell again. Then I throw up. I throw up blood mixed with yellow liquid. I am in the middle of Toopkhaneh Square. I am trying to get myself home, running and running. I am telling my wife: "I have been freed. Everything has been a lie. A nightmare."

Then I stretch myself out and my wife starts massaging my feet. Why is she crying? Why is she wearing black? I plead: "Wife, let me die …"

She says: "No, no. You must live."

And I slowly open my eyes. It is pitch dark. I am in a place like a hospital. My feet are tied to the bed. An intravenous drip is attached to my hand. And again, I descend into darkness.

When I return to my senses, I am back in my cell. It takes a while before I recall what happened. The cell light is off. So it must be day. I am cold. The shivering begins again. My whole body is aching. I sit up with difficulty. My need for the bathroom is horrific. I stand up with difficulty. My head is spinning. I touch the wall for balance. I manage to pull out the IV line. My hands have swollen and are aching badly. I try to look out through the hole in the cardboard. I bang on the door. The shepherd guard arrives immediately. He gently grasps me under my arms and lays me back down on the bed. He goes out and comes back with a bowl filled with warm water.

"Rub your hands and feet."

I look down. The bandages have been removed. Warm water – what pleasure. I rub my feet. The shepherd guard is squatting beside me: "Why are they doing this to you?"

I have no idea. I shake my head.

"Bathroom …"

"You are not allowed to leave your cell. Do your business here. You know how."

The shepherd guard laughs and leaves. I do my business into the bowl. I am all ears for the door. I fear you might turn up, Brother Hamid. But no. There's nothing. I push the bowl aside and stretch out.

There is the sound of knocking from the left wall, behind which is cell number fourteen. Someone is doing Morse code. I am not familiar with Morse code. Randomly, I knock on the wall. Again, there's an answering knock in Morse code. Again, I knock on the wall, willy-nilly.

Who's in that cell? What does he want to say?

During the Shah's time, when the prisoners used Morse code, they also kept an ear out for the guard. The knocking is bound to be heard in the silence of the block. But no guard comes. Then there is silence. I don't know how much time passes before I hear the shuffling of slippers and I jump up with the speed of lightning. You are coming for me, Brother Hamid. But no, the door to the next cell opens. I hear whispers. I force myself to stand up. I go to the door; I place my ear against the door. I can't hear anything. I try to adjust the cardboard on the door and then I notice that there are some tiny holes in it. I put on my glasses. I look through the holes and see you, for the first time, Brother Hamid. How young you are and how thin. You have made the prisoner in cell fourteen lean against the wall. He is blindfolded. You don't even reach his shoulders. He is saying something and you are listening. And this image stays with me for eternity. I turn away and stretch myself out on the bed.

The sound of shuffling slippers arrives later that night. The door opens. It's your voice: "Get out!"

I first put on the blindfold. You grab me under my arm and help me reach the bathroom. You tell me to leave the door open. You also help me back to my cell. When the door closes, I find a piece of screwed-up paper on the floor. I open it. It's a tiny instruction grid for Morse code. The light is still on. I hear the sound of tapping on the cell wall. I work out the meaning from the grid:

C … o … m … r … a … d … e

Comrade in resistance …

Had I not seen you with the cellmate next door, the phrase would have meant something very different to me. But I realize that this is another way of extracting information. That night, I remain silent. The next day I respond in Morse. I have no secrets; I say what I have already said in the interrogation. Two days later, when someone else is put into that cell, the Morse code stops. Much later, I see the report of the Morse code episode in an envelope in my file.

The cell door opens: "Who's Houshang?"

I put on my blindfold. I hang onto the end of the stick and set off. I sense that someone is accompanying us. We go to the room downstairs. The guard makes me sit on the bed. Suddenly, I collapse. I shiver. I feel sick. All the pain is returning in waves. I am about to stand up almost against my will when a hand is placed on my shoulder, making me sit down. It's you, Brother Hamid. You must have observed all my movements. I say in a shaky voice: "Hello."

You answer kindly: "Hello, good boy."

Then you start walking. I can see your military trousers from underneath the blindfold, I am watching you walk up and down and your words are being carved into my brain one by one: "We really had no idea that Mr Khamenei liked you that much, Mr Asadi. If he finds out that we have punished you, he will certainly be upset. But our problem is that we don't know whether what you have written about him is true or a bunch of lies. It had better not be lies. But if it's true, it will change everything."

"I swear to God it's true, Brother Hamid."

"God? So you believe in God? Never mind. Take the paper and write a letter to Mr Khamenei. We will give him the letter. If he confirms …"

You fall silent. You must be watching my movements and waiting for my answer. To be honest, I am happy. Very happy. I nod my head in agreement. You give me a pile of paper and a biro.

"Write the letter on a separate sheet."

And you laugh: "Of course you are not going to write about lovey-dovey stuff to Aqa. And for us, write about the trip to the Soviet Union. I want every detail. I really don't want to have to bring you back down here."

Then you grip my sleeve and make me stand up. You walk with me to the room upstairs. You gently pat me on my back: "Knock on the door when you have finished writing the letter."

Chapter 12

Defending Khomeini in the Heart of Moscow

I lifted my glass and shouted: "Viva Khomeini!"

And the foreign journalists had all laughed at me. I went out for a walk. The domes of the famous St Basil's Cathedral emerged in the distance on Red Square. Postnik Yakovlev built this amazing church on the order of Ivan the Terrible. When work on the cathedral was complete, Ivan ordered that its architect be blinded, to prevent him from creating a similar building for anyone else. The terrible tsar and the great artist are now both long dead. The church's colourful cupolas face Lenin's mausoleum, a reminder of the end of another era of notorious oppression. Like Iran, Russia has long been a breeding ground for oppression, in the name of the king and the crown, the church and the cleric, and the people.

"Stop writing. That's enough."

It's not you, Brother Hamid, giving me this order. It's my wife's worried voice, repeating the doctor's orders. I collapsed again yesterday. The French doctor arrived immediately. He examined me again, and again pronounced: "There is no physical cause or problem."

My wife explained that I had been revisiting the torture chamber in my mind, and the doctor had insisted that I stop writing.

But I must write. I must finish writing this.

Moscow, winter/summer 1980

"Come in, KGB agent!"

It was like a game. Mansour Taraji, who died while I was writing this book, would keep repeating it, and we would quickly turn into a lane to lose any KGB agents who might be following us. It was winter 1980. Winter in the Moscow sense of the word – with people ice-skating on the frozen surface of the Volga River.

We had reached Moscow in the evening. A black car had been sent to meet us and was waiting for us at the bottom of the airplane steps. An exceptionally good-looking Russian man who, unlike the one we saw in Kabul, had a diplomat's face and manner of dressing, came to receive us. We got into the car and for the first and last time in my life, I left the airport without being searched. The car passed through the large and frozen Leninsky Boulevard and delivered us to the Rossiya Hotel, a hotel reserved for foreign guests. We rested and then at eight o'clock in the evening joined our host, who spoke Farsi fairly well, in the restaurant.

A special dish of cow's tongue in aspic and a few glasses of Russia's famous vodka kept us warm and cheerful until the early hours of the morning. Mansour told our host that we had come to interview Gromyko. He said that this would probably be impossible but he would do his best to arrange it. He left after we had arranged a meeting for the next day to visit the Kremlin and Lenin's mummified body.

After he left, we walked out into the street, watchful for the KGB agents that Mansour was convinced were tailing us. Scenarios from the espionage films that were so popular during the Cold War and which, in my view, played a significant role in the collapse of the Soviet Union, kept playing in my mind. We reached the wide Leninsky Boulevard. The domes of the famous St Basil's Cathedral in Red Square could be seen in the distance. We walked towards the square, and passed two guards who looked at us in astonishment. Except for a boy and a girl who were locked in a loving embrace,

Red Square was empty. Greater and more silent than anything I could have imagined.

The next morning we went to Lenin's mausoleum. As usual, there was a long queue in front of the tomb. Our Russian companion took us to the head of the queue, pulled out a card, and we were immediately ushered in. Our walk past Lenin didn't take more than a few seconds and didn't trigger any emotion in me. Later on, while I was in prison, I watched footage of his statue being pulled down, and in exile, I watched a documentary about his mummification. On both occasions I recalled that moment, and asked myself: "What calibre of man was he?"

From there we went to the Kremlin Palace. We passed through a tall, medieval-looking gateway, visited Lenin's office and left.

That night, the same Russian took us to the Bolshoi Theatre. I saw smartly dressed men, and women drenched in perfume and wearing revealing evening dresses hand over expensive fur coats to the cloakroom attendants before entering the hall. The scene reminded me of Tolstoy's *War and Peace*. We had front row seats and watched an astonishing adaptation of *Don Quixote*. That is the most beautiful memory of my first visit to the Soviet Union.

The next day, we received news of Gromyko's adamant refusal to be interviewed, and we took the first flight back to Tehran, flying via Delhi.

My wife and Rahman were waiting for me at the airport. After hugging and kissing each other on the cheeks, Rahman immediately warned me that the situation had worsened while I was away. He listened with keen interest to my report about Afghanistan and the situation there, as did Kianuri the following day. A few days later I went to visit Khamenei, who appeared almost indifferent while he listened to me, and was not interested in hearing Babrak Karmal's message.

I want to stop right here, after only a few lines about that trip. I haven't done anything illegal, and besides, all this is already known to one of the country's highest officials. Even though I am now weak and my body is broken into pieces, I'm terrified of describing an incident that might be used in building a court case against me.

When we were in Afghanistan, they were in the process of replacing their ambassadors. Hafizullah Amin's government had appointed most of them and therefore they were seen as opponents of the new regime. One of them was the then Afghan ambassador to Tehran who, if I am not mistaken, had given an interview in which he had criticized the Soviets' presence in his country. He had not returned to Afghanistan after the change of government, but had fled to the West. While I was in Afghanistan, it had been arranged that his replacement would call me upon his arrival in Iran.

One spring day in 1980, there was a phone call for me in the *Mardom* office. It was the new ambassador. After informing Kianuri and getting his agreement, we arranged a meeting and I went to the Afghan Embassy. The ambassador was a very young man, and looked like the rest of the Parchami men. We agreed to remain in contact so that he could pass news and information about Afghanistan to me for the paper.

At our final meeting, he agreed to meet with a Party representative. The meeting was to take place at the Taryani Cafe, which was close to the embassy. In order to ensure that the two men identified each other correctly, I was supposed to sit at an adjacent table. On the agreed date, I entered the cafe slightly earlier than planned. I sat down, and opened my newspaper. Habibullah Foroughian,[54] the Party's representative, arrived exactly on time and sat down near me. The ambassador arrived a little bit later and joined Foroughian. They shook hands and started a conversation of which I didn't hear a single word. Since I had done what I came to do, I asked for the bill. While I was paying, I noticed a man entering the cafe. He looked very familiar. I wracked my brain and quickly recalled a Moshtarek guard from the Shah's time. He carefully looked around the cafe, left and then returned with another man.

It was being said at the time that although Savak had been disbanded the year before, Savak's anti-communist faction had been
left untouched, and was cooperating with the Islamic Republic.
There was no doubt that the meeting was being watchᴬd. I didn't
leave, and instead waited until the meeting was over. The ambassador left and a bit later, Foroughian stood up and walked quickly
past me to the door, with some men hurrying after him. I followed
to see what would happen. At the first traffic crossing, Foroughian
rushed up to a shared taxi stop, and ignoring the etiquette of the
queue, jumped into the waiting taxi, taking the last empty seat
in the car. By the time the men tailing him reached the car and
grabbed hold of the door handle, it had already set off. They were
too late.

On my way to get a taxi back to the *Mardom* office so I could fill
Kianuri in. I spotted the agent from Moshtarek Prison in a phone
box. He was dialling a number. I stopped and listened. When the line
was connected, he said: "He escaped."

He hung up the phone and hurried off, looking worried. I went
back to the office to tell Kianuri what had happened, but Foroughian
had already told him everything. This was the incident that I was
frightened of writing about. So I didn't write it.

That summer, the Olympic Games was to be held in Moscow. I had
wanted to attend the Olympic Games ever since I learned to play
football, and this seemed like an excellent opportunity to me. I talked
to Rahman about it. A few days later Kianuri called me and said that
my Olympic trip had been arranged. I would be attending the
Olympics with a female reporter and Javid, a well-known footballer
on the national team. On the day we were due to fly to Moscow, the
Soviet National Olympic Committee made a last-minute change
and announced that they could only accommodate two people, the
female reporter and myself.

The Olympic Games had started two or three days earlier. The

giant Russian plane was completely full. At Larnaca, all the other passengers left the plane while we were kept on board, together
with three heavily built men who must have been the plane's security staff.

At Moscow's newly built airport, the highly polished floor
reflected our steps. We handed over our passports to the official in
charge. He carefully scrutinized them and said something in Russian.
We responded that we didn't understand Russian. I said this in
English and my colleague in German. The official picked up the
phone and made a call. A bit later, two men dressed in Red Army
uniforms arrived. They separated us and asked us individually, one
in English and the other in German, who we were and what we
were up to. We explained that we were reporters for the Iranian
Tudeh Party's press and had arrived to cover the Olympics. Their
attitude was unfriendly, and they left. Three security officials arrived,
and again they asked us the same questions, separately. They wanted
to know why we had arrived after the Games had already started.
They asked to be shown the National Olympic Committee's
invitation letter and our Tudeh membership cards. We explained
that the conditions in Iran had delayed our trip and for security
reasons we had not been able to bring our membership documents
with us.

The three individuals, who were members of the Soviet
Communist Party's Youth Organization, took us with them and
handed us over to three middle-aged men who officially interrogated
us on behalf of the KGB. They asked the same questions in an angry
and aggressive tone. They kept using telephones and walkie-talkies,
speaking to each other and with some other party. There was clearly
a problem, but we had no idea what it was. We were both getting
angry, and protested that we were representatives of a "fraternal
party"[55] and should not be treated like this.

Eventually they asked us to open our suitcases to be searched. The
official in charge examined every single item in our suitcases very

thoroughly. He pressed the buttons on my binoculars a few times. He opened my camera and removed the film. He rubbed my shaving cream onto my hand and moistened it with his saliva until it started to foam. I could see out of the corner of my eye that they were pulling out my colleague's underwear piece by piece, and that her face had turned red with anger.

They took our money and counted it carefully before handing it back to us. After an hour or so, we were escorted to the exit surrounded by some security officials, and put on a bus. We were the only passengers, apart from an official and we didn't know where we were being taken. When we reached Leninsky Boulevard, I realized that we were in the city centre. The bus stopped outside a large hotel. The official accompanying us handed us over to someone else. We passed through the hotel's three checkpoints and found the Party's representative in the Soviet Union waiting for us on the other side. He explained to us what had occurred. We had arrived at night and a number of days after the Games had started. The offices in charge of guests had been closed at the time and the entire Olympics committee had been off-duty. The security officials had looked everywhere for someone to verify our names but had not succeeded in finding anyone so they had decided to send us to prison for interrogation. The bus had been about to set off towards the prison when they had finally found a contact who had verified our identities.

We took deep breaths in our luxurious rooms and then went down to the hotel's glittering dining room for dinner.

The menacing atmosphere of intense security aside, Moscow's Olympic Games resembled an aristocratic party. The Soviets had done everything in their power to put a glorified image of their country on display.

The tables were filled with food and dozens of women, dressed in the latest fashion, were on hand to serve the guests. However, I found it intriguing that the many waiters available attended the guests unwillingly and only after being called. None of them spoke any language apart from Russian. I also noticed them hiding bread, boiled eggs and cold meats under their uniforms.

America had boycotted the Olympics but hundreds of foreign reporters were present in Moscow, carefully observing everything. I went to watch various events during the day and in the evening I phoned in my reports to Tehran. The hotel's telephone hall was large, with many telephone boxes. Telephone numbers were handed in to the very beautiful, multilingual girls who were in charge of dialling them. The first time I handed over the newspaper's telephone number, I sensed disdain in the Russian girl's manner. I felt seriously offended. After all, we were all communists, members of the same family. The following night, watching the hall from above, I noticed the same look of disdain on the part of the majority of the girls and the waiters towards the third world reporters. In contrast, Westerners were given a great deal of attention. I was suffering – I was learning the truth about life in the country that had given birth to socialism.

The second night, I went to the hotel bar. A large crowd of foreign reporters were drinking themselves into a state of oblivion, and the free alcohol was loosening their tongues. I knew some of them from Tehran and the days of revolution. They crowded around me, eager to talk about the situation in Iran. They were all intensely against the revolution while I defended it. Initially they assumed that I was joking but when they realized that I was serious, the discussion became heated. I remember that eventually I lifted my glass and shouted: "Viva Khomeini!"

And they all laughed at me.

One day, a young, almost shabbily dressed woman stopped me while I was leaving the hotel. She looked Vietnamese. She spoke in an unfamiliar language, asking for something that I didn't understand. The next day, the same thing happened again. Eventually, she pulled a battery out of her pocket and pointed at the hotel. I went inside and bought her a battery. When I returned, there was no sign of her.

The next day, I saw her again. I gave her the battery and her eyes lit up with happiness. Gesticulating with my hands and eyes, I made her understand that I wanted to see where she lived. I wanted to understand what was going on. I couldn't believe that there were women in the Soviet Union in such desperate need of a battery. When she understood me, her eyes went dark and she ran away.

This happened just before we were taken to the Lenin museum. Each of our small groups had a Russian guide, ours was a tall young man. When we reached the museum, we saw a very large picture of Leonid Brezhnev prominently displayed on the front of the building. The young man said quietly: "It wasn't like this in Lenin's time."

We looked round the museum and watched a subtitled film about Lenin's life. Lenin was stroking a cat, responding to journalists' questions and describing the future of socialism. The guide sitting next to me kept saying: "But that's not how things have turned out."

When the other journalists had dispersed, I asked the young guide to show me around the city. He agreed. We went to a park. It was a bright, sunny day. Beside a statue of Yuri Gagarin, the first Soviet astronaut, the young man began to tell me what life in Russia was really like.

Then we walked into the city to a statue of Philex Dejensky, the founder of the Soviet security system and a fairytale-style hero of communism. The young man pointed at the statue and said: "Our lives are in their hands."

I was reminded of that young man when the Soviet Union fell apart.

One afternoon, I suddenly felt uneasy. I was walking away from the huge Lenin Stadium after watching a running race when I felt anxious without any obvious reason. When I reached the hotel, I went to the communication hall. I handed in the Party's office number and waited. An unfamiliar voice came on the line. I said that I was phoning from Moscow and wanted to speak to one of the editors. The voice said: "He's not here," and hung up. Something must have happened, so I asked for the number to be called again. This time, someone else picked up the phone and said: "We have arrested your fellow spies." And again, the line was cut off.

We didn't have a telephone at home. An idea suddenly occurred to me. I went to the telephone girl and asked her to please tell them that she was phoning from Germany, not Moscow. The girl hesitated a bit but then took the phone number. This time a third person picked up the phone. I said: "I am phoning from the Islamic Association of Frankfurt and would like to give you a press release."

The person at the other end of the line happily related that Hezbollah had raided the office of the traitor Tudeh Party and had obtained evidence of espionage. I put down the phone. So my uneasiness had not been without reason.

Later, when I had got back to Tehran, I was told that the day after my telephone call, *The Islamic Republic* newspaper had announced: "Following the raid on the Tudeh Party office, Brezhnev had personally called to register his objection."

From Moscow I went to Frankfurt. My wife had arrived a few days earlier. Sadly, on the way to Frankfurt, she had miscarried. We stayed in Frankfurt for a few days. We returned from our trip abroad to days of peril and torture.

A few days after my return, a letter arrived for me from the Party's organization. It was Javid's letter of complaint. He was very upset, protesting that factionalism had occurred within the Party, which is why he had been prevented from visiting the Soviet Union and the Olympic Games. I wrote a response, and underlined that "Our friends in the National Olympic Committee in the Soviet Union had reduced the number of guests at the last moment, which is why only reporters were allowed to attend."

I am in the room upstairs, writing to Khamenei with my swollen hands. I can no longer control my bladder. I knock on the door. The guard appears, like a genie. I hand over the letter. I say that I need the bathroom. He tells me to wait. He leaves, and returns: "Put on the blindfold, come on."

We go out. He tightens my blindfold. He hands me the tip of the stick. We enter a toilet block. I couldn't have done my business sitting down, even if I were used to it. I wash my face several times with cold water. I see my reflection against metal. My beard has grown. For the first time in my life, I see myself with a long beard. There are knocks on the door. I am taking too long. I put on my blindfold and go back out. The guard tightens my blindfold. Then he hits me hard on my head:"Damn you, you piece of filth. Were you pissing standing up?"

I do not yet understand what great importance peeing while standing up has in Islam. I'll find out later on, in Evin prison.

You come and take my writing away with you. The guard brings me food. I am allowed to lie down. But I can't relax, constantly listening out for the shuffling sound of slippers. I turn and twist my wounded body on the blanket, trying to sleep. I draw my knees to my chest to protect my throbbing feet. I press my broken teeth together. When my left shoulder touches the floor, the pain makes me miserable. I lie on my right side. I see my wife's eyes. She is looking at me, worried. I let myself drown in the darkness of her eyes.

The warmth of sleep had not yet swallowed me up when something makes me jump. At first I don't know what has alerted me, and then I hear the shuffling sound of slippers. I can't believe it. Two people are whispering to each other. The door opens and I hear your voice: "Stand up, useless wimp!"

I stand up. I put on my blindfold. I set off. I am scared. I am shaking. Night visits mean torture. What am I supposed to confess to this time? You grab hold of my jacket hem. We go to the room downstairs. You put me on the bed.

"Have you remembered anything new?"

I say: "I have said things ... even ..."

I want to say: "I have even confessed to your words."

Fear stops me in my tracks. You say: "You have left the trench but you have not yet thrown down your hand grenade. Pull up your blindfold."

I do it. You hold a piece of paper up to my eyes. It's the letter that I wrote in response to Javid's complaint. You pull down my blindfold again.

"We know everything! And the comrades have become very talkative, singing like nightingales."

A question has filled my brain: "Where did they get hold of the letter?"

Later on, I learn that the letter and other documents had been found after the arrest of one of the advisors to the Party's Central Committee, when his house had been searched.

I say: "But I have written about this."

"No, as I said, you have not yet thrown your hand grenade. This, 'our friends', who are they?"

"Our friends?"

This time you give me the paper. Your voice suddenly turns angry: "Look carefully."

I look. The sentence is my own sentence. My signature.

"Our friends in the National Olympic Committee."

I say: "Our friends meaning the people in the Soviet National Olympic Committee who wanted to reduce the number of people coming on the trip."

"Do you have Russian friends, Mr Asadi?"

"No."

"So what do you mean by 'our friends'?"

I am still searching for an answer when you take hold of my arm and, as if suddenly remembering something, you ask: "You definitely don't know who Khosrow is?"

Khosrow? You have also arrested my brother? But he has nothing to do with the Party. He is not political at all.

You hit me on my head with several slow hits.

"Khosrow? Comrade Khosrow?"

I suddenly remember the pieces of paper, they were the colour of the skin of yellow onions, that used to arrive at the *Mardom* office. They were about people's lives and sometimes workplace matters. Written on all of them was the name Khosrow. I used to think that it was Rahman who, while writing about the Party's history, was also writing these. I said:

"Ahhh, Khosrow."

"Do you know him?"

I say: "I think he's Rahman Hatefi."

You said: "We've figured that out. We are figuring out the rest. We'll get to 'our friends' as well. You poor sod, you still keep playing games. The others are telling us everything about you."

You become silent. This too is part of the interrogation. A silence that is a hundred times more horrific than talking or even the whip. When you start talking again it feels like a thousand years have passed: "By the way, would you like to see your dear comrades?"

Chapter 13

Visiting the Dead

The 1980s were called the "Decade of the Great Terror" in Iran. The "Spring of Freedom", as Iranians dubbed the months immediately following the 1979 Revolution, turned out to be very short, just like the Iranian spring itself. The bloody clampdown on both armed and unarmed opposition groups that had begun in the summer of 1980 reached a climax in 1983. By the beginning of that year, only the Tudeh Party remained, which after joining forces with Fedayeen had become Iran's largest leftist political party. But from the start of the decade, important events had been taking place under the skin of the city that eventually culminated in its decimation.

Vladimir Kuzichkin, the KGB's Intelligence Officer at the Soviet Embassy in Tehran, and the Russian contact for the Tudeh Party, disappeared in 1982, and later that year reappeared in London. Having defected to Britain through the British Embassy in Tehran, he shared his insider information with MI6. In a secret meeting that took place in Islamabad, Pakistan, an MI6 agent in turn handed over the information on the Tudeh Party and its leadership to representatives of the Islamic Republic of Iran.

With this information in hand, the Intelligence Officers of the Revolutionary Guards Corps intercepted a member of the Central Committee of the Party as he left one of the KGB offices in Tehran that operated under the cover of a commercial company. They copied the communications that he was carrying from the KGB to the Tudeh Party, and threatened the lives of his daughters if he were to warn the

Party. *These letters reached Khomeini, who immediately issued orders for the arrest of the Party's members.*

And so here I am in prison, writing my "confessions" for you Brother Hamid. And this is what the elimination of the Party means.

Throughout the night, a storm is raging, the wind howls and the lashes of the whip are hitting heaven and earth. Through the whole night I have revisited that horrific winter of 1983. I have been wrestling with ghosts. It's been a week since the doctor ordered me to stop writing, but this fearful night has taken me back to you, Brother Hamid. I have returned to write my thirteenth letter. You must have had many such nights of pleasure, torturing the innocent to their graves. And you perform your prayers with profound purity of heart.

Moshtarek Prison, 11 March 1983

I feel as if I am in a timeless place, a nowhere place, when a heavy blow hits my side, making me jump. I put on my blindfold. I no longer bark only when it's time for writing. I have become like Pavlov's dog.

It's you saying: "We've got a meeting with the comrades. They can't believe that this is who you really are."

You drag me down the stairs. We enter the courtyard. The freezing cold is making my whole body shake, opening up my wounds. I hear your voice: "It's time for you to throw down your hand grenade."

I try to make my brain interpret this sentence. We enter a corridor. I guess it's the same one that leads to the bathrooms. I don't know whether I am right or not. We pass through turnings, or maybe you have made me swirl around myself. My impression is that I am walking along a timeless nowhere tunnel. I don't know why, but I'm reminded of Tabari's words. Recently he had kept saying:

"We are moving along a dark tunnel in the blind hope of some direction."

Then we apparently reach a courtyard. You say: "Wait. Now lift your blindfold, but don't turn around."

I do as I'm told. It's as if a light has been switched on.

Without my glasses and in the dim light I see the vague contours of some coffins that have been lined up against the wall. What is their purpose? Where are we? Am I dreaming? Your voice is filled with pleasure: "The comrades are sleeping here."

A tremor goes through my whole body. I have always feared corpses and am frightened now. I have always fled from corpses and I want to flee now. I didn't even dare to look at my own mother's face after she died. A famous song comes into my mind: "They are taking the dead from street to street …"

And your voice: "Right, I am going to choose one of them, the one you like best."

The image of corpses being carried flashes through my mind. There's the sound of something being opened. Is it a door? Wooden? No, metallic. You grab my head and move me along.

"Do you know him?"

I look down at Manuchehr Behzadi's[56] moon-shaped face. In my imagination, he's opening his eyes for a moment and then closing them again. But no, the eyes were closed. Involuntarily, I sink to my knees and throw up. This man, who is lying so still inside the coffin, used to be the editor-in-chief of a newspaper. Quiet, literate and a man of few words. He loved his family, his daughters. Now you have forced him to sleep, for days on end, inside a narrow wooden box, one of the most ingenious devices in the service of the Islamic Republic where, apparently, there's no torture.

You hit me hard on my head: "Stop playing movie games! Useless wimp!"

You make me stand up.

"You piece of filth!"

You drag me along while you speak: "It's your turn now. You are getting it and you'll be sleeping comfortably alongside the others. The British agents together with the Russian agents."

My body is shaking. I keep feeling like throwing up but fear is stopping me. We stop. I sense that we are in Under the Eight.

First we will show you your wife and then we'll give you the coffin next to hers.

My knees cannot take it anymore. Unwillingly, I have doubled up. I am trying not to throw up. You grab me under my arm and make me stand up: "You are going to your cell. You have only one option. Hand over the hand grenade, okay?"

I can't hold myself upright. I sink down. You are being kind. You are sitting down yourself. I lean against the wall. I keep feeling sick, my stomach is in my mouth. I hear your voice: "You are now going back to your cell. This is your last chance."

I start to get up. I am desperate to get to a bathroom. Diarrhoea is about to join the vomit. You won't let me go. You are holding me back. You are laughing and asking: "Did you recognize Comrade Manuchehr?"

I shake my head.

"Was he dead or alive?"

At last you hand me over to the guard and leave. When the shuffling sound fades out of earshot, my fear lessens and I say to the guard: "For God's sake ... bathroom."

I am lucky that it's the shepherd guard. He takes me to the bathroom. I run to the toilet. When I get out, I go to the sink and throw up. I am shaking and throwing up. I re-enter the toilet and relieve myself. I get out and place my head underneath my country's most refreshing, coldest water. To no avail. The vomit and diarrhoea keep coming in waves. The guard takes me back to my cell. He gives me a bowl and leaves me. I shake until dawn. I throw up into the bowl. I relieve myself inside the bowl.

Manuchehr's face appears. That man who was, in the truest sense of the word, decent, sleeping inside the coffin in his prison clothes. His face has no colour. Asleep, unsmiling. A tomb which is both gravestone and grave is one of the achievements of a revolution that does not know torture. Everything is done in line with Islam, and Shari'a law.

"You must throw in your hand grenade."

I can see the line of coffins in my mind's eye. They have names engraved over them. The names are spinning and becoming one.

First we will show you your wife.

I can see my wife's face. She has gone to sleep forever, and she has averted her eyes from me in the eternal night. I hit my head against the wall. I throw up. I wish the night could be endless. I fear the morning. I don't know what "throwing in my hand grenade" means, but I suspect that there will be more torture. My whole body is aching. Toothache has made me restless. My feet are wounded. I can't hold my back straight. When my shoulders touch the ground, the pain makes me cry out. In order to sleep, I sit down, leaning against the wall. What do they want from me? I have written down everything about my activities and my life. The final stages of our activities were obvious. We had defended them. We had nothing to hide. We weren't even spiteful. Many of the groups had announced a war and had mentally prepared themselves. But we had shouted "Imam, Imam," until the last day. I had shouted right in the heart of the land of infidels, right in the centre of Red Square: "Viva Khomeini!"

The door flies open with a terrifying bang. I jump. No, it's not you, Brother Hamid, you who my heart longs to never see again. It's time for the morning visit to the bathroom. I who have shitted myself. The guard throws me a clean uniform: "Change your clothes."

We go to the bathroom. The waves of vomit and diarrhoea keep coming. My empty stomach is only throwing up bitter-tasting liquid and making terrible noises. I wash my underwear with dishwashing detergent under the cold tap. I put on the clean clothes and return to my cell. They have brought in breakfast. What pleasure there is in hot tea. It moves over my broken teeth and when it reaches my stomach, it comes up again. I put aside the red plastic cup. I lean against the wall. My whole existence wants you not to return. But I know that you are coming back. And something inside my head makes a thudding sound. Like a woodpecker pecking a tree. Then there is an aching. How I long for you to come here and find me dead. The headache has settled in my temples. It stays there and will accompany me for many long years. Even now, it pays me a visit now and then.

The loudspeaker has been turned on. It's seven in the morning on 11 March 1983. Ayatollah Prozac[57] has begun talking. I cannot believe it. A month has passed. Automatically I touch my beard. It's grown full.

Night comes but there's no sign of you. The food arrives. We go to the bathroom in the evening. The corridor is covered in blankets. Everyone's feet are in bandages as if we have been wounded in a war. My underwear is dry and I put it on. We return to our cells. The lights go off. I stretch myself out. I try to sleep. It's not happening. Headache. Suddenly I miss my pillow back home; it was always clean, and scented with perfume. Toothache. I am back home, flossing my teeth. I hear my wife shouting: "You have made everything dirty, Houshka."

My wife and I had just finished reading Alexei Tolstoy's *The Road to Calvary* trilogy, and she had taken to calling me Houshka after one of the book's characters.

Aching shoulders, wounded feet, but worse than everything else is the constant dread that is wandering around my soul, directionless. As soon as my eyelids begin to droop, I think I hear the sound of shuffling slippers and jerk awake. But there's no sign of you. The night, the whole night is spent in pain and with the nightmare of the approaching sound of slippers. In the morning, one of "God's fathers" opens the cell door: "Who is Houshang?"

I answer: "That's me."

That's me? I feel like I am running away on my wounded feet, distancing myself from myself. If I dare to turn around, I'll see Houshang Asadi sniggering at me.

I am holding the tip of the stick and am being dragged along. If the guard comes to pick you up, that means your situation is not very dangerous. We cross the courtyard. The guard is not giving up: "Why haven't you called yourself Ali? Why not Muhammad?"

He's shouting from the depths of a culture that has come to power and, like an idiot, I am failing to get it. A few years later, in Ghezel Hesar prison, the cultural official theorized about the guard's folkloric question: "From our point of view, you intellectuals, the Houshangs, the Kiumars, and the Nimas,[58] you are all polluted."

Door, stairs. First floor. Right turn. First room. The usual chair. I sit down, facing the wall. I take off my blindfold and wait. The door opens two or three times. No, it's not you. Someone comes in, asks my name and leaves. Then, suddenly, a hand hits my shoulder and I hear your voice: "How are you, little lion?"

When did you get here? I hadn't heard the sound of shuffling slippers. Maybe you had come in before me and were watching me. The sound of the shuffling slippers allows me to prepare my body for defence. You, who in your own words are "a master of making people talk", have taken away this small comfort from me, the prisoner.

I blurt out: "Hello."

This time you answer: "Hello, good boy."

I hear the sound of a chair being dragged and then your voice: "Put on your blindfold. Get a move on!"

I do as I'm told. I see from underneath the blindfold that you are seated on a chair in front of me. You are wearing the same military trousers. You have your boots on. I see a pair of hands that have tortured me. You start talking. Your voice has become very kind: "It is clear from what you have written that you are very attached to the revolution. We too have given up our lives for the revolution. I myself was a student at the University of Science and Technology. If I had done one more year, I would have qualified as an architect. But I delayed my studies because the revolution was under threat."

You pause. A long pause. Then you say: "What beautiful long hands you have, Mr Asadi."

You must see me trying to hold my hands together and maybe you have noticed that I am embarrassed. Then you say: "No, this is not a good place. Let's go to a better place."

You do not bother to get a stick, but grab my hand and make me stand up. I am being dragged alongside you. I cannot hold my tongue: "You are polluting yourself."

You say: "Is your hand wet?"[59]

I am dragging myself and moving. You keep saying: "Watch out ... get on the stairs ... to the left ... right ..."

We pass through a triangular courtyard. I feel the sun's warmth. My feet are making a slurping noise over melted snow. I shake from the inside. We are on our way to the room downstairs. But no. We walk past Under the Eight and walk up the stairs. You hold me under my arm and are helping me. What astonishing kindness. My whole body is aching. Going up the stairs has become harder than ever. The same stairs that I ran up with open eyes and a gun in my hand on the day of the revolution's victory. I pause when we reach the balcony. You let me catch my breath.

During one of these pauses I hear a curious conversation. First I see a white chador. Then I hear a woman's voice: "Brother, allow me to go to my cell."

A harsh voice, which must belong to an interrogator, asks: "Where have you got hold of these two pathetic bits of branch?"

The woman's voice is pleading: "Please, Brother. I will put it into a glass so it can grow roots."

We walk on and lose track of the voices. Who was that woman?

Where had she got hold of two pathetic bits of branch? She wanted to put them into a glass and let them grow roots inside this house of death and lashes to help her stay alive. We walk up the stairs. The woman's voice is there again and she is pleading and crying. We walk up the stairs and reach a place where we lean against the railings. I feel the sun's warmth and see from underneath my blindfold a courtyard covered in snow.

"How many days have you been without the sun?"

I cannot tell. I saw the sun for the last time on the morning of the sixth of February. A bird is singing faraway and I hear the distant, very distant, sound of traffic. I imagine the streets around me, which must be filled with passers-by, life and shouting. It's your voice that is bringing me back to reality: "Look, Mr Asadi. We did not plan to put you under pressure. This is your own interpretation. We didn't want this to happen, even before Mr Khamenei read your letter and put in a special request on your behalf. To you, we are a backward people."

I said: "We never regarded you as backward. We defended you."

You carry on talking: "But we too have a heart, are humans. It is true that we punish in line with the Shari'a law but our heart is not in it. We too know something. We have evidence. How else could we have rounded you all up in one day? Our intention is to save you. If I were in your shoes, I'd save myself. Islam's door is open to everyone who repents.[60] Getting information is not that important to us. We'll get it sooner or later. You saw Comrade Manuchehr. He came to his senses and returned to his cell. Had it not been for the Ayatollah's request, it would have been your turn to go to sleep in his stead."

A wave of vomit is coming up. Your blows are raining down on me, one after another. You immediately strike again: "By the way, we are aware that your wife is running here and there trying to save you."

You grab my hand and we set off. A door opens and everything goes dark. We walk down the stairs. There's silence until we reach Under the Eight.

"Now go to your room. If I were you, I'd save myself."

You must have signalled to the guard with your hand because he's coming and taking hold of my sleeve. You say: "I am telling you one last time. Throw down your hand grenade. Tell the truth. If you take one step towards us, we'll take a hundred steps towards you."

Then I hear the shuffling of slippers. You are leaving. The guard says: "Watch what's in front of your feet."

I step over the railing and enter the block. A hand is touching my back. It's you.

"By the way, would you like to see your wife on the night of the Eid holiday?"

Chapter 14

Drinking Hard Liquor in the Islamic Torture Chamber

The torture chamber: a metal-framed bed with a metal-spring base but no mattress, a wooden chair, a rope hanging from a hook in the ceiling. And on the chair, a bottle of Parmoon.

Every time I feel like a drink, I am reminded of that bottle of Parmoon and of you. I have to drink more and more to forget what kind of drinking companion you were. I drank the last drop from the blue bottle so that I could die. So I could be saved. I drank every drop. In one go. Without cucumber yoghurt.[61] Without taste. No, with the taste of the pain that was running through my body. With the bitterness of suffering and the sweetness of death that was coming to take me away. I don't know whether you drink when you are on your own. No. No. You are pious. You don't touch alcohol. You certainly perform ablution before you perform torture. You pray. You are not like me, I who am still washing away my sorrow with a glass of spirits or a pint of beer. You have prepared yourself for the intoxicating streams running through paradise. You are expecting God to offer you a fine, fair houri in return for each strike of your whip. And for now, your purity is no hardship, for you take such pleasure in the beating and killing.

Yes, lovely Brother Hamid, my fourteenth letter is about drinking in the torture chamber where you were the one with the whip. Think about it. If you had written about the other side of the drama that you watched unfold, in which you played such a big part, together we could have written a timeless masterpiece.

Moshtarek Prison, 12 March 1983

The final hours of the night. I should celebrate my wedding anniversary. The light has been turned off, so I know it's past eleven o'clock. I lean against the wall. I search with my hands for the two pieces of sugar cube that I saved from breakfast. We married five years ago. Where is my wife now? Is she, too, inside a cell, remembering our wedding? I close my eyes. I fantasize about holding her hand. In my fantasy she is saying: "You are very tired. Sleep ... sleep."

I wake up to the sound of the door opening. A guard takes me to the bathroom.

"Knock on the door when you have done your business."

I go in. There is no mirror. I try to see my reflection against the metal cubicle wall. I wash my face. My scalp is itching. I wash my hair with some of the dishwashing detergent that stands in for soap at Moshtarek, and rinse my head under the cold water. The water at Moshtarek prison comes from one of Tehran's oldest springs and is among the coldest, most refreshing waters of the world. My head almost freezes and my shirt gets wet. I knock on the door and the shepherd guard arrives. I am taken back to my cell. The guard leaves and comes back with a clean prison shirt for me.

As always, the door opens suddenly: "Who's Houshang?"

There is no one else in the cell, except me, so I must be Houshang. I stand up and we set off. On the way, there's the usual argument: "Why have you called yourself Houshang?"

As soon as we reach the courtyard, someone grabs my shirt collar and punches me hard in the stomach, and when I come back to my senses, I find myself on the metal bed. A fist is hitting my face. A voice is saying: "Start it, Brother Haykal."

"Karbala, Karbala ... We are on our way ..."

Punches and kicks rain down on me. Together they drag me into a standing position and then hit me so that I fall against the metal bed and the bed's springs dig into my body. I hear the heavy breathing of someone I cannot see and words are tearing at my ear and burrowing deep inside my brain.

"Karbala, Karbala … We are on our way …"

And you are hitting me again. Suddenly a fist lands on my mouth. It's Brother Haykal. Do you remember him, Brother Hamid? You both hit me, and the two of you are laughing.

I don't know how much time passes before I hear your voices. You are circling me: "Spy. Torturer. Useless wimp. Savak agent. We don't need evidence. He's the evidence. He's a piece of filth. His stink is everywhere."

Then you leave. I hold my head in my hands. I listen carefully. There's no sound. I pick up my blindfold. My clothes are covered in the blood that's spilling from my mouth. I spit and a broken tooth falls out. I feel a piercing pain in my molar teeth. The torture chamber is the size of a cell. A room where I will be a guest for a long time. Its walls are covered in blood. I can vaguely see the shape of a rope hanging from the ceiling. A black chair and a metal bed.

"Put on your blindfold."

I put it on. The door opens. Someone drags me out, pulls me up the stairs and throws me into a room.

"Wait until your interrogator arrives."

I am sitting and waiting for you to arrive, Brother Hamid. You are preceded by the sound of shuffling slippers. You put a pile of paper on the desk: "This time I don't want anything vague, or wishy-washy. A lot of things have changed in the last few days. You have to get straight to the point, right now. We want facts."

And you leave.

You are right, Brother Hamid. It does seem like there's some sort of chaos going on. Doors are opening and closing. From that night onwards I keep hearing the terrible sound of screaming. You leave and I start writing.

I don't know, Brother Hamid, how many hours I've been writing. I am eager to finish quickly. My face is burning, my mouth is full of blood. A pain for which there's no cure has afflicted my poor teeth that have broken under the onslaught of your fists. Even as I write, I spit out bits of tooth. I am frightened to knock on the door. I tell myself that you'll be coming back soon and I'll be able to go to the bathroom. But you don't come. I can hear the incessant sound of shouting coming from the corridor. Doors keep opening and closing. I guess it's one of those days when interrogation takes up the whole twenty-four hours and you and your colleagues take confessions in three shifts.

When I'm taken back to my cell, the light is on and will not be switched off again.

From that time of endless light, that was also a time of endless darkness, all I remember is insults, shouting and lashes. Nights ran into days. First I lost all track of time, and then I lost myself. The one that was me remained forever in that torture chamber, and another me left; a me whose creator was neither God nor nature, a handcuffed me, a lashed me, a beaten, broken me.

The overwhelming pressure makes me knock on the door. After a while someone appears and asks from behind the door what I want. I answer. He says he has to ask. You are in charge, Brother Hamid. They even have to ask for your permission for me to go to the bathroom. You must have given your permission because the guard comes and takes me away.

I take off my blindfold in that life-saving toilet, I put on my glasses, and I see my reflection in the metal cubicle wall. I am horrified. Blood has dried on my face. My eyes are swollen. I rinse out my mouth and touch my teeth. Two molar teeth, one on the right and one on the left, are gone and a front tooth is loose.

The guard knocks on the door. The bathroom time is short. I do my business and we return upstairs and again I start writing. I write more quickly, using few words.

All my teeth are aching and it has made me restless. I keep standing up and walking. Then I sit down and write. Then I walk again. I knock on the door. Someone comes. He asks from behind the door: "What's up?"

I say: "The pain is killing me."

He says: "Keep walking. The marks of punishment will get better."

I say: "My mouth, my teeth."

He laughs: "Have they managed to lower your pain threshold? Who's your interrogator?"

I answer: "Brother Hamid." And he leaves.

And I walk. The sound of shuffling slippers arrives. I put on the blindfold and face the wall. "Finished?"

I say: "My teeth."

"Shut up, useless wimp."

You pick up what I have written so far and then leave. I am being left behind, with my toothache. I am left behind with the blank paper. I should finish quickly. I should write quickly, maybe then they'll take me back to my cell and do something about my teeth.

Eventually, someone comes. He takes my sleeve silently and leads me away. The cold in the courtyard is piercing. I shuffle over snow. It's clear that it has snowed heavily. My socks are soaking wet by the time I reach you. You say: "You'll see my true face now. You'll understand why they call me 'The Torturer'."

There are many torturers in this world, with whips, and handcuffs, just like you, and with your way of thinking – if someone doesn't share your views, you must kill him. With the wounds of the whip, the tip of the pen or the lashes of the tongue.

You say: "Take off your socks."

I take them off.

You say: "Are you writing the truth? Or shall I start ..."

"I have written the truth!"

And I am afraid. I assume you want me to write about the organization. About the Party members, about my wife and ... But I am mistaken. As usual, you are talking to me in code. Meaning, you are indirectly telling the prisoner what you want to hear.

"I am going to start. I want the truth about how you became a Savak agent. Open and close your hand ..."

And in the blink of an eye I am thrown onto the bed. The springs are cutting into my flesh. You are tying my hands. Another person, who must be Brother Haykal, is tying my feet and it is starting ...

"In the name of the Heavenly Fatimeh ..."

The lash descends.

"Karbala, Karbala ... We are on our way ..."

And you are striking. The blows hit the soles of my feet and echo in my head. I don't know how many lashes you will administer. You must have been given an order in line with Shari'a law and you will not exceed the lawful number of allocated lashes.

I am yelling. Something is being put into my mouth. It's my wet socks. Were you aware that due to sinus problems I can only breathe properly through my mouth? I am suffocating. The socks are putting pressure on the broken teeth. I prefer being lashed to being gagged. For the first time it occurs to me to open and close my hand. I do just that. A hand removes the socks; it's as if I have just emerged from under water.

"Right. First confess it verbally."

I can only hear my own voice with difficulty: "About what?"

"How you became a Savak agent and why you infiltrated the Party."

There's a piercing sound in my brain. These words are more painful than the lashing of the whip. You must be bluffing. When the whip strikes, I cry out. The socks are stuffed back into my mouth and the blows continue. I tell myself: "I'd rather die than accept this lie."

The blows descend until I escape into deep darkness. When I come round, I am seated by the side of the bed, whining. The soles of my feet are on fire. I can't lift them. I touch my feet. They are bleeding. I hear your voice: "Now stand up and move around. It's good for you."

Later, I will come to understand that walking has a special place in torture. Interrogators have been taught exactly when to stop whipping the feet to prevent nerve cells from dying. That's why they make their victims walk and move their feet; it's to keep the cells alive. Doing this to swollen feet is a new form of torture as well as preparation for the torture session to come. Victims who are aware of this try to avoid walking and I, without knowing anything about it, always tried to avoid walking. I just couldn't walk on my feet. You are whispering in my ear: "You must have been given thorough training, little lion. Keep walking."

You are calling me little lion. Whenever you are feeling well, I become little lion and you, The Torturer.

And I walk.

And then, loud and deafening: "Karbala, Karbala … We are on our way …"

Again, two people grab me roughly and throw me onto the bed. They tie my hands and feet. They push the socks back into my mouth.

"In the name of the Heavenly Fatimeh …"

And the whip descends. The more I twist, the more the rope puts pressure on my hands and feet, cutting into them.

"The more resistance you put up, the more obvious it becomes that you are keeping secrets."

This is another lesson in the science of torture. And I am suffocating. I can't even twist myself around. A heavy weight is pressing me down. I hear your voice: "Sit further up, Brother Haykal, so he can't move. This one, he's well trained."

And the blows rain down on me with great force. And I don't

know when I drown in darkness. The intense burning sensation in my feet brings me back to my senses. I have been untied. Someone is rubbing something on the soles of my feet. It's the guard/doctor. When he finishes his task, he grabs me under my arms and makes me stand up: "Have pity on yourself. In the end, everybody gives in."

And he takes me out of the torture chamber. A few steps further, and he hands me over to someone else. I hear the guard's voice: "Your interrogator wants you to walk. Face the wall and just move your feet around."

I start moving my feet. I move them slowly. They are very swollen. I hear someone being dragged along and thrown into the room downstairs. A little while later, there's yelling.

The voice of a woman.

The voice of a man.

The piercing cry of a woman.

The yelling of a man.

I am moving my feet and listening to the yelling. I feel a strange pressure in my stomach. I try to look around me under the corner of my blindfold. With my eyebrows I manage to push the blindfold up a tiny bit. Over there, I can see the vague shadow of iron bars and a cooking stove with a perpetually steaming kettle on top of it and next to it, a chair. I free myself, as if automatically. And then I hear the sound of my bowels emptying themselves and I fear someone might come. I am embarrassed. I hear a voice. It's not the shuffling of slippers. It's the stamping of boots. A hand is touching my shoulder. It's the guard. Laughing he says: "Seems you haven't moved your feet properly. I am leaving so you won't be embarrassed. Keep moving your feet."

And the drama carries on. I am tired in a horrible way. I lift my hand. I hear a voice from a distance: "What's up?"

I gesticulate with my hand that I want to go to the bathroom. The guard walks up: "Keep moving your feet until I've asked your interrogator."

He leaves and I move my feet. The yelling has stopped. Once or twice I squat and then stand up until a hand grabs my sleeve and takes me with him. We pass by the blankets that carpet the corridors. We reach the bathroom.

"Do your business quickly and then knock."

The guard leaves. I take off my blindfold. I splash a fistful of water onto my face. My feet are swollen and burning. I sit down with huge difficulty. But then I cannot make myself stand up. I delay it as long as I can; the toilet is my best refuge. But I cannot stay here for eternity. I go out. I am looking for something to see my reflection in when someone bangs on the door.

"Put on your blindfold."

I do as I'm told. Someone comes and asks my name. I answer. He grabs my sleeve and takes me away. He's dragging me, rushing along. I am forced to run after him. We leave the block. I recognize the pool in the middle of the courtyard. We skirt it. We enter another corridor. A voice says: "Put your hand on the one in front of you."

I do as I'm told. The line is moving slowly. There's whispering. Everyone is trying to figure out who is in front or behind him.

"Where are they taking us?"

A stupid hope is lighting up my naive heart: "They are releasing us!"

I see myself running down the street on my wounded feet. The queue stops somewhere.

"Pull up your blindfold."

I pull it up. I see a sturdy, laughing man. He hands me clean clothes for the bathroom and he asks: "Do you want a pillowcase?"

I ask, astounded: "Pillowcase?"

I don't have a pillow. He shrugs. When steam reaches my nostrils, I realize that we have come to the bathroom. We stand behind the same black, plastic curtain. Then we enter the shower. The showers are the same ones that Khamenei and I used to wash ourselves in. But something has changed. The Islamic Republic's showers have a showerhead. The time allocated to showering is ten minutes. Washing when one's feet are swollen and blood is running out of one's mouth is sheer torture. But warm water revives one's body. You feel as though you have suddenly left hell and entered paradise. I pick up the soap and rub it on my head. It feels good to be clean. I haven't finished washing my hair when a very familiar voice whispers my name. It's you, Brother Hamid. I answer: "Yes, that's me."

"Hurry up and get out. Who told you to come here?"

I have hardly finished getting dressed when you grab my hand and drag me along. You are hitting me over the head and dragging me. You keep saying: "Useless wimp … Savak agent … Torturer …"

I am wet, very wet, and the cold air is making me shiver uncontrollably. We go through the courtyard and around the pool. We go into the room downstairs. You throw me onto the bed and start punching and kicking me. Then, once again my feet and hands are tied to the bed.

Your voice: "In the name of the Heavenly Fatimeh …"

"Karbala, Karbala … We are on our way …"

And the lash descends. It descends. It cuts into the soles of my feet and makes my clenched teeth burst in pain. I open and close my hand. The blows stop. A hand pulls the gag out of my mouth.

"What is it? Do you want to talk?"

"Bathroom …"

The same hand shoves the gag back into my mouth.

"Shut up useless wimp. If you mention the bathroom again, I'll give you shit to eat."

And the next blow makes my body convulse. This time, when I come to my senses, I find myself sprawled across the bed with bandaged feet. I sit up with difficulty, trying to remember where I am. I pull off my blindfold. My eyes wander around the torture chamber. A metal-framed bed with a metal-spring base but no mattress, a wooden chair, a rope hanging on a hook from the ceiling. It is hard to see what's sitting on the chair. I squint to read: Parmoon.

My mind is searching for a connection. The blue bottle of Parmoon. My thoughts are wandering and wandering and eventually reach our little home. Every weekend my wife and I clean the house. We are doing the dishes, my wife is washing up and I am drying. The connection is there. Parmoon is the same liquid we used to use to disinfect the bathroom and the toilet. I can hear my wife's voice: "Wash your hands carefully. It's poisonous."

The door opens and the smell of food wafts in. The guard puts down the plate of food. I say: "I am thirsty."

He goes away and comes back with a red, plastic cup of water. I take it and drink it all. I say: "Bathroom ..."

"I have to ask your interrogator."

He goes out and doesn't come back. I cannot eat. My whole mouth is aching. It's a different kind of pain to that of my feet. I feel the salty taste of blood in my mouth. My brain automatically starts analysing incidents and words. What do they want from me? Why do they focus so much on this Savak issue? Are they themselves Savak agents? Are they the men from the Revolutionary Guards Corps? I can't find an answer.

The sound of shuffling arrives, which means it's you, Brother Hamid. Automatically, I look for my blindfold and put it on. You stop in the doorway and say: "You still don't want to talk, useless wimp?"

"I don't know what else I am supposed to write."

This answer has come from my subconscious and later I come to understand that the answer is the beginning of something that the interrogator is expecting, but he pretends that he doesn't expect it. You say: "You are going to remember what you need to say right now. I didn't want us to get to this stage. It's your own fault."

Then you grab my hands and pull them behind my back. For a moment I feel the coolness of the handcuffs on my wrists and a piercing pain shoots through my shoulder. I am expecting you to throw me onto the bed with my hands handcuffed. I prepare myself. But you are doing something I cannot see. Then you say: "Stand up."

I stand up with difficulty. I feel that something has been tied to the handcuffs. Suddenly I find myself hanging in the air. I am swinging in the air, with my hands handcuffed behind my back. You grab me, Brother Hamid, and pull me down. When the tips of my toes almost touch the ground, you release me again. Meanwhile, you are talking: "Everyone is mute at the beginning. Then they all turn into nightingales. When they put up a lot of resistance, we make them bark like dogs. Collect your thoughts and think until I come back."

The sound of shuffling slippers and the closing of the door. And the pain starts from the wrists, reaches the soles of the feet, and fills up the whole body. It is not possible to describe the quality of the pain. It's a different type of pain, different from the whip, or when your teeth are broken right inside your mouth. Each pain has its own taste. The toothache is salty. The whip is red. It burns. It hits the soles of your feet and sets your brain on fire. The pain of handcuffs is bitter. The rope keeps moving, which intensifies the pain. You feel as though your shoulders are being ripped apart. Your heart beats frantically. Your mouth dries up. Becomes bitter. Something bitter, bitter as poison, spills through your body. You force yourself to hold still. But you twist again and the rope turns again. Your whole confidence, your sole hope, focuses on the tip of your toe, which is connected to the ground, a place you used to stand on. And this point of connection, psychologically speaking, is the most important and the most horrific thing about the hanging torture. It means that there is a place to which you can return. You can stand firmly on it. No suffering. You will get back to being yourself. And the condition for you to return to that place is to talk. The graduates of the faculty of torture know exactly how much the body can endure, how to give the body just enough rest. When to get you back on the floor. When to open the handcuffs. To give you a taste of what it's like to not be handcuffed, to be standing on the ground. Your options are either to talk or to yell. I am yelling. Yelling.

And sometimes you come in, Brother Hamid. You take me down without a word. You open my handcuffs, and that is the most painful moment.

Your wrists and hands feel dead. To get back to normal, you move your hands, and you rub your wrists. Your shoulders have frozen up, and cannot return to their usual position, they feel as if they will burst with pain. The torturer makes you stand up and makes you walk. Little by little, everything turns into a habit. Your body fills with the pleasure of release, and just then, you are thrown onto the bed again. In the blink of an eye your hands are handcuffed behind your back once more and before you know it, you are hanging in the air, and only the tip of your toe reaches the floor. Or if you are hanging by your ankles, the top of your head.

And I am yelling. Yelling. I feel like a thousand hours, a thousand nights have passed. Maybe it has been less than five minutes. Or maybe five days. When you are hanging, time loses all meaning. You are twisting inside a black hole.

Then, unexpectedly, the door opens. Someone gently unties you. You realize from the smell of food that it's mealtime. From the type of food you can work out whether it's morning, noon or night. You swallow your saliva with difficulty. Your whole body is terrified. You know that this, being untied, is only a temporary reprieve. It is going to come to an end. And this is another type of torture. Eating also offers some respite. Experience shows that Brother Hamid is also in love with this time of the day. Usually, it takes a long time for him to return. In addition, you are allowed to take off your blindfold.

When I take off my blindfold this time, I see the blue bottle of Parmoon on the chair. The sound of shuffling arrives. I put on my blindfold. You pull my hands behind my back, Brother Hamid, and bark: "Which side? Which hand do you want on top?"

How unbalanced one is hanging this way, one hand pulled over the shoulder from the front, the other pulled up behind your back, and then both wrists handcuffed together, before being strung up from the ceiling. Usually they alternate which arm is pulled over the shoulder, to increase the pain. This time you let me choose. You laugh and say: "See, contrary to what you think, there's freedom in Islam."

But I cannot even make use of this freedom. My right hand cannot reach my left hand from the back, so you always handcuff me in the same position. I ought to let you know, it will bring you so much happiness, that my left shoulder was permanently damaged under your care.

Two months ago, when I was rushed to a Parisian hospital, they wanted to put a line into my left hand, but I instinctively shouted out: "Not in my left hand! No! Don't hang me from my left hand." The nurses didn't understand what I was saying. When my wife explained to them, they rolled their eyes in astonishment and said: "*Ah bon! Ah bon! C'est vrai?!*" ("Well, well, is that true?")

Yes Brother Hamid, I told you that you'd entered my life for good. When you lock the handcuffs, you give me advice. You soften your voice: "Be reasonable. Write. We know the truth. But we want you to write it down yourself. Who sent you to Savak?"

And you haul me up again. I am left hanging between the air and the floor. I yell. I am tied and untied a number of times. One time I say: "Bathroom …"

You accompany me yourself. You open the door. I delay my business to catch my breath. You bang on the door. "Hurry up, useless wimp."

I put on my blindfold. I want to wash my hands. You don't let me. You grab my sleeve: "You are worse than shit!"

You drag me out.

"Next time you mention the bathroom, I'll dip your head into a pile of shit."

I assume you mean to threaten me. But later, I will understand what was going through your head at that moment. We return to the room downstairs. You tie me up again. Again I am unable to make use of my Islamic freedom. When you lift me up, you say: "You cannot fool us the way you fooled the Party. Write the truth."

This code giving prepares the prisoner to move towards what the interrogator wants, step by step. The truth according to your interrogator enters your brain with tiny, little details. And just when you are lifting me up, you fire another shot: "The Tudeh people are talking, singing like nightingales. But you Savak agent, you haven't opened your mouth yet. But you will."

And you leave. I remain and your words are circling around in my head. I throw them up with hatred but they return painfully. From my wrists, the soles of my feet, my mouth. I didn't know and I don't know how much time passed. I am tied and untied several times. I can only tell whether it's night or day from the food. In the daytime, there's usually rice or a stew. At night its eggs and potatoes. Experience teaches me that at night you return later. Your mouth usually reeks of the ugly smell of onion. Savak interrogators used to enter the torture chamber drunk on alcohol. What made you intoxicated? Did you drink from the mystic cup? Or did the smell of blood get you drunk?

At dinnertime, the guard unties me briefly. I am allowed to take off my blindfold. Again I see the Parmoon bottle. I hear my wife's voice: "Be careful, it's poisonous."

Something goes through my mind like lightning and turns into a decision in a second. I close my eyes. No. Sooner or later, they'll figure out that I have told the truth. No, I'll be hanging from the ceiling again. I have to "confess" to whatever it is that Brother Hamid wants me to confess to, and I still don't know what that is. I move closer to the chair.

The guard comes in and ties me up. He covers my eyes with the blindfold and leaves. I push myself towards the chair. I inch forward, little by little. I am all ears. I lift my blindfold with my eyebrows as much as I can. It seems like a thousand years have passed before I reach the chair. I move the blindfold against the chair. It's been pushed up enough for me to get a vague impression of everything. I hit the chair with my head. The chair falls with a bang. I think everyone must have heard the noise and will run for the room. But there's no sound. The Parmoon bottle has dropped onto the floor and is calling to me like a saviour. I lie on the floor face down. I wriggle across the floor inch by inch and reach for the bottle. I grab it with my mouth. I sit up again with great difficulty. My shoulders are pulled back. I lower my head. I place the bottle between my knees and open the lid with my teeth. I put my mouth over its rim. My ear is to the door. There's no sound. I say goodbye to my wife and to life and swallow the contents of the bottle in one go. A flame of fire rushes down my throat. My body is burning, from the tip of my tongue to the depths of my intestines. I drop the bottle and collapse on the ground. Lying on my back is not possible because my arms are handcuffed behind me. I turn and lie face down on the cold floor. Relief is within reach. I am dying and being released from this hell. Something resembling sleep comes over me. It's death. I am dying bit by bit and how sweet this feels. I see my wife's crying eyes and Rahman comforting her.

I don't know how much time has passed when I am kicked on my side and a voice says: "Who said you could sleep, useless wimp?"

In my mind I think I'm dying, and can't answer you. You turn me around with your foot. I open my eyes and see you for the second time. Involuntarily I mutter: "I'm getting rid of you …"

You give me another hard kick in the ribs, and then flip my limp body onto my front with your foot. You lean down and put on my blindfold.

"What shit have you eaten, idiot?"

"Poison …"

You must have looked around and seen the Parmoon bottle on

the floor. I hear the sound of slippers running down the corridor, and then the sound of many shoes arriving at a run. Brother Hamid must have shown the Parmoon bottle to someone. There is the sound of laugher. Hands grab me by my handcuffs and throw me onto the bed. I hear your voice, Brother Hamid: "What you have just swallowed was alcohol, you idiot. Do you know what punishment Islam specifies for drinking alcohol? Haj Aqa is here and has ordered eighty lashes."

And you start. This time you count while you strike me. I don't know what number you reach before I faint.

Chapter 15

Woof, Woof. I am a Spy

My little dog is yapping. Licking my feet. He wants me to take him out. His name is Sonny. He is my little boy, kind and loyal. He has no idea that under the pressure of the whip I too became a dog. He is the opposite of my broken, wounded and devastated self. But all this has nothing to do with my beautiful dog. He has no idea that once I had to bark before I was allowed to speak.

On this stormy Parisian morning, I am writing my fifteenth letter to you and to history, and am forced to return to the most bitter days of my life. To the time when my battered body was shaking on the torture bed, and my soul was running away to avoid surrendering to the devil.

Moshtarek Prison, 12 to 18 March 1983

You have left and I am twisting and turning on the blanket. My shoulders are in agony. My shoulder blades want to break away from my body. I want to find some calm, to sleep for a few minutes. But it's not possible. I sit up with difficulty. I lean my head against the wall. The toothache has returned. I press my hand against the wall and stand up. I walk on my feet with difficulty. I get tired quickly and struggle to sit down. I am all ears. You might come back at any moment.

First we'll show you your wife in her coffin. She's like my own sister. She's looking very pretty.

By the way, would you like to see your wife on the night of Eid?

My wife's image appears. Then I see the row of coffins. I read the names, one by one. I know all of them. I have worked with all of them. Like me they wanted to help Iran reach a better tomorrow. Now they are sleeping inside their coffins. Back then, I had not read or heard anything about the coffin torture. Only later would I hear the full story.

The door of repentance is always open …

Repentance, repentance. How remote and how hateful a word.

Repentance. Life. Revolution. The words repeat inside my brain and become one. I stretch out. I hold my head, which is feeling hot, between my hands. I try to get your words out of my head, Brother Hamid. I hear the voice of the woman prisoner:

"Dear Brother, please let me take these to my cell …"

She wanted to take two small tree branches into her cell.

Yes, life is beautiful …

We were walking along a dark tunnel. There was no light. I could hear the voice of my wife calling me from a distance, and I opened my eyes. I am in my cell. Cell number fifteen. The cries of a woman reach me from the room below.

Our aim is to save you. If I were you, I'd save myself, Mr Asadi. The door of repentance is open to everyone in Islam.

I sit down. A faint light is appearing at the end of this dark tunnel: it's going to end. They are not going to hang me. They are not going to bring in my wife. They are going to believe me. They are going to believe that I have written everything I know. There is only one thing I haven't written about. I am going to write that too. Even though I was only a witness, nothing more.

The whip descends.

"In the name of the Heavenly Fatimeh …"

The sound coming from the tape recorder is even louder than the sound of the lashes: "Karbala, Karbala … We are on our way …"

The whip strikes: "Spy!"

"Yes. I am a spy. A British agent."

He must still have my unintelligible handwriting in that damn file. He is laughing out loud.

I am confessing to being a British agent.

I stand up and try to push aside my thoughts. Anxiety or stress now triggers floods of urine. A souvenir that has stayed with me. I have smuggled an empty dishwashing detergent bottle from the bathroom into my cell, and I relieve myself into it. Behind the door, facing the wall, careful to not let the guard see me. I used to urinate into the food bowl, but once the guard came in while I was emptying the urine filled bowl into the toilet. He grabbed my collar from behind, turned me towards him, shouted: "Infidel …"And punched me in the face.

I had to think of another solution. Eventually I emptied the plastic dishwashing liquid bottle into the toilet. I put it under my clothes and took it to my cell, concealing it from the guard. The bottle had become my saviour and I would get into trouble with the guards over it many times. No matter which guard it was, and whether they would beat me or not, they would all make me take the bottle and throw it into the toilet. It would then be ages before I could get a new bottle and secretly take it back to my cell.

"Throw in the bottle!"

"Throw in your hand grenade!"

I had only ever seen hand grenades on the day of the revolution. My brother had given me a box of grenades that he had found in an empty barracks. And I, in turn, had given the box to Rahman. Rahman said that he would take the box back and hand it in to the revolutionary army. Later on, I found out that he had hidden them.

If you take one step towards us, we'll take a hundred steps towards you …

A thought occurred to me. Well, I'll just lie, as a tactic. I'll lie. I despised myself. I was frightened of my own thoughts. I will have to do prayers. Hold a rosary in my hand. They'll call me Haj Aqa. Haj Aqa.

I walk. I push my thoughts aside.

By the way, would you like to see your wife on the night of Eid?

How I long to see my wife. How I lust for her eyes. How she feared that they might arrest me. I remember the words that I had exchanged with Amir Nikayeen on one of the last days. I don't know whether he too had been arrested. He had said: "They will imprison and kill us."

And I replied: "Or maybe worse, they will make us repent."

And Amir's eyes had filled with tears and I was amazed. You, Brother Hamid, are opening the coffins one by one; you are laughing a devilish laugh and are saying: "Do you recognize this one? It's Amir, right?"

And this one …

And this one …

Would you like to sleep next to your wife?

The final coffin is empty. It looks just like an Islamic coffin. Wooden with a tin plate. Dressed in my prison uniform, I get inside the coffin. You sit down on the coffin.

Save yourself, Mr Asadi.

A wave of sickness brings me back to my senses. I am shaking. I sit down and start shivering again and feeling sick. I throw up into the food bowl. I tell myself: I'd rather get into the coffin than repent.

And I'm shivering again and throwing up. When the door opens, I feel that my body can't take it anymore.

"Who is Houshang?"

It's the guard. He is taking me straight to the room downstairs where you are waiting for me.

"Hey, hey Mr Asadi, You've got yourself into a frenzy again!"

The guard pushes me onto the bed.

"Woof, woof."

The two of you are laughing like devils. You are saying:

"Woof, woof. You're late …"

I am shivering. Someone is dragging me out of the cell and I try to pull myself up: "I am going to repent. Repent."

I don't recognize my own voice. But you are indifferent, and say: "Thanks for taking the trouble. After all, you are saving yourself for the hereafter. Your business is with God alone. But we, we have to give the people justice."

I had stepped into the devil's trap that terrible morning.

"Go and take a rest in your room. We've got lots to sort out together."

When I return to my cell, I find a copy of the Qur'an, a religious book called *The Ornament of the Righteous*,[62] a prayer rug,[63] and a prayer stone.[64] I am so tired and broken that I drop down on the blanket and lose consciousness.

I am in the middle of a nightmare; you have taken me to Toopkhaneh Square and have put me on display. A crowd is applauding.

You are saying: "If you hadn't repented, these people would have torn you to pieces."

The sound of Qur'an recitations is being broadcast all around the square. As if loudspeakers have been placed on all the old buildings and have been connected straight into my ears. I lift myself up into a sitting position with difficulty and encounter a new problem. The cell's loudspeaker, which has been placed high up out of reach at the junction between the wall and the ceiling, is broadcasting Qur'an recitations. The cell door opens and the guard's voice mixes with the recitations:

"Who is Houshang?"

I put on the blindfold and set off. It's bathroom time. I pass by the blankets and notice bandaged feet throughout the corridor. I go to the toilet. I get out and wash my face.

"Well, don't forget to perform your ablution."

It's the guard. I look at him, astonished.

"You don't know how to do it, right?"

And he instructs me. I had seen my father perform his ablution, and my mother and my grandmother. I had seen Khamenei do it and Sheikh Karroubi. For me, performing ablution meant sitting by the side of the pool in the freezing winter, when the whole of the old square was woken up by the sound of the muezzin's dawn call to prayers. I had lived thirty-three years in such company and been this removed from it. The guard finishes his instructions and we return to the cell.

"You probably don't know how to pray either."

He mixes his voice with the voice of the recitations and teaches me how to pray. I repeat the guard's words and perform the very first prayer of my life.

After he left, the broadcasting of Qur'an recitations continued, and from that day on, they are broadcast every day, from dawn 'til dusk. I finish my lunch in disbelief. My heart and soul are not in tune with what I am doing. When I was taken to visit shrines as a child by my mother I would obediently kiss the gold-painted door handles before entering. When leaving the shrine, I would walk backwards and again kiss the door handles. I acted as expected, but I felt no emotion. I had the same lack of feeling again now, in my prison cell.

"Who is Houshang?"

It's the same guard. The same conversation is being repeated, along the same lines, with a new ending: "What name have you given your father?"

I don't even bother to explain that I hadn't named my father. I say: "Mahmoud."

"Your mother's name?"

"May her soul rest in peace. Her name was Fatimeh."

"So what's your new name going to be?"

"My new name?"

"Yes, of course. Houshang is a communist name."

It begins to dawn on me why he has been so sensitive about my name. We reach the stairs: "Well, you know the way to the room. Don't forget to think about your new name."

I walk up the stairs with difficulty. This is the longest walk I have ever done. There are fifteen paces from the top of the stairs to the interrogation room. I am moving from one world into another one. I enter a room. I say hello. No one answers. I lift my blindfold. The room is empty. Two chairs and the sun, which is streaming through the window. I sit down facing the wall until your arrival.

"Hello."

"Hello, good boy. Now pull down your blindfold and turn around."

Your voice is much kinder than yesterday. I put on my blindfold and turn. You have seated yourself opposite me. You seem to be wearing the same clothes. There is some paper on the arm of the chair.

"Look, I want to do you a favour. The kind of favour I have never done for anyone else."

Then you tear up the paper and give it to me.

"This rubbish you have written down! Now we have to start again, from scratch. Imagine it's the first night of your interrogation. Write down the date at the top of the page. Write down the creed.[65] Then your life's political direction. Complete, correct, and precise."

"The creed?"

"You don't know it? The guard will teach you."

I look at the pages. It's my own handwriting. I put them on the arm of the chair. You take them and replace them with blank pages.

"Name on the top of the page with the date. You have to sign each page at the bottom. This is your last chance. Don't even think about screwing up. All you have done is to repent. Most of your comrades repented on the first day. So many of them have repented that we are running out of prayer rugs."

"Tell me what you want me to write and I will write it down."

I realize that you have been waiting for this moment but you are pretending you have not and are feigning anger: "Man, we want the truth. The things that you know about. Spying, England, Russia, Afghanistan."

This is your method and I am becoming more and more familiar with it every day. First I learn about the plot in your film script, and then I fill up the pages. Your words, which are the plot's outline, become intelligence material as soon as I write them down.

You are leaving and I start writing. No lie could be bigger than the lie that I have told myself, and the sleeve of my shirt is still wet from my first ablution.

I write down the date of my arrest on the first page, 6 February 1983. I leave an empty space for the creed and when the guard comes in, I hurriedly fill that in. Then I recount the dramas that you have requested. A summary of the plot scenario that you have repeatedly outlined in an indirect manner, and which is now being completed on paper in my untidy handwriting.

According to the convoluted and rather far-fetched script that I was obliged to produce, the KGB and the CIA worked together during the Shah's time in Iran. The *Kayhan* newspaper office was one of the main locations where they exchanged information, and *Kayhan*'s editor-in-chief was their representative. I joined Savak through him and in return received a good salary. After my release from prison in 1975, Sonia was given orders to approach me. She was my mistress and had planned to marry me. On the 1977 trip to England, I had gone to the BBC. There, I had joined MI6, the British Secret Intelligence Service, through her. She was also a member of the Freemasons. I was given orders to infiltrate the KGB in any way I could. This I was able to do through the auspices of the Tudeh Party and it took place during the 1980 trip to Afghanistan and Moscow.

When I had finished writing this plot down (the original draft is in my file, and I would love to see it one day) my one and only concern was that my case would now be considered complete and I would be hanged. I told myself that I would have a chance to defend myself in court and to explain that I had only concocted the story in order to end the torture.

Every day now, as soon as my breakfast is finished, I am taken to the room downstairs. I race through my dawn prayer and wolf down my breakfast under the constant pressure of the endless Qur'an recitations and the fear of interrogation. I have become constipated. A thousand types of pain have taken hold of me, from my head to my toes. The relentless headache that started on the night of the coffins continues to torment me. The guard puts me on the bed. Then I hear the sound of shuffling feet. You enter, Brother Hamid. I say hello and woof, woof.

You laugh and take me by the arm and we go to the room upstairs. Once, you even put a dried fig into the palm of my hand on the way up the stairs. You recite the rest of the plot either on the way or inside the room, and I write it down. The confessions are not putting anyone else in danger. Only me. I am thickening my file out of the fear of torture.

By now, I am just like Pavlov's dog. In the time that passes when you take away my writing to read it, or when I am eating lunch, or performing prayers, my mind becomes active and works on completing the story you want me to tell. I shouldn't restrain myself. If I am silent, there will be the final punishment, meaning lying in a coffin. Yes, you have turned a hopeful young man into Pavlov's dog and a multiple agent.

One evening, when I get back to my cell, the loudspeaker is broadcasting the Qur'an recitations and the guard has left me a copy of Sayyed Ali Khamenei's *Learning to Pray*. I start reading. I am trying to learn. I memorize sentences in Arabic. With difficulty, I make myself move about on my feet so I can walk and repeat the sentences and memorize them the way I am used to memorizing things. I have not yet uttered the first sentence when a wave of terror washes over me. All my aches and pains come back to life. I sit down and close the book. I find a solution, a solution that I later discover has been used by many other inmates. Instead of reciting Arabic words, prayers or verses, I start counting. I counted so it looked like I was praying and studying. I couldn't double up or bend down for prayers anyway. As soon as I sat down, a murderous pain would shoot through me, making me collapse on the floor. Sometimes these situations made me laugh, other times I would cry.

But I would do my ablution with proper pomp and ceremony. I knew the guards would be watching and report back. And you Brother Hamid, you were preoccupied with more important matters. My business with God was my own affair. You were busy completing my file.

I have barked and I'm in the room upstairs.

"By the way, did you say that you knew Khosrow?"

"Yes, he's Rahman Hatefi."

"Crap. But never mind. Have the names and addresses of all the members of the secret network ready by the time I get back. Including organizational structures, especially the military wing."

You walk out. I crumble. The secret network? The military wing? Immediately I am reminded of Khamenei's hints to Kianuri. But I am sure that Navid has been dissolved as was stated in the final notice. The only individual I knew to be a member of the secret network was Rahman. Rahman's role has been revealed.

You return very quickly: "Have you written everything down?"

I am sure the secret network is no longer active.

You laugh out aloud.

"Man, you believe that once you say 'I repent, I repent,' we're going to believe any sort of rubbish you say. Get up, come on."

You grab my sleeve and drag me along. You are pushing me down the stairs. Before I can blink, I find myself seated on the metal bed. My brain is working automatically. Nothing is more frightening than the descent of another blow. I bark.

"If you write any more rubbish, 'woof, woof' is not going to help you. First you will be punished and then you will join Comrade Manuchehr."

And you throw a pile of papers and a biro onto the bed and leave. I pull up my blindfold. The walls are bloodstained. The horrible bleach bottle is still on the chair. My mind starts racing. I assume that every secret network has an open part and a military part. The military section must include the air force, the territorial army and the navy. And so I draft a probable structure.

On each branch I put five people who are linked to each other horizontally. I give them names, changing the first names and giving them surnames that I still remember. For example, instead of Yusef Mohammadi, I write Mohammad Yusefi and so on. When I draw the invented military wing's chart, I pull out the page. I redraw it neatly on another piece of paper and cross over the original page and put it into the pocket of my prison shirt.

As soon as I hear the shuffling sound of slippers, I put on my blindfold and hold out the page in your direction. There is silence. You must be reading the chart. Then, without saying a word, you leave and you don't return for a long time. While you are gone, the guard brings in food and I go to the bathroom. Then the guard takes me to the room upstairs. You are waiting and your voice has become gentle again: "Sit down, little lion, sit down. Why didn't you write down all the information at once, giving us and yourself a break? Now redraw the charts before I get back."

You leave and I redraw the chart, copying it from the original draft in my pocket. When you come back and pick up the charts, you hit me on my shoulder: "Well done!"

You sound happy. I have saved myself. No, I have put an even heavier pair of shackles around my ankles. I am killing myself for fear of death.

You leave and you don't come back. A long time passes before the guard comes and takes me to my cell. Qur'an recitations are being broadcast. I can't even sleep anymore. I go to the bathroom. I perform my ablution. I return. I do my numeric prayers and am so exhausted that I faint. The next morning the guard comes for me as soon as I have finished breakfast. He takes me to the room downstairs. There is the sound of shuffling slippers and then you. I say: "Hello."

You don't answer. Meaning, you are angry.

I say: "Woof, woof."

You take me upstairs. You don't say a word. You send me off to the room. I wait for a long time before you come. Then you stand over me, and you are almost shouting, happily chanting: "The case of Khosrow has become clear. The secret network has become clear. Everything has become clear. The military wing has become clear."

You say this and then leave. I take off my blindfold. Your words are echoing in my head: "Khosrow ... Secret network, military wing ..."

Are these new pages for the film script or the truth?

I am happy that I haven't related what I myself view as my only crime, which is my part in setting up a meeting between the Afghan ambassador and Foroughian. Besides, if what you are saying is true, then you must realize that I was totally ignorant of what was going on.

Eventually you return. I say hello. You respond. This means there's peace. You put a piece of paper on the arm of the chair: "The filthy Tudeh Party's infiltrators are in all the government departments."

There's a brief silence and then you say: "Write about everyone. Apart from the Imam and Mr Montazeri. They could all be infiltrators. Even I could be."

And you leave. I hadn't taken this issue into consideration. I stand up and as usual, walk slowly, gingerly. My feet are slightly better but from my head, which is perpetually aching, to my teeth and my shoulders and my feet, everything in my body is hurting to varying degrees. Sometimes I can't bear it any more. Sometimes the pain makes me faint. I keep walking and trying to remember the names of anyone who had ever said anything even slightly fishy about the government. I write down the names on the interrogation paper. I tell myself: "Fuck them. Let them think these guys are also in the Tudeh Party."

Then I add "information". I link them to the Party this or that way. I fill up several pages and am beginning to relax, thinking that I have done today's "confession".

You come and pick up the papers. You stand behind me. There's silence. You must be reading and then I realize you must have finished because you ask: "Is that it? Are you sure you haven't kept back any secrets?"

A shiver goes down my spine and my feet start burning. In exactly the same place where they still burn twenty-five years later.

Chapter 16

The Coup and the Bullshitters

Coup d'etat? Coup d'etat? Coup d'etat?

You were after a coup d'etat on those spring nights of 1983. We have reached those nights in this, my sixteenth, letter. No other phrase has been stranger to me. Who wanted to stage a coup d'etat? The Party? Nothing could be more ridiculous. Even if I had known about the secret network at the time, I wouldn't have believed this story. I now understand that extracting coup d'etat confessions was another stage in the Islamic Republic's metamorphosis. With the clamping down on the Tudeh Party, the regime had begun to eliminate the forces that defended the revolution but had a non-Taliban outlook. It was the same conspiracy theory that you used to destroy Ayatollah Montazeri's leadership, Brother Hamid. Then you moved forward, step by step and eventually took up the Taliban's arms and Al-Qaeda's banner.

Moshtarek Prison, 19 March to 1 April 1983

Spring has arrived, and the nights of the new Iranian year. I haven't been interrogated for a couple of days. The spring air carries the noise of the crowd in Toopkhaneh Square where a hundred years ago Sheikh Fazlollah Noori,[66] the intellectual figurehead of Brother Hamid and his fellow believers, was hanged. No one can stop the spring air from moving. It is now entering the cell, through the thick prison walls, via the rusty barbed wire. Everything is reflecting the change of the season.

I think it's New Year's Eve.[67] When the lights go off, I take it as a sign that the New Year has begun, and force myself to sit up, with great difficulty, leaning against the wall. For the traditional New Year's ceremony, I need seven items beginning with the Farsi letter "seen" or "s". In most Persian homes, these would include an apple, some wheat grass, garlic and other items beginning with "s", as well as a goldfish in a bowl of water, symbolizing life, arranged on a table in the living room. Of course, I don't have these objects to hand in my cell, so I substitute them with sugar cubes and bread. I break the bread into seven parts. I imagine my wife is sitting next to me. I stare at the "fish", which is bobbing up and down in the imaginary waves, and moving the apple's reflection in the mirror. The cannon shot[68] heralds the New Year, and we embrace each other.

For the first time, I spend New Year's Eve in prison. I was just about to go to sleep, with tears in my eyes, when I hear the shuffling sound of slippers. Food has been brought in. I try to sleep. I have to twist and turn until a part of my body accepts the pressure of my weight on it. I have just had a brief opportunity to catch some sleep when the sound of shuffling slippers wakes me up. I fall asleep again. I see my wife in my dream; she's wearing white and is telling the American businessman on board the Greek boat: "I am prepared to wear a sack over my head as long as my country is free and independent."

The businessman is laughing out loud and fish are leaping out of the sea. In my sleep, I feel something warm moving across my face. I brush it aside with my hand. I am in Toopkhaneh Square. Kaveh Golestan[69] is taking pictures. Brother Hamid is pointing at me with his hand. Some people are shouting. They run towards me.

"Death to the communists!"

I cover my face with my hands and turn my back. Some people dressed in black and holding a red flag are pointing at me:

"He doesn't pray! Death to those who do not pray!"

Something is running across my chest. I jump up, terrified. A warm thing is moving inside my clothes. Terrified, I rip off my clothes and shake them. I can't see whether a creature has got into my clothes or not. Reluctantly, I put my clothes back on and sit up against the wall. My eyelids have just begun to droop when I feel something is moving up my hand. Automatically, I grab it and crush it. The stomach-churning heat of a cockroach's body makes me feel sick. I have just closed my eyes again when I hear the door lock being quietly turned. The door opens slightly and a voice says: "Hey! Stand up, come on ..."

It's you, Brother Hamid. In the darkness, I dig my blindfold out of my pocket and put it on. I touch my other pocket – my glasses are there. I put on my slippers and walk out. You are waiting for me outside the door.

"How are you? Fine?"

Your voice is very gentle, but I am more afraid of the kind tone of your voice than of your anger. I grasp at straws: "If you have lots to do for me, I should perform my prayers first."

You laugh: "No. You'll be back in time for the dawn prayers."

We pass by Under the Eight. We enter a triangular courtyard. The cold wind is making me shiver. The spring air comes from the snow-capped Alburz Mountains, bringing with it the sound of the water springs. You sit me down in a corner. There's a prolonged silence.

"How are you? Fine?"

I answer: "Thank you."

"Pain anywhere?"

I say: "From head to toe. I have asked the guard for a doctor a few times. He said that I would need your permission."

You are saying: "No. What I mean is do you have any specific illness, like a heart condition or something to do with the lungs or whatever."

"None."

"Are you sure?"

"Yes."

You say: "I have not yet had the chance to ask about your family. I only know that your father is very pious."

"Yes, that's correct."

"Your mother?"

"She passed away."

"May her soul rest in peace. How many brothers and sisters do you have?"

I answer.

"How many uncles?"

I answer.

"Aunts?"

I tell him.

"Their names?"

I tell him: "Simin Taj, Mahin Taj."[70]

"Do you visit your aunts?"

I answer: "No, it's been years since I last saw them."

"Are you sure?"

"Yes."

"You haven't met any of them recently?"

"No."

"Do you know their telephone numbers?"

"No."

"Do you have any godmothers?"

"No."

You say: "Right. Lift up your blindfold now and have a look at this."

I do as he tells me and see a piece of paper.

"Put on your glasses and have a look."

My wife's familiar handwriting comes to life in the moonlight. There are no more than a few lines dancing about in front of me. They say:

My dear husband. I love you and am worried about you. I have sent you some pills with this letter. We were all in the garden, together, and thought of you. Give me a call if you can; you can find me through Aunt Pari.

I read the letter a few times. Later on I discovered that my wife, who had been trying everything to find me, had sent this letter together with the pills that I needed for an eye problem, to the address of the Revolutionary Guards' headquarters.

"Now take off your glasses and put on the blindfold."

You take the paper from me.

"Right? Did you get the secret code?"

"The secret code?"

"Yes. The secret code. Didn't you say you do not have any serious illness? What are the pills for, then?"

"I had forgotten it, with all the pain that I am having. Besides, it's not an illness. The pills are to improve ..."

"What about your aunt. Didn't you say that you haven't seen any of them recently?"

"Of course."

"So who's Aunt Pari?"

"We used to call our friend, Mrs Parvin, Aunt Pari. Since we didn't have a telephone at home, we used to use hers in emergencies."

This is what I explain to you, Brother Hamid.

You are saying: "Let's see."

"Let's see" is a filler expression that smells of death. You take my hand to lead me down to the room downstairs and push me onto the metal bed. I bark automatically.

You say: "Shoo, shoo."

Then you handcuff me. While hanging me up in the air, you whisper gently into my ear: "Things have remained untold. The important things have remained unsaid."

And you leave. I am hanging in the air in the middle of a spring night, and limitless pain, from my head to my toes, is joining up. I yell so much that you have to come back. I am both dreading the shuffling sound of slippers and am waiting for them. The hands that have tied me up are also the ones that can untie me. As soon as you arrive, I say: "Woof, woof."

"Right. Speak up."

No, there was nothing. From the moment I was strung up, my mind had been focusing on the meeting between Foroughian and the Afghan ambassador. I say: "I forgot a very important spying matter."

By now you have noticed that I am blowing matters of little significance out of all proportion. You say: "Okay?"

"I arranged the meeting between Foroughian and the Afghan ambassador."

You reply in a mocking tone: "What an important story. Wait a moment."

You leave and I don't know how long it takes before you return. Judging by what you say, you must be reading through the confession of someone who had already explained the whole story. Then you say: "Don't bother wasting your time, Mr Asadi. We know everything. We even know about the main purpose of that meeting. But you don't happen to know the purpose, right?"

I say: "No …"

You laugh. You whisper in my ear: "Do you remember the first night and your first slap? We have returned to that moment: coup d'etat!"

And then you leave, again.

Coup d'etat? Coup d'etat? Coup d'etat?

That phrase completely threw me. I still couldn't work out who might be planning to stage a coup d'etat. The Party? Nothing could be more ridiculous. Even if I had known about the Party's secret network at the time, I wouldn't have believed this story. I now realize that extracting coup d'etat confessions was just another stage in the Islamic Republic's metamorphosis. With the clamping down on the

Tudeh Party, the regime had begun to eliminate all the forces that were defending the revolution but had a non-Taliban outlook. It was the same conspiracy theory that you used to remove Khomeini's designated successor Ayatollah Montazeri.

My memory is not helping me in concocting a lie that will get me released. I just keep yelling. You come back a few times. You untie my hands. You make me shake them. If I don't do this myself, you grab my hands and pull them hard. Every time I ask for the bathroom, you ignore me. The walk to and from the bathroom is the biggest chance for relaxation, it is the path from hell to heaven. Eventually, you let me: "Hey, go to the bathroom. At the end of the day, I'll give you your own crap to eat."

The guard, who's a bathroom specialist, accompanies me. He tells me to leave the toilet door open. He's standing and watching me. He immediately starts shouting: "Finish and come out!"

I finish. Even now when I remember that guard my bowels give up. He's taking me back, quickly. This time we pass through the courtyard and walk up the stairs. I take a breath. I am feeling relieved.

It turns out the coup d'etat story is a lie. Or at least, I don't know about it.

We are not going back to the interrogation room. We are two floors above that room. Again, I can see from under my blindfold a group of people dressed in military uniform, sitting down and reading some papers. Someone grabs me under my arms and takes me to a room, which seems to be large hall.

"Lift your blindfold. Open those blind eyes of yours."

It's you, Brother Hamid. I do as I'm told. You hand me two pages of interrogation results.

"Read."

One of the main Party leaders has confessed that the Party had intended to stage a coup d'etat.

Then you show me a video clip. Another Party leader is saying the same thing.

You pick up the papers and take me downstairs. We walk slowly and again you have become gentle: "We know everything. The military wing. The weapons. Everything. Everything. We are finding out all about the ins and outs of the coup. You bastards assumed that Iran is like Afghanistan …"

We go to the room downstairs. You string me up and then leave. The blow is sudden and incapacitating. The words on the paper run before my eyes. I see images of the Party leaders, hanging from the ceiling, and confessing to a coup d'etat. My mind refuses to cooperate and fails to come up with any lies. The thought of the Party launching a coup is as ridiculous as saying that Lenin is going to enter the room to untie me. Our Party's strategy has been to maintain the policy of "unity and criticism", even if we find ourselves facing the noose. Besides, even if there were plans for a coup, what have I got to do with it? They have arrested the main leaders of the Party, and they even have the intelligence guys. Compared to them, who am I to know anything about the coup? These thoughts are meandering through my mind and I just keep yelling, and am now shouting "O Master of the Age!"[71] Maybe it's my father's voice, reaching me through the years and resonating through my mouth. I keep yelling until I faint. Then they bring me back to my senses. They forcefully shake my hands and then hang me up again. The only solution left to me is suicide. As I am hanging between the ground and the air, I think that I should save myself in any possible way. First, I try to push myself towards the wall so I can hit my head. The rope is too short for this and the increased pressure adds to the unbearable pain.

You keep coming, Brother Hamid. Following the strict rules of interrogation, you are obliged to untie my hands at specific intervals. You make sure I shake my hands, and as soon as the muscles come back to life, you tie me up again and leave.

"Your comrades started talking after the first threat. The more resistance you put up, the more obvious it is that you are keeping an important secret."

I don't know whether it's day or night when you come back and untie me, and leave me unhandcuffed. I assume from the smell of kebab that you have ordered something special for me to prevent my body from collapsing. The prisoner has to be kept alive, he must have enough energy to talk. This is the best time for me to put my thoughts into practice. I say my goodbyes to life, to my wife and to the spring. I break the lens of my glasses. The same glasses that were trampled under the feet of the crowds inside the police station's weapons arsenal on 11 February, the day of the revolution's victory. First, I cut the veins in my wrist. Then I swallow the bloodied bits of glass and calmly stretch myself out on the floor. I feel the blood oozing out of me. Now, when I look at the scars on my wrist, I am reminded of that time when I found death to be so much sweeter than life. I wet my hand with my blood and drag myself close to the wall and write: "I am neither a Savak agent nor a spy. The confessions were taken from me under torture."

I imagine they'll publish my photograph along with my confession of being a Savak agent and a spy, and that this nightmare will follow me into death.

When I regain consciousness, I find myself unable to move. At first I assume I have been buried. But no, I can hear a familiar voice. People seem to be talking in whispers. I open my eyes. Next to me there is a thin, white curtain, and behind the curtain are two people, talking. You are one of them, Brother Hamid, and my whole body shakes in terror.

Then I realize that an intravenous drip is going into my hand. My wrists have been bandaged and tied to the bed. The guard/doctor sticks his head round the curtain and smiles. Then he comes to take my blood pressure, checks my heartbeat, and unties me: "Put on your blindfold ..."

I stand up with difficulty. I put on my blindfold and am being handed over to you on the other side of the curtain. "Woohoo, Mr Hero."

You take my arm and help me walk into the prison courtyard. I can feel the sun. I smell the scent of spring and hear the sound of a bird singing somewhere. Then it gets dark and we walk down the stairs.

"Obviously you are hiding a serious secret if you are even prepared to die for it."

In a voice sounding as if it is coming from deep inside a well, I say: "I don't know anything. My previous confessions were all fabrication …"

You are laughing: "We shall see …"

When we reach the Under the Eight, I hear a cry from the courtyard: "Bring in Mrs Amiri."

Amiri is my wife's surname. Initially, I don't understand the meaning of these words. Then, the words connect to each other one by one in my brain and I see my wife being dragged along, her hands handcuffed.

We enter the room downstairs. You make me sit on the edge of the bed. The unfinished death has given me new courage. I am not barking.

You hand me a tall white bottle.

"Drink this."

Inside the bottle is a thick, tasteless white liquid. You force me to drink it. Then you put a plate next to me. You pick something up from it and give it to me.

"Eat all these potatoes. Wash them down with the water."

I touch the potato. It's large, unpeeled, and covered in mud. With my fingers I touch the plate. It's full of raw potatoes. You hand me a jug: "Go, fill this up with water and come back. Whatever shit you need to do, get it over with. You'll be here for quite a while …"

I drag myself along, the jug in my hand, and enter the block. The left side has been all but emptied of people; apart from a figure wrapped in a black chador, sleeping on a blanket. My legs are shaking. So far I have not seen women in this block. I drag myself to the bathroom. I fill the jug with water and return. I stand over the woman and look at her from underneath my blindfold. There is no one in the corridor. I whisper my wife's name: "Nooshabeh?"

The woman, who's been lying on the blanket, collects herself upon hearing my voice, but she's not speaking. Again, I say: "Nooshabeh?"

I hear the guard's voice: "Why have you stopped?"

I start moving again, and go to the Under the Eight. My hands are shaking and the water is spilling. The guard is taking me into the room downstairs and we sit down on the edge of the bed. You say: "Start eating."

I pick up one of the raw potatoes and bring it towards my mouth. I can't bring myself to bite into it. You say: "If you wish, I could call your wife to clean them for you."

And you cram the potato into my mouth. I take my first bite and taste the mingled flavours of mud and raw potato. I chew with my broken teeth and force myself to wash the potato down with the water.

Later I find out that they had realized from the wounds on my lips that I had swallowed the broken glass from my lenses and were trying to clear my stomach. The white liquid was a laxative. I don't know how many potatoes I have swallowed when a woman's piercing screams make a shiver go down my spine. I can hear the sound of whipping from somewhere, and the woman screaming. You say casually: "I don't think your wife is going to put up as much resistance as you."

The first movement of my bowels is imminent. All of a sudden the pressure is intense and accompanied by a cramping stomachache. I grab my stomach and gasp out: "Bathroom!"

It's as if you've been waiting for this moment. You snap the hand-cuffs around my ankles and before I know it, I am hanging from the ceiling by my feet, with only the tip of my nose reaching the floor. On cue, my bowels start heaving. A dreadful warmth is trickling down in the direction of my head and reaches my neck. My only solution is to yell. When I fall silent, I can hear the cries of the woman who is crying: "Help me …"

I don't know how much time passes before you come back and untie me. I take off my filthy underwear and trousers, still hearing the cries of the woman (my wife?) in the background. You give me another pair of trousers and again, I am up in the air, hanging, turning. This time, my filthy trousers and underwear are put underneath my nose and mouth. A new wave of bowel movements grips me. Again you untie me so I can change my trousers. Every time I am strung up, my mouth and nose dive deeper into the excrement, and every time I take a breath, the foul-smelling discharge enters my body through my nose and mouth.

This goes on until I finish eating all the potatoes, washing them down with three jugs of water. My stomach is throwing up everything it contains and my mouth is pushing down what the stomach has discharged.

You have at last lived up to your earlier promise, Brother Hamid: You are forcing me to eat my own shit.

Four or five days later, when you untie me, I have no heart or energy left for resistance.

"Say 'I ate shit.'"[72]

"I ate shit."

"Again: 'I ate shit.'"

"Now bark, spy."

"Woof, woof."

"Sit down on the floor, dog. Walk on all fours and bark."

I do as I'm told.

By the time you untie me, I am utterly, totally broken. I am wracked with waves of vomit and diarrhoea. My headache intensifies. I am cold and shaking uncontrollably. I am empty. I have nothing left to lean on. That is exactly why there's repentance. Repentance holds a special place in Islamic theory. It is one of the tools of interrogation. For both the prisoner and the torturer. The prisoner wants to be freed. The interrogator, who under huge pressure relies on Islamic compassion, wants to get into the inner world of the prisoner by forcing him to repent. The whip and the handcuffs are there to overcome the prisoner physically. Repentance is there to overpower the soul. It's as if you open up your own chest to allow a spear to strike through to your heart. The interrogator knows very well that claiming to repent is yet another lie told by the prisoner, another role acted out by the prisoner. He also understands that confessing to having repented pulls away the ground from beneath the prisoner's feet, breaking him.

The ideologically driven interrogator takes pleasure both in extracting confessions and making use of confessions. This type of interrogator, be they employees of a Stalinist system or the likes of Brother Hamid, reach their climax when intellectuals throw themselves at their feet, repenting and laying down the banner that represents their worldview. To repent is to be both disarmed and to be hanged. As soon as one repents, the benefits and advantages that come from repenting are relegated to the hereafter, and to God's judgement. The interrogator is in charge of the earthly rewards of repentance, and if you repent, he stops torturing you, he gives you freebies, allows you visitors or keeps promising you that you'll be allowed visitors. The interrogator always wants the prisoner to take yet another step to prove that his repentance is authentic. And eventually, a point is reached when the prisoner turns up in the execution square, firing bullets at his own wife, mother and father.

I cannot eat food. I cannot even drink water. Everything smells of excrement. Everything has become shitty. My stomach is discharging and my mouth is vomiting. Deep inside, my lungs are filled with shit. Your diagnosis, Brother Hamid, is that I am acting out a new role. You distrust the Baluch doctor as well. The poor man is pleading with you in that accent of his. You order them to grab hold of my hands and feet and throw water into my mouth. Water mixed with compote, and I throw all of it up.

I have lost track of time, space and myself. I have difficulty even recalling my wife's eyes. Instead I hear her cries; she is hanging from the ceiling and screaming. The only person I interact with is you, Brother Hamid, only you. The sound of shuffling slippers is nearing. For days you don't let me go back to my cell. I am either in the room upstairs, in the corridor outside, or in the room downstairs, a place close enough for you to push me quickly if you are in a rush. We sit down on the bed. I say: "I ate shit."

I am on all fours, crawling and barking and telling you the story of a coup. Step by step, you communicate to me your ideas, bringing other people's written confessions so I can add interest to the soup, adding oil and onions so I am not returned to the ritual of eating my own shit. You must be doing the same thing to others, too.

I am no longer myself. I have become what you tell me, Brother Hamid. And you tell me that in May 1982, the British instructed me to arrange a meeting in Tehran with the Soviet representative. The meeting place was Paprika restaurant, at the top of Villa Road. The British had come to an agreement with the Mujahedin to launch a coup with the support of the Tudeh Party. I made sure the news of the agreement reached Rahman and to ensure my complete safety, I broke off all contact with the editorial staff at *Kayhan* and stopped going to the newspaper office. A few days prior to my arrest, the British representative arranged a rendezvous with me in his car under the Hafez Bridge and announced the designated day for the coup, which was 1 April 1983. He told me that the Soviets had informed the Party via a separate source.

I now realize how my previous confessions have been used. The words of a *Mardom* reporter – who nine months prior to his arrest had severed ties even with the editorial desk, who had no serious, organizational responsibilities in the Party, and was totally unaware of its secret network – would not be considered evidence by anyone. But the situation changes if he's a British spy who is also an agent for Savak and the KGB. I can't believe such a ridiculous story even for a moment. I have no doubt that the Party is incapable of launching such a coup; besides the Party is not getting along with the Mujahedin. You insist that this is the truth, and of course I am not sharing my thoughts with you, Brother Hamid. In order to help you develop your film script, I'd report to meetings between the British, the Soviets and Kianuri, and you would insist that I had been in charge of delivering information to Rahman. So I wrote down what you wanted me to write down.

I drink a bit of water and compote juice. I am breaking into pieces, day by day. I smell of shit. I think I've got lice. I drag a particular blanket around with me wherever I go. I put my slippers under my head and go to sleep. I sleep in Under the Eight, outside the room downstairs or in the room upstairs. The room upstairs is best; it's warm and I can see the ghost of my face reflected in the metal wall of the bathroom.

I am fully at your service, Brother Hamid. I, who have become your tongue. You read me the Party leaders' confessions to the coup. Moshtarek Prison is full of hustle and bustle. Work is going on, day and night. The sound of crying can be heard. The business of extracting confessions is going well. Then it's time to determine the coup regime. You become animated and say: "Congratulations Mr Asadi, you have become the head of both the radio and television."

"I?"

"Yes, you. The coup regime has given you the chair."

I say: "The most responsibility I would be given would be that of a reporter for a newspaper."

You say: "Don't be modest, please."

And you show me someone's handwriting, I don't know whose, but he has introduced me as the head of the radio and television. Okay, I accept this, and become a TV boss. There are other officers identified as well. If my memory serves me right, Kianuri is to be the president, Amoui the commander of the air force, Shaltouki the commander of ground forces, Hatefi the minister of culture, Khodayee the minister of intelligence, Kayhan the minister of labour, Amir Nikayeen the minister of agriculture.

According to this plan, the Soviet forces will be entering via the Afghan and Tajik borders. The Mujahedin are being organized by the British.

Chapter 17

The Night of the Coup

Ali Shamkhani[73] *was the deputy chief of the Revolutionary Guards Corps back then. He had asked me: "The coup story, is it true?"*

I had insisted it was a lie. He slapped me on my ear, then shook me hard. Later, whenever I saw him smartly dressed in his post as minister of defence in Khatami's reformist cabinet, my ears would make a whistling sound.

I spent the whole night of the supposed coup twisting and turning, between sleep and wakefulness. You came and went, and each time you hit me on my head. My tooth is still aching as it did on that night, even though it was pulled out yesterday. No pain relief seems to work on it. It's cold and I am writing. Do you remember, Brother Hamid? That night you were wearing a mask. The rest of them were also wearing clothes that revealed their true nature: you all looked like members of the Ku Klux Klan.

Moshtarek Prison, the night of 2 April 1983

How many nights have I spent sleeping outside the door of the room downstairs or the room upstairs? I don't know. You have been kind and haven't taken away my blanket. During these days I struggle to drink water and eat compote. I try very hard not to throw up. You are right, Brother Hamid. Shit has taken over my whole body, has even gotten into my heart. Since the eat-your-shit ceremony – I don't even know which day of the month it is – I have written down whatever you wanted me to write.

I'm huddled under my blanket, in the corner of the room upstairs. I hear the sound of doors being opened and then closed. Some people pick me up and take me off somewhere, then bring me back. The door opens and I can hear the shuffling sound of slippers.

"Face the wall. Put on your blindfold."

I do as I'm told. Someone grabs hold of my hand. Removes the blanket from my shoulders and takes me away. It's you, Brother Hamid, dragging me to the room downstairs and hanging me up. You say: "You don't have much time until I feed you shit again. Tell us the exact time of the coup."

I bark.

"Shut up, useless wimp. Stop acting."

"First of April."

For the first and last time, you make a confession: "That's the one I told you."

That is the one.

My mind is not working. The coup, which from the beginning was organized by you, Brother Hamid, has no external existence in my mind. I mean, what sort of coup is it when its leaders are already in prison? Could its date change and the report of the changed date reach me? I am totally quarantined.

You say: "Wait now, I'll be back in a sec …"

You leave and return a bit later. You untie me. You move my shoulders. It feels like they are being split from my body. You place me on the bed. There is an awful smell and I don't know where it's coming from. I assume it's me and that I have shitted myself again. I touch my trousers. My stomach has nothing left to digest. You are watching my movements and say: "You have eaten your own shit. Now you have to eat your comrades' shit."

And you hand me something. It's a spoon.

"Pull up your blindfold."

I pull it up. A red plastic spoon is in my hand and there's a bowl next to me. I realize that the awful smell is coming from there. You say: "Please, help yourself."

Even now I cannot believe it. With a shaking hand, I am dipping the spoon into the bowl. I feel sick and want to throw up. With a shaking hand, I lift a spoonful. Bring it closer to my mouth. My whole body is crying out "no"; I throw away the spoon. Four strong hands grab my head and push it into the bowl.

[I have broken into a sweat and cannot write down the rest, how spoonful by spoonful ...]

It's good medicine. The correct date of the coup becomes clear: "The third of April."

You explain that all the comrades have confessed the correct date and you are counting on me to confirm it.

"Eighth of April?"

"No."

Why did I say no? I myself have absolutely no idea why.

"Fifth of April?"

"No."

"Third of April?"

For no apparent reason, I blurt out:

"Yes."

Why did I say yes? Again, I don't know. Maybe deep down my brain is looking for a memory linked to this number.

And I hear you running and running. The last chance to foil it is this evening, 2 April 1983. I only know this because the date has been shouted out.

The guard takes me away. He allows me to wash my face and gargle as much as I can. Then he takes me to the room upstairs. There's a huge commotion. Yelling can be heard from behind all the doors. In the corridor, he makes me stand, facing the wall. I hear the continuous sound of blows. Someone is being slapped in a rhythmic and uninterrupted manner. I hear some people coming along the corridor. They walk past me, quickly. The guard takes me to a room and sits me on a chair. He tightens my blindfold. I hear some people entering the room. A chair is being moved and placed in front of me. Suddenly, in the dark and out of the blue, my jaw is being hit hard, on the same spot where I pulled out the broken tooth yesterday. There's a pause for a second and then the subsequent blows …

[My whole body is shaking in the cold of exile. It takes me two hours to regain composure and get back to writing. I have to finish this.]

I don't know how many blows. Heavy and without pause, finishing off my already broken teeth. I am about to collapse when it stops. From behind my back, a voice says:

"Lift up your blindfold."

It's your voice, Brother Hamid.

I take off my blindfold.

In front of me, I see Ali Shamkhani, dressed in the Revolutionary Guard uniform. He's the one who's been doing the slapping. He asks in a thick, southern Iranian accent: "Do you recognize me?"

"I don't have my glasses."

He moves his head forward.

"Now?"

I nod my head.

"Who am I?"

"Mr Shamkhani."

"I have only one question. The coup story, is it true?"

I say: "No. It's a lie."

The blow descends hard.

"It's a lie?"

"Yes."

Another slap: "It's a lie?"

"Yes."

Then I hear your voice, behind my back, Brother Hamid: "He's playing games again. He's one of the seasoned ones."

Shamkhani is standing up. But it is you, Brother Hamid, who says: "Put on your blindfold, useless wimp."

I put it on. You pull me up and drag me along. You are dragging me to the room downstairs. I have found strength for a moment. I tell myself: "I'd rather die than accept this."

As if you have read my mind, you say: "Let's see whether it's a lie, Mr Hero …"

And I am not a hero. When I am hanging from my feet, a bowl of shit placed under my mouth, I yell: "Woof, woof. It's true."

You untie me and take me upstairs. Again, I sit on a chair and take off my blindfold at your request. Ali Shamkhani is standing in exactly that same spot. He says: "Tomorrow's coup, is it the truth or a lie?"

I pause. A hand grabs my hair from behind and Ali Shamkhani's slaps hit my face, right and left.

"It's true."

Shamkhani stands up and says: "Take him upstairs."

And leaves.

We set off. This upstairs is different from the usual upstairs. It's so far away. Eventually we arrive. I sense I have entered a large hall. You, Brother Hamid, push me down onto a chair. I hear a whisper from somewhere. I lift my head slightly. I use my eyebrows to push the blindfold up as much as I can. It's a large hall. That's all I can see. The sound of shuffling slippers arrives. You grab my sleeve and drag me along. We walk up two or three carpeted stairs. I see a number of black chairs. You, Brother Hamid, are putting me on one of them.

"Pull up your blindfold."

I lift it up.

The room lights up. I don't turn round. I am on a raised dais, three steps above the ground. I'm sitting behind a wooden table. In front of me are television cameras and next to them some people wearing the Revolutionary Guard trousers with their faces covered. Just like the Ku Klux Klan. I hear your voice, Brother Hamid, from behind me: "When I lift my hand, you'll start. Just the same things you have already confessed to. Introduce yourself, briefly. If you feel like it, ask for forgiveness at the end."

You move your head close to my ear: "Or else, we will have to go downstairs."

The sound of slippers walking away. I see a thin, masked man walking down the steps and joining the rest. A few words are exchanged. A hand is raised. The lights are turned on and the cameras are running. I can see myself on the monitor screen next to me. My beard has grown bushy, it's reddish. It has not yet turned white. I stroke my beard. Later I find out that in the first sample recording the look and dress of the confessor does not matter. You, Brother Hamid, lift your hand. And I begin: "In the name of God, the Compassionate, the Merciful ..."

I first introduce myself and then explain the film script. My hands are shaking. Below, the Ku Klux Klan crowd is watching me, with their black masks on. Shamkhani is in the middle of them. I don't know why my voice is shaking. My wife's image appears in front of me and she's crying. I see Rahman, whose face has gone red up to his ears. And suddenly, a terrible weeping causes me to break down. The lights are snapped off. You, Brother Hamid, pick me up and throw me down the steps. Then you kick me in the stomach. I crumple.

In the corridor, I huddle under my blanket, sobbing. I hear voices. Shouts. I later learn that that night all the Party leaders, except for Kianuri, confessed to a coup. I don't know what time it is when the guard arrives, grabs my sleeve, and drags me after him. We walk down the stairs. We pass through the courtyard. But we are not going to Under the Eight. I don't know where we are. The guard makes me sit down in a corner and says: "Pull the blanket over your head and don't move."

I am shivering in the cold. I push the blindfold up on my forehead. Slowly, slowly, I lift my head over the blanket. I am leaning against a wall along with two other people, each of us covered with a blanket. The distance between us makes it impossible to talk or identify one another. I pull the blanket back over my head and try to sleep for a few minutes. My mind has closed down, completely overwhelmed by events. I guess that they want to take us to the garden. Brother Hamid has repeatedly questioned me about it, and in the end this is where the imaginary coup was designated to take place. Except for one occasion, I have only been to the garden in times of danger. If Rahman were to find out that I had been to the garden accompanied by the Revolutionary Guards, he'd do something about my predicament. But how? Myself, the self that I used to be, is pushing aside all the torture, the prayers, the shit-eating, and is grasping at flimsy straws of hope. Eventually someone arrives and grabs my sleeve. I am handcuffed and forced into a car. A voice says: "Put your head down." I do as I'm told and a blanket is dragged roughly over my head. A while later, the car starts moving. I am trying to figure out where we are going when a voice says: "Lift your head."

I lift my head. The street lamps have not yet been turned off and there is a faint glow on the horizon. The car moves through the traffic on a rainy spring morning, joining other cars, taxis, and trucks in lots of different colours. Since I can't see without my glasses, I am forced to squint to see better.

On the way, Brother Sedaghat, who is in charge of the operation, says something in code language into a walkie-talkie. The Hillmans all pull over to the side of the road, and a large number of people, dressed in both Revolutionary Guard uniforms and civilian clothing, get out, place their weapons on the ground beside them, and start performing the dawn prayer in the rain.

When the prayer is finished, the cars all move off towards the garden. The Hillmans come to a stop, a short distance apart. Mine is right in front of the gate.

Brother Sedaghat announces: "Get ready. We have been ordered to shoot you all right here, in front of the gate."

He leaves, his walkie-talkie in his hand. I have pressed my head against the window and am watching this unbelievable scene. A large number of guards are running towards the ruins to the north of the garden, their guns at the ready. Gradually, it dawns on me that there must be a coup underway, and that the garden is its centre. The one who is me and who has raised his head from deep inside me, is tempting me: "Get out …"

I am scared. The me that is me is saying they'll hang you without hesitation. Sooner or later. Maybe your wife will be rescued. Maybe Rahman. I pull the door handle with the handcuffed hand. It opens. I put my feet outside. I hesitate, but the me who is me makes me get out. As soon as I reach the gate, it opens. Brother Sedaghat is dragging along Mash[74] Akbar, the gardener. Poor Mash Akbar, fear has made his eyes pop out. Brother Sedaghat asks me: "Who told you to get out of the car?"

"I am sorry, urine …"

"Is this the gardener?"

I say: "Yes. That's Mash Akbar."

Brother Sedaghat asks him: "Do you know this man?"

He says: "No."

"Tell Mash Akbar your name."

It is clear that he doesn't recognize me. I don't have my glasses on, I have a long beard, and I'm wrapped in a blanket. The me that is me is saying:

"Mash Akbar. I am Houshang Asadi."

Mash Akbar shakes his head. They take him back into the garden, and tell him there has been a theft, and they need to search the place. They set about searching the whole garden, even digging up the floor of the little pool, looking for the weapons they believe must be hidden there in readiness for the coup. The driver walks back towards the Hillman. First he sits on the back seat and closes the door. Then he gets behind the wheel and calls me over. I walk back and get into the car. They close the doors. It is now light. Brother Sedaghat returns with Mash Akbar. He puts him into the car too and tells the driver to drive. We set off, passing through back roads before reaching a surfaced road. Brother Sedaghat is saying: "Why did you lie? We kept telling your interrogator that it was a lie but he insisted that it was not."

I say: "I told Mr Shamkhani that it was a lie."

Brother Sedaghat replies: "We are going to take you on a picnic so you can learn to stop telling lies."

Then, laughingly, he turns to Mash Akbar: "We've got just the place for a picnic; Mr Asadi knows the place very well."

Mash Akbar, who is shaking in fear, is looking at me. I say: "It's me alright. It's just that I've grown a beard."

I am sure that even if he hasn't recognized my face, he will definitely remember my name. I am confident that he will phone Rahman's sister-in-law, who in turn will get in touch with Rahman. My heart fills with joy. Brother Hamid's ridiculous game is now working against him.

Years later, I discover that Rahman, accompanied by my wife and the poet Siavash Kasrai, had gone to the garden for the thirteenth-day picnic following the New Year. Mash Akbar had in fact told Rahman's sister-in-law that day, and she had passed on the news to Rahman. Rahman and Ali Reza Khodayee had analysed the information and had come to two conclusions:

the story of the theft could be true, and this was why the guards had searched the garden;

it was a sign that the situation in the prison was very bad, and that forced confessions had been taken from the Party members.

Even though his Russian contacts had informed Rahman on 1 April that confessions had been extracted from the prisoners, unfortunately they failed to read the situation correctly. That information, coupled with the raid on the garden, if accurately interpreted, could have alerted the remaining Party leaders, including Rahman, of the great danger they were in. Rahman sought out Farajullah Mizani, known as Javanshir, who was the Party's second-in-command and had not yet been arrested. Whatever the outcome of their discussions, no action was taken. Just twenty-three days later, the Revolutionary Guards, having extracted confessions from the political prisoners, launched their final assault on the Party and rounded up all the remaining key members in the early hours of 26 April 1983.

Why did they just sit there, twiddling their thumbs and doing nothing? I don't know, but it seems that Mash Akbar never told Rahman and my wife that I had been taken to the garden on the day of the raid.

The Hillman is moving fast. Once again I decide to end my ordeal. I inch my way very slowly towards the door. I grasp the door handle and glance at the horizon. I say my farewell to life. I see my wife's eyes; I see her running across the pedestrian crossing in the middle of the road, and pull the door handle. The door will open and I'll be cut into pieces on the asphalt road, turned wet by the rain. I may even go under the tyres of the two Hillmans that are following us, carrying two other people wrapped in blankets. The door won't open. I pull harder. It's not opening. I hear the sound of the driver's laughter: "That door is locked, Mr Asadi. Now lower your head."

I lower my head. The wet blanket is pulled over me. An hour later, I am thrown into a corner of the room upstairs. I know what is coming. The old caretaker doesn't know what picnic means, but I do. I rub my head against the wall and pull off my blindfold. I catch sight of an electrical socket. I move towards it. I hit the corner of the handcuffs against the socket frame and pull it off. I pull out the two cables, the red and the blue. Once again I say my farewells to my wife and life, and stick the sides of the handcuffs against the cables. I have had two full months of being tortured by you, if we add the nights of torture, I guess it might even add up to more than two months.

When I come back to my senses, I am all but a corpse, stinking from head to toe. First of all, I see a cockroach, high up on the wall. I guess he's frozen in that position. It's a large, brown cockroach. I am shivering with repulsion. I take off my prison shirt and fold it into a ball. With all the force of my broken body, I throw it up so it hits the cockroach, but the cockroach doesn't fall. It is holding onto life with all six legs. I throw my shirt again and again, until eventually it falls off. Steve McQueen ate his cockroach. I put a glass over it. I cover the glass with my clothes. I wait until it's time for the bathroom visit and I throw it out of my cell. It sticks to the ground. I lift my foot. I cannot kill it. I cannot kill you either, Brother Hamid. I cannot kill anything. The cockroach flees, running up the wall. I have had a terror of cockroaches ever since that night.

When the door opens, I assume it is you, Brother Hamid. But it's a man asking me whether I need some tidying up. I leave the cell and sit down on a wooden chair. The barber is a middle-aged man who does his work in absolute silence. I tell him to cut my hair and my beard very short. He does just that and a huge pile of hair falls onto the floor. I want to free myself from all the filth and the shit. When the barber finishes, he asks for money. I say I have none. He grunts and says he'll pick it up next time. As chance would have it, my turn for the shower room is the next day. I scrub myself in that brief spell of time. I would have pulled off my skin, had it been possible. But filth has reached the depths of my soul, the veins of my heart. I cannot eat. I am throwing up. I have to force myself to swallow water.

There is not a single healthy part of my mind left. I have gone crazy. I keep praying, from morning 'til night. I pick up Khamenei's book and perform prayers from it. I consult the Qur'an to tell my fortune. All I get is bad news. Whichever bit I look at, there's talk of killing. Kill them. Kill them. I cannot find in the Qur'an the compassion that Khamenei mentions in his book. I am all ears, waiting for the shuffling sound of slippers. I realize that I should be preparing myself. I plan story after story. I invent crimes that the Soviet Union intended to commit. I recall Tabari's words about Soviet plans and their power, and turn each one into an incident. I am working on the stories and am ready to bark when you arrive. To hand them over to you. For you to read them and not hang me from the ceiling again.

To read them and not whip me again. To read them and not feed me shit again.

But you do not come. Apparently you no longer have time. In your own words, you were busy rounding up the others. You are spreading your net to trap the military wing, the secret network, the leadership.

Once a week they bring in the nail clippers. They hand them out and collect them up afterwards. One of the guards usually asks: "Do you have any nail clippers?" If you say no, he moves on. A thought goes through my mind. When he comes back to collect the nail clippers from me I will say no to him, I will tell him that I do not have them. Then I will try to separate the sharp bit from the rest of the clippers. I'll put it under my prison clothes and sharpen it with the clipper's file. After all, I can't eat anything. I can only walk with difficulty. My thought is that when I get to the point of total weakness, I will cut my wrists at night, under the blanket, and in the morning, when they arrive to unlock the door, the deed would be done. And this idea becomes the comfort of my life. I have no doubt that they'll present me as a spy, and will publish it in their newspapers and stick it to the walls. My only wish is to somehow make my voice heard in the outside world. To somehow manage to tell my wife that I have not been a spy. To tell her that I am who she knew me to be. In love with Iran. I don't want to leave anything to chance. So I set to work writing on the door and walls of the cell. I am writing to my wife. When they come to take away my corpse, they'll put someone else into the cell who will read these words, and that way they will reach my wife.

I sharpen the knife at night. Then I put it under the mat they have placed in front of the door. I hide the rest of the nail clipper somewhere else. I fall asleep, in love with death. Sometimes I hear the sound of shuffling slippers and feel that something is crawling over my hand. I jump. It's a nightmare.

I wake up in the morning to the sound of an Arab, Abdul Basit.[75] I go to the bathroom, doing my ablution with pomp and noise. I perform my prayers. I have learned them. Khamenei had told me inside one of these cells: "Under an Islamic government, not a single tear would be shed by the innocent."

And now I have learned to pray through reading his book, he who is now Iran's president. And I am not crying. The tears come later. I pray. The bits that I cannot remember, I count instead. Then I read the Qur'an like a book of fortune telling. I go to sleep. I write on the walls: "I am not a spy. I am not a spy. I am not a Savak agent. I had no idea about anything. I, I, I have gone crazy. I am trying to sleep. I can't. The cockroach is waking me up."

In the daytime, when they bring in the food, the smell makes me sick. I eat a little bit of sauce. I make a promise to myself to stay in control up to the last moment. A mixture of madness and reason.

The official in charge of the shop arrives once and knocks on the door. He is selling soap, toothpaste, dried figs and underwear. I have no money to buy anything. I wash my hair in the bathroom with the dishwashing detergent. I dry my hair with my blue prison shirt. I wash my underwear under the tap with the same detergent and then wait until it dries so I can wear it.

Once, I find some used dental floss in the bathroom. Somebody must have dropped it. I, who used to floss my teeth three times a day, am in my third month of not having flossed. I pick it up. From the depths of my heart, I revolt at the thought of putting someone else's floss into my mouth. My reason is telling me that I have no other option. I place the floss under the running water and wash it with detergent about ten times. Then I bring it to my mouth. I can't do it. I wash it again. I close my eyes and press it into my mouth.

Days pass but you no longer come for me. I have scratched one line per day on the wall, and am counting the days and months. My feet are slowly getting better. My headache has become chronic and will accompany me for many long years. My broken teeth are also still with me. I am not eating and I am getting weaker by the day. I can hardly stand.

There's no longer any sign of your love for me, Brother Hamid. You have forgotten me. The film script that you forced on me has turned out to be meaningless, and you are holding me accountable for it. You and the rest of the interrogators hate me. What great luck. You don't trust me a bit, an even greater piece of luck. Both times you called me up to ask about my brother, you didn't believe a single word I said. You arrested him on the same day as me. My brother, who has absolutely nothing to do with politics. He is kept in prison for three years, until it eventually becomes clear that he is just my brother, and that is his only offence.

Chapter 18

Return from the Grave

I spent the whole of last night walking around inside a castle with white walls and muddied corridors with no roof. You were wearing a tie, Brother Hamid, and were laughing and guiding me. Paul Auster's words come to my mind; I was reading him before I fell asleep: "I am a dead man who's writing the memoirs of a dead man."

His dead man is Chateaubriand who wishes he could get out of his grave in the middle of the night to correct his memoirs.

I picked the book from the shelf by sheer chance. I needed a powerful place to lose myself in. I, who am but an ordinary man exiled to the land of Chateaubriand, spent the whole night escaping from the grave of sleep, just like him, and corrected my memoirs in my sleep. I retrieved forgotten senses. The tooth that was pulled out was aching. My heart was burning, again.

I got up to write my eighteenth letter to your Eminence.

Moshtarek Prison, spring/summer 1983

The Qur'an recitations stopped three days ago. In the morning, when I go to the bathroom, the corridor is empty. I return to my cell and go back to sleep, but am soon jolted awake by the sound of crying; there is pandemonium outside. The window of my cell overlooks a small, brick-paved courtyard, the same courtyard where members of the Revolutionary Guards Corps play football in the summer. They have opened the doors of several large lorries, and simply emptied their human cargo into the courtyard. Underneath my window, a girl keeps crying and saying: "I am innocent."

In the afternoon when I go to the bathroom, the corridor is jam-packed. They have arrested the rest of the Party's leadership.

I realize that this could be a good day for dying. After all, I have become so weak that I can hardly get up, and I can't walk without leaning against the wall. I have filled the walls of my cell with as much writing as I can muster. Someone is going to read it all eventually and ensure that my wife hears my words. I decide to do it tonight, when the lights go off. But when dinner comes, so does another prisoner, dressed in blue.

As soon as he enters, he says: "They have betrayed us!"

His name is Reza. He explains that the Party had a mole inside the Revolutionary Guards Corps and they arrested him early that morning. They confronted the traitor informant with their evidence and he had admitted to it. Then he walks around the tiny cell, looking into every nook and cranny, and finds the little razor hidden underneath the mat. He asks: "Do you want to kill yourself?"

I don't reply.

He says: "They'll do it anyway, with a bullet."

With great enthusiasm he eats my dinner, which I haven't touched. He puts some leftover uncooked pieces of bread inside a cup and places the cup inside the jug.

When the door is opened for the nightly bathroom visit, he exchanges greetings with the guard. (Over the next few days I notice that he knows most of the guards.) I go to the bathroom. I perform my ablution out of sheer angst. He stands and mocks me. Suddenly, the door opens while he is throwing the leftover bread into the rubbish bin. The guard rushes in and hits us both hard on the head. He says in a thick, Turkish accent: "You bastards are throwing away God's blessing?"

In accordance with I don't know whose fatwa,[76] throwing away the inedible raw dough from the bread had been classified as a sin, and in the prison the raw dough has to be eaten along with the bread. One of the guards has a curious sensitivity about this particular Islamic rule and he watches to make sure no one is throwing away any bread.

The lights go off and we go to sleep. I am jolted awake, my body in the grip of violent convulsions. I'm shivering uncontrollably. I feel my joints disconnecting. I think my knees are coming apart. I was right. This is the night of death. Had Reza not arrived, I'd have used the little knife and they would have found my body at dawn. Reza takes my pulse. He leaps up and bangs loudly on the door: "He's dying!"

Sobbing, I say: "Leave me alone. Let me die."

He answers: "We must be killed with a bullet, like true soldiers."

He bangs and bangs on the door until they open it and two guards come in. They want me to put on my blindfold and stand up. I'm desperately weak. I have absolutely no energy. My muscles won't obey me. In the end, they grab me under my arms and half carry, half drag me upstairs. I find myself on a hospital bed, semi-conscious, hovering between life and death. I see the face of the guard/doctor. My vision blurs. It seems he's treating someone else as well. I can hear another voice:

"He must be given this injection, and he needs to swallow the pills. But most important of all is his blood sugar. He must be given compote for some days."

The guard/doctor asks me: "How many compotes should I get you?"

I have no idea how many. Feebly I shake my head. He asks: "Do you have money in your cell?"

I open my eyes with difficulty.

"I don't have any money."

Brother Heydari puts his hand into his own pocket, pulls out some money and gives it to the guard. I think to myself that it is very late to have to go out and buy compote. I wonder where the nearest shop is. The guard leaves and a little later, returns with apple compote.

The next day, first thing in the morning, they take Reza for interrogation. When he returns, he is laughing. He's got a strong physique. He hits his chest with his strong fists and says: "They have betrayed us; they have told them everything."

Towards the afternoon, Brother Davoud arrives. He's brought me a shirt and a singlet and some cans of compote. He says: "They cost 90 Tumans [about $2 at that time], but they are a gift from your interrogator."

You are embarrassing me, Brother Hamid. I've got to see you some day so I can repay you the 90 Tumans. If you read these memoirs, feel free to go and see my father and ask him for the money. In fact, come to Paris and let's have a beer. My treat.

Reza buys me oranges and dried figs. The figs and the compote are bringing me back to life. As usual, when I'm angry I start bingeing on food. Or maybe this is my body's natural reaction to the period of starvation. We eat so many figs that it is becoming a full-time occupation.

A few nights later, they give us rice and chicken for dinner. It's very tasty and I, who have now started demolishing my food in a rage, wolf everything down. When the lights go off and I get under the blanket, I feel my stomach churning. I sit up. I hear the sound of frantic banging on one of the cell doors. Then another door. Knocking on doors at this time of the night is unprecedented. Just then I feel my stomach spasm, and as a wave of discharge threatens, I rush to knock on my cell door too. A little later, a guard opens the door. He is supporting his back with his hand and yelling: "Run!"

I stagger to the bathroom. The chicken we had been given that night had gone off and the whole block was suffering from a serious case of diarrhoea.

I get up. I take my little dog out. There is frost everywhere. We walk to a lake. The elegant swans seem to rise up from the surface of the frozen water. The pillars, domes and minaret of a newly built mosque have surfaced. It's still just concrete and resembles Moshtarek Prison. I imagine Brother Hamid, dressed in buttoned-up diplomatic attire, standing on the top of the minaret and inviting the infidel world to share in Islamic fairness and compassion.

We walk across frost-covered grass. We reach a little wall that slips down towards the water like a white snake. My boy and I step over it. I want to get to a place where I can yell forever. A flock of white birds are seated on the railings. I stand still and facing the sun, I start screaming. Screaming.

My little boy is scratching my legs. I look at him. His father's cries have astounded him. He's looking at a sobbing, old man. A man with unkempt hair and a beard streaked with white.

Yes, Brother Hamid, you had gone. You had caught a lot of prey in your net, and finally you left me alone. I must confess that from this point on you stopped tormenting me. Later on, you just swore at me a few times.

I was left alone. I had no idea that this loneliness would last for two years, and that cell number fifteen would become one of my homes.

My headache has become chronic. I tear off a strip of my shirt and tie it around my head like a bandana. I wet it under the tap every time I go to the bathroom. Little by little, the headache becomes part of me, like the toothache, like the shoulder ache, and the piercing pain in my feet, my feet on which the lashes have left their marks, which are slowly getting better. I can now move my hands almost comfortably and have started doing some gentle exercise. The pain is lessening, but you can still see the bruises on my wrists from the handcuffs. I'll be keeping your souvenirs for the rest of my life. The handcuffs' mark on my right wrist. The trace of the cut that I made with the lenses of my glasses on the left one. The marks of the rope you tied my feet with. The burning pain in the soles of my feet. My wounded heart. The smell of excrement in my nose. The marks of the whip all over my back. Doctors always ask me: "Were you born with these marks?"

I answer: "No, but I'll take them to the grave with me."

That night, when I go to the bathroom, I fill up my jug as usual and am on my way back to my cell when I hear the voice of one of the main Party leaders being broadcast over the loudspeakers, announcing the Party's dissolution. I stop automatically. My knees are shaking and suddenly I collapse. I manage to get back on my feet, and drag myself to my cell. The Party leader's confessions[77] are being broadcast and a deathly silence fills the block. When the loudspeaker is turned off, there is absolute silence for a few minutes and then someone, somewhere, starts crying and suddenly, the whole block is shaking with the sound of weeping. The prisoners are crying in their cells. They are crying in the corridors. There is no other sound, apart from the sound of weeping. I lean against the wall of my cell and my whole body is shaking. Someone is shouting: "Look what we wanted to achieve, and look what has happened ..."

Again, a wave of crying starts and slowly dies down to intermittent sobs. I feel as if the ground underneath my feet has been pulled away and I am going down. My heart is empty and I have nothing to rely on. Everything has gone to the wind.

I recall the early golden days of revolution in the summer of 1981. Men and women, boys and girls, had come together in political organizations, with their heads held high and their hearts filled with the hope of freeing Iran. The Party members were happier and luckier than everyone else. The anti-imperialist, anti-oppression revolution was progressing under the leadership of Imam Khomeini. The American Embassy had been seized. Farmland was to be distributed to farmers. Workers were to have unions. We had to take this historical turn alongside the revolutionary democrats in order to reach socialism. From each according to his ability, to each according to his need.

The age of imperialism was on the wane, the sun of socialism was rising on the horizon. During the ceremonies, which were held surrounded by members of Hezbollah who carried self-flagellation chains, we used to hold hands and sing:

> The Tudeh Party is going to make us victorious
> Tomorrow is on its way, after today has gone.

My wife was bound to cry at some point during the song. In which cell was she being held? Later, I would learn that on that horrific night, she had placed her head on Firoozeh's shoulder and both of them had sobbed. They had seen the footage of the confessions, while I had only heard the voices. The golden days had gone with the wind now. We had been a small group of Party members. We used to come together almost every night. We spent holidays together. We used to go for walks together. We used to play together. We used to make a circle together and shout: "Death to America!"

Years later, quite by chance, I came across a very short roll of 16mm film that had been recorded on an old-fashioned cine camera back in those halcyon days. How happy we were. How young. How hopeful. We were on a calm island in the middle of a stormy sea. I am reminded of the words of Bahram Danesh, an old soldier who was hanged during the mass killing of political prisoners in 1988. He was seventy-eight. "We are tiny sparrows, twittering on a branch in the middle of a wild jungle full of predators."

On that spring night of 1983, my world collapsed inside me. Not long before, I had pretended to repent my beliefs under horrific torture and now those beliefs had turned to ashes. When the lights were turned off, the sound of the last cries were still audible.

I felt absolutely defenceless. For the first time in my life, I felt the need to pray. I put the prayer stone on a piece of paper and with a mixture of astonishment and excitement, I stood in front of it to

begin my prayers. That night was the first time that I felt so vulner-
able that I sought refuge in prayer. The God that I prayed to was a
creation of my own mind. Years later, I see him again in a hospital in
Paris, just before a heart operation. How different this God is from
the God of prison. That God resembled Brother Hamid, he was
dressed in black and was holding a whip. This one has light green
eyes and resembles the doctor who operated on me. I moulded God
in the shape that appealed to me. Just as I saw the Party the way I had
shaped it in my mind. I suppose everybody does this, whether con-
sciously or unconsciously.

I am alone in my cell. No one bothers with me any more. So I am left
alone with loneliness. The Qur'an, the prayer book, and *The
Ornament of the Righteous*. I start reading. I try to discover the truth in
the Qur'an. Maybe we have all been wrong. Maybe everything is
contained in the Qur'an. I am also reading *The Ornament of the
Righteous* very carefully. One section of this book, which offers a very
thorough examination of sexual issues, astonishes me. For any man
left alone in a cell, reading that section must be arousing. It's only
merit is that it is realistic, it is unintentionally drawing me back to the
real world, a world from which I have been cut off now for four
months.

I soon realize just how much I appreciate this involuntary
solitude in cell number fifteen. The chance to read and to think,
think, think …

Then the old feelings return, and the sorrow of the sunset fills my
heart. I have read somewhere that this feeling of tightness and alienation has it roots with the Africans who were stolen from Africa and
taken to Western shores. Every night, when the sun goes down, they
are filled with sorrow. Outside prison, I seek a cure for my feelings of
alienation in drink. But here, I seek refuge in prayer. A strange
thought occurs to me: alcohol shares some of the same intoxicating
qualities as prayer. Later on, my thoughts expand and I discover that

sin and the avoidance of it create similar sensations of pain and pleasure. There is little difference between Zorba the Greek and the oppressed of the past. Belief and disbelief also share these attributes. And I take more and more refuge in prayer. There's no one around to take any notice of this, so my newfound dedication to prayer cannot affect my future. When the prisoner repents during the interrogation, he has reached the stage where he is completely broken. The expert interrogator is aware that the act of repenting is a farce, but nevertheless the act of confession still has a powerful impact on the prisoner. He is broken inside, and for the interrogator this means he has accomplished his objective. The interrogator is the one who discovers the path towards spiritual meaning: he turns an infidel into a believer.

And cell number fifteen becomes my home. In the evening, the guards play football outside the window, and their shouts intrude on the comforts of solitude. One night, just when the lights go off, I hear a cry from the courtyard below: "Everyone! Look at what they are doing to us!"

It's Rahman's voice. He had said many times that he felt like shouting out right in the middle of Toopkhaneh Square, telling people who he really was, yet he had no choice but to hide his membership of the Tudeh Party. And that night, it was as if he was crying in the middle of Toopkhaneh Square. He was either on his way to or from the torture chamber.

Two years later I will find out that the following day his lifeless body had been found inside his cell. He had torn open the veins in his wrists with his teeth.

I don't know how I would have reacted had I been aware of Rahman's heroic death that night. Or what I would have done had I known his body had been left outside the window of my cell for forty-eight hours.

A few days later, a guard opens the door and takes me with him without a word. We walk up an old stone stairway. A door opens. The guard orders: "Take off your blindfold and go in."

I do as I'm told. The door closes behind me and the sun's glare hits my eyes. I find myself in the fresh-air section on the roof of Moshtarek Prison, which has been carefully covered and enclosed with metal bars. Pigeons have perched themselves on the bars. The sky is blue and a hot summer sun is shining. I cannot bear standing up. I sit down and lean against the wall. It takes a long time for my eyes to get used to the light.

Day by day, I am losing myself in the intoxication of prayer. The Arabic words are becoming meaningful. There is a short distance between atheism and true belief in God. Theism and atheism are two sides of the same coin, and when the two become absolute, they change shape, turning from spiritual tools into material means. When my hand reaches for the book, I read a passage that says that for mystics, saying a prayer is like drinking wine in paradise. A famous mystic had said about his lengthy prayer sessions that it was as if wine was bubbling up in his mind. Everybody moulds his God in the way that appeals to him.

One day, a tall guard turns up. He's in charge of the library. He gives me a list of books to choose from. Two days later, I receive two books of poetry, one by Rumi, the other by Hafez. I drown in the poetry, it washes away the filth of my days. My heart grows sadder and I pray even more. It doesn't matter what time of the day it is. As soon as I become sad, I perform my ablution and pray. I am somehow finding refuge in not having a refuge. Then I seek refuge in poetry.

One day, I spot this poem by Siavash Kasrai scribbled in tiny letters in pencil in the margin of the book I'm reading:

Though once again they've closed the tavern doors
Though they've smashed our bottles
Though they've extracted
   from lips, repentance
   from hands, the glasses
Tell the vice patrol to be on the lookout
As I'm still drunk with wine every night.

I read it. Ten times. A hundred times. After a while I hear my wife's voice: "Houshka ... Houshka ..." But no: she is not calling the Houshang who is sitting here; she wants the me who has been lost. I am just a puppet.

The following day is a Friday. I have had nightmares the whole night. At the end, I am standing on the top of the cliff from which Steve McQueen jumps at the end of *Papillon*. My wife is down there, in a boat. She's shouting: "Houshka, Houshka, don't be afraid. Jump. Jump."

I wake up with a jolt. I am full of sorrow, from my head to my toes. I knock on the door and go to perform my ablution. In the middle of my prayer, the door suddenly opens. I am prostrating so I do not lift my head. Someone kicks me hard on my side with his boots:

"Useless wimp, is this the time for prayers?"

I recognize your voice, Brother Hamid. You who have forced me to repent.

"Put on the blindfold and face the wall."

I do as I'm told. I sense that you have seated yourself by the door.

"What are you up to these days?"

I explain and you listen and then ask: "Need anything?"

"Of course I do. I've been here for a long time. Aren't you taking me to court?"

You sigh and say: "I've been waiting for this longer than you have. When the sentence is passed, I would like to shoot the final bullet myself."

There is the sound of a door closing. For a while I just sit there, blindfolded and facing the wall. Then I lift the blindfold. My restlessness intensifies, coming over me in wave after wave.

Who was I? What have I become?

What wonders that heartless kick did for me. The man who had thrown me into hell with the cut of a lash had pulled me out of it with a kick. For which one of these acts will he be rewarded and which punished? Would the God on whose behalf he was administering the lashes, and handcuffing me, and feeding me shit, reward the repentance that he had ordered, or would he reward the repentance that he had triggered inadvertently? My repentance, though initially false, had now become my refuge.

What place does this incident have on his path of leading me to God? How easy is it to simplify the complexity of a man's existence and to prepare the scales of oppression for the sake of political expediency?

You save me, Brother Hamid. I am clawing my way out of a dark tunnel. There is a light at the far end, and even if it's the light of the final bullet that you have promised to shoot, even so, it still signifies release.

I am returning to myself, I who am no longer that self. It's as if a hat made of lead has been lifted from my head. The wind of tomorrow is touching my face, burning my wounds and setting fire to my heart. The fire is warming me and the whole of my past is coming back with the warmth. Childhood, hunger, and poverty. Youthfulness and running. Hope and revolution. The hungry are rising up, and changing the world.

My whole soul has been ploughed. Dust and excrement have been mixed. Stray weeds and perfumed herbs. I am running over this newly ploughed ground on my wounded feet in search of myself. No, I want to sow myself in this field. I am still thirty-three years old and if I come out of here alive, I can be myself again.

I return to the world and rediscover myself. I randomly open the book of Hafez's poetry, and my eye falls on this poem:

Spring and its lovely flowers have come and gone,
And you, who has broken his promise of repentance,
Watch the beauty of the flower and uproot sorrow from your heart,
Tell the story of the wine, and the beauties,
Listen to Hafez, the wise man who knows.

I start to shake. I read the poem, maybe a hundred times. I imagine the sound of my wife reading it in her pleasant voice. And all I want is to be myself again.

My life inside cell number fifteen slips into a routine. Bathing once a week, and before bathing there's the distribution of nail clippers. Fresh air once a week. Hair cut once a month. Brother Rasouli, the tall, young guard, gives me books. But only morally uplifting ones.

I am reviewing my old life, bit by bit, while I am living this life in my cell. I don't know how often I succumb to feelings of regret. Sorrow fills me. I weep, and eventually I decide, not knowing that this is going to be the most difficult decision of my whole life, that I want to remain independent. I want to stay alive without causing harm to anyone else.

And inside me, blood is raining, wind is blowing, there's a storm and the icebergs are breaking up, like in Pudovkin's film *Mother*[78] when the water forges a path through the ice. *The Downpour*,[79] arrives and it's as if I am looking for something inside that abandoned storage room. I am searching for myself. I am paddling with my feet and hands from dawn to dusk. I bob up and down in the water. I have a fever. The sites of my wounds ache. My feet are burning with a piercing pain. I tighten my bandana. I press against my teeth with my fingers. I lean against the wall. I sit down and stand up. I don't know when it is that my tears become a flood and drown my eyes. It's a spring that first starts with a slow trickle before bursting its banks. I sob for hours and spill out all the filth that they have pushed down inside me. I am not even aware that I am sobbing loudly and reciting passages from *Jean-Christophe*:

Life! Oh Life! I have understood. I have been looking for myself in you. My being crumbles inside me, air is entering from the inside of my wounds, I am breathing and am discovering you, oh life!

There are loud knocks on the wall. Behazin, the book's translator, is in the cell next to mine. I fall silent. He says in a loud voice: "My son, whoever you are, be calm."

I sit down. Some time passes. Is it a minute or a year? Then, an old song surfaces from somewhere and is running over my lips:

> I went with you, and returned without you,
> From her abode, O my crazy heart!
> I hid, in the ashes of sorrow,
> All those hopes, O my crazy heart!

Oh my crazy heart, Oh my crazy heart, Oh my crazy heart! Now I am weeping and singing. I feel released from my chains. The ice in my soul melts away. The stone in my heart cracks open. I become myself and come out of myself. All of me comes out, and spins around. All life rises ...

These days, I have a new guest in my cell.

Hussein Abi had finished performing his prayers at the Imam Reza shrine[80] in Mashhad and had prayed to God to find him a good wife to relieve him of his loneliness. He had just turned thirty. He was short and stocky, with a big, round belly. In Mashhad's bazaar, everybody knew him as Hussein Abi, Hussein the Blue. He was mad about football and supported the Blues and was dead against the Reds.[81] He was walking and thinking about the noon prayers he was supposed to perform after lunch, and about returning to his little shop, when the sound of sobbing caught his attention. He walked in the direction of the noise and saw a woman draped in a black chador. She was crying and her shoulders were shaking. He hesitated, rubbing his hands awkwardly, and asked the woman in a shy voice: "Excuse me, Sister. Are you alright?"

The woman explained that she had lost all her family in an Iraqi attack in the south of Iran and that she herself had fled, fearing rape at the hands of Iraqi soldiers. She had come to the city of Mashhad to seek protection under the auspices of Imam Reza, the city's patron saint.

Hussein Abi told her that if she wished, she could stay with his old mother for a couple of days. The woman accepted the offer as if she had been anticipating this sort of invitation and set off with Hussein. Hussein, who was a traditional, religious man, walked ahead and the woman, whose name he didn't know, followed him. From time to time, when Hussein Abi turned his head to check whether the stranger was following him, he noticed under her chador the outline of a good figure, and this would make him feel restless; he saw a pair of sparkling eyes that made his heart soar. The walk to his home took a long time because Hussein Abi had chosen an unfamiliar route to avoid bumping into his business colleagues.

Fatimeh Khanum, who was called Fati, ended up staying with them. Hussein Abi's mother told everyone that the woman was a distant relative and had come from the south, having lost her family in the war. The beautiful, olive-skinned Fatimeh Khanum, who was a woman of few words, soon found her place in the community. And then, one day, the neighbours heard the news that Hussein Abi had quietly married her.

Hussein Abi was madly in love with his wife. He loved her more than he loved the Blues and believed that she was a gift from Imam Reza.

In the first year of their marriage Fati Khanum gave birth to baby girl. She looked fresh and beautiful like a bunch of flowers and they called her Ziba, or Beauty. Three years later the little girl became sister to a new baby girl, Rana.

It was on the night of Rana's birthday that the family heard loud knocks on their door. The house was soon filled with men and machine-guns. Fatimeh Khanum and her husband were both taken away.

When Hussein Abi, my new cellmate, reaches this part of his story, he becomes silent and tears run down his face. When he first arrived in the cell, he was extremely agitated and depressed. He didn't talk, didn't eat, and didn't walk. His feet are still in bandages and it took him days to warm to me and to talk to me in his thick Mashhadi accent.

The prisoners are tortured from the moment of their arrest, and Hussein is asked to provide information about organizational matters. He has never been exposed to this type of vocabulary before, so he doesn't understand and has no answers for them. And since he is not answering their questions, they assume that he's a real professional. They send him to Tehran and even under torture in Tehran all he does is to call out God's name in praise. Eventually, Fatimeh gives in to torture and starts talking. When she is brought face-to-face with her husband, she says: "I've been telling you lies, Haj Aqa. My family is alive. I am an active member of the Peykar organization.[82] When the rest of them were arrested, I fled and came to Mashhad with a fake ID. That's when I met you. Divorce me. I am not into politics anymore. I have fallen in love with the simple life that I've been leading with you. Go away and look after our children."

A cleric, who is present at the meeting, says: "This woman is forbidden to you. She is a communist, a polluted infidel."

Hussein Abi answers: "My beloved saint, Imam Reza, gave her to me as a gift. She was married to me in line with the Prophet's traditions. You, who are torturers, cannot forbid me what God has allowed me. I have no idea what this Peykar thing is about. I am not going to leave without my wife. If you make me leave, I'll go straight to Mashhad's main market, and I'll shout and yell, and set fire to myself and my children, there and then."

This ordinary man had fallen for a communist woman. He doesn't care about her real name, whether she's a Muslim or an infidel. Every time he says her name, he cries. He says: "The feet of my wife, the mother of my children, have swollen to the size of pillows."

I, who am usually a supporter of the Blues, suddenly decide to back the Reds and day in, day out, Hussein Abi and I argue over the relative merits of the Blues versus the Reds.

Two weeks pass. He stops performing his prayers. He knows Khamenei, but now can only insult him.

Early in the summer of 1983, they come for him one incredibly hot day and take him away.

Where has he been taken? What's going to happen to him?

I am afraid for his wife, a woman I have never met, and for his two beautiful daughters.

Chapter 19

My Wife's Voice and her Eyes

The Islamic Republic has now turned Moshtarek Prison into a propaganda museum, displaying statues of Savak torturers wearing ties. Maybe they are hoping that the Islamic Republic's very own torturers will be forgotten.

This is my nineteenth letter to you, Brother Hamid. You, who have deprived me of even the minimum prisoner's rights. For nine months, you didn't let me hear my wife's voice. Even though you had completed your interrogation of me and of all those connected with me, you still kept me locked up, and led me to believe that my wife had also been imprisoned.

Moshtarek Prison, winter 1983

The cell door opens on the morning of 20 December 1983. A tall man dressed in civilian clothing, with a group of guards standing respectfully behind him, asks me how many visitors I have had so far.

"None."

"How often have you had phone calls?"

Again I answer: "None."

He looks at the guards, astonished. And says: "When were you arrested?"

I answer: "The sixth of February 1983."

He frowns, surprised, and asks: "Are you sure you are not mistaken? You haven't even had a phone call in all this time?"

I say: "No."

He asks my name and writes it down on a piece of paper. I suspect it's for visitors. I say: "My wife has also been arrested. I just want to see her."

He writes down my wife's name and leaves. He returns a little later: "Have you given us your wife's name correctly?"

I repeat her name.

"We don't have anyone by that name."

I am so happy that I nearly grow wings and fly. I realize that my wife has not been arrested after all.

"It's very strange that you have not had phone calls. After three months, everyone ..."

He swallows the rest of his words and leaves. It doesn't take long for the guard to come for me. I put on my blindfold, grab hold of the stick and set off. In the courtyard, when you grab my arm, I realize that once again I've been given the honour of visiting you.

"Hello."

You reply: "Hello and fuck you. Why didn't you ask me to let you make phone calls, useless wimp?"

Then you take me to a place where the sound of ringing telephones can be heard: "How can we contact your wife? Give me the numbers."

My heart swells with pleasure. I am feeling certain that my wife has not been arrested. I start giving you numbers of places where my wife could be found. You take down the numbers, Brother Hamid. I can hear the sound of a telephone ringing. You say: "Not in. They have all disappeared into the rat's hole."

You ask for another number. I give it to you. You hit my head twice, it feels like bombs have been dropped on my head.

"During interrogation, you couldn't remember a thing. But now, your brain is working like a computer, useless wimp."

Suddenly, I recall the telephone number of a close friend. My dear Reza, who last year fell silent for good in Vienna. He had an intensely clear insight into things and no inclination towards any

political group. He knew most of them and was critical of their outlook. On one occasion, he asked me: "So why are you supporting
the clerics?"

I said: "Because they are opposed to imperialism."

He laughed out loud and said: "The clerics are anti-everything.
Why have you picked on their anti-imperialism?"

His wife was a descendant of a daughter of the grand poet of the
constitutional revolution, Mirzadah Eshqi, who was assassinated at
home. A lovely and very cultured family.

In that darkness in which I was losing hope of getting hold of my
wife, I reluctantly give you their number. The phone rings a few
times and you, Brother Hamid, are handing over the telephone to
me. It's the lovely voice of dear Firoozeh, Reza's wife. Upon hearing my voice, she cries out enthusiastically: "Where are you, our dear
Houshang?"

Suddenly, I feel my throat contract in a sob. I compose myself. I
say that I want to get hold of my wife so I can talk to her. But
Firoozeh keeps asking: "Are you okay? Have you been harassed? Is
your health okay? I can't believe it!"

Eventually, it becomes clear that by sheer coincidence my wife
had visited her the night before and they had arranged for her to call
Firoozeh today. You, Brother Hamid, who are listening to the
conversation through another receiver, are slowly whispering into
my ear:

Arrange a call for the day after tomorrow at four in the afternoon.

I do as he says. When I put down the phone, you hit me hard on
my head: "Who was that whore of a woman who kept saying lovely
things to you?"

I say: "But you are a Muslim. Why are you saying such things
about a married woman?"

Again you hit me on my head: "Do not lecture me about moral-
ity, useless wimp!"

And you pull at my hand and take me out of the room.

"So what is this woman's business?"

I explain that she is not at all political and has only a straightforward friendship with us. You say: "Sod off. Go now. Tell the guard about the day after tomorrow."

I return to my cell and sit down in a corner. Firoozeh's voice has brought the first breeze of freedom to my soul. But even now, when her name is mentioned or when I speak to her, the thought of that revolutionary Muslim brother's dirty insult makes me shiver.

Fear and excitement are my companions for forty-eight hours. I am excited that my wife has not been arrested and that I will soon be able to hear her voice from the freedom of the outside world. I also fear that this might be another trap. I imagine you have discovered Firoozeh's home address from the telephone number. That there has been a raid and she and her children have been detained. Fear doesn't leave me. After forty-eight hours, I am allowed to speak to my wife for four minutes. After saying hello, we both just cry. You are holding the other handset in your hand, Brother Hamid.

From this time onwards, a monthly ten-minute phone conversation is added to the life of the prisoner in cell number fifteen. We are rounded up in the courtyard. We are made to stand up or sit down, blindfolded. Later, a guard calls us out, one by one. He takes the phone numbers.

He keeps one handset and gives me the other one. The phone call cannot stray beyond saying hello and enquiring about each other's wellbeing. Even hinting at torture is absolutely banned, causing the phone call to be terminated. For anything aside from greetings and questions about health, a separate permit is required. When I ask them to allow me to ask my wife to bring me a pair of glasses, they agree, but only if I say to her: "My glasses have fallen off and broken."

On a sunny March day, we are called up. We place our hand on the shoulder of the person in front of us in the line. Exactly thirteen months after my arrest, I am permitted a visit. We set off, our eyes blindfolded. We walk on roads for a short distance. We stop. They tell us to take off the blindfolds and put them in our pockets. We walk on again and soon find ourselves beside a large gate, which I later understand to be the entrance to the Swiss school on Palestine Road. It's the place closest to Moshtarek Prison, and also to the King's Palace, which at that time had not yet become the headquarters of Ayatollah Khomeini. When the prisoner queue enters, the courtyard suddenly takes on the atmosphere of a meeting place in a desert. The yelling and cries of the wives and mothers rise up from the ground. Children are shouting, searching for their fathers, searching faces to find the one familiar to them amid all the people dressed in blue. Whenever someone finds a loved one, they embrace him and cry, showering him with kisses. The mothers hit their chests with their fists, the fathers use their walking sticks to try to clear the way to their offspring. It really is like Judgement Day, the last day when the dead are brought back to life. The scene repeats itself each time a new line of prisoners arrives.

We enter the courtyard, and I am taken to the right, up a long staircase. I enter a place like a classroom. I sit down on a school chair next to somebody else. A little later someone calls out:

"Houshang!"

I hear the voice of the person next to me ask: "Which Houshang? There are two Houshangs here."

My God. It's Amir (Houshang) Nikayeen. With his beautiful, humanist smile.

The guard is saying: "That one."

And is pointing at me.

As soon as I stand up, I see my wife. Wrapped in a black chador she is dragging herself towards me. She stands still and says: "Is this my husband? No ... What have you done to him? What have you done to him?"

She sees me with my bushy beard, bloated stomach, dressed in my prison uniform and slippers, and for a moment she's horrified. She throws herself into my arms and shouts out for everyone to hear: "I love you!"

She hands me my new glasses. I put them on. For the first time in months I am able to see everything clearly again.

When we walk down the stairs, we see people dressed in the blue prison uniform filling all corners of the courtyard. Blankets have been neatly spread on the ground and a guard is seated in the middle of each one. Like the rest of the people, my wife and I sit down on opposite sides of a blanket. After thirteen months and in the company of total strangers, what else could we say apart from repeating, yes, I am well and how are you? In the middle of this exchange, I ask her: "How is uncle?"

Apart from Rahman, we had no other uncle, but I had not seen Rahman in the crowd. My wife shook her head. I don't know what would have happened had she told me then and there that Rahman was no longer with us. Would that have made a difference to the way I felt or the decision I had made? The visit ends too quickly. I return to the prison with a box of sweets. On the way back, the men whisper to each other and share the news that ten individuals from the Party's secret organization have been executed.

The lines I have carved on the wall to count the days, the pigeons' cooing, the spring breeze and the pleasant air all tell me that the New Year holiday is almost upon us. For a second time, I am to be your guest on New Year's Day, Brother Hamid. I am not permitted to see anybody apart from the prison guard. I am only allowed to hear my wife's voice once a month. Each time, after the excitement of going to the telephone, I am plunged into the deepest depression when the phone call ends. I return to my cell and I spend my days crying and memorizing poetry.

I've been quarantined, and kept completely cut off from the outside world. I read the Qur'an from cover to cover many times. I read

The Book of Eloquence again and again and finally, the long journey of my quest for truth leads me back to Rumi and Hafez. By now, I understand full well that the path that I had taken in the past was of no use to me. I am a poet. I don't belong in politics. I had lost myself in

politics but am rediscovering my lost self in poetry.

I don't even have access to newspapers, although the "news" is broadcast every day at two in the afternoon. I have reviewed my life a thousand times and my resolve has grown with every day that passes: "I'll try to stay alive, if I can do it without hurting others. I shall be independent and have nothing to do with politics. If I can, I'll write, and finish what needs to be finished." Then I become agitated. I feel I am running out of time and my creative energy is going to be lost forever. My spirits sink. I throw myself against the walls and the door. I want to be taken to the court soon. I want them to make up their minds: either finish me off or let me find a way to the future.

I celebrate New Year's Day alone and preoccupied. For this New Year's ceremony, I seek out seven items beginning with the letter 's'. For *sabzi*, greenery, I use a green leaf. I have been saving an apple (*sib*) for just this purpose, and I have a safety pin (*sanjaq*) and a piece of wire (*sim*). I use the butt of a cigarette (*sigar*) for another 's' and a piece of soap (*saboon*, though it is not the right 's'), so I have most of my seven items starting with 'seen' ready for the New Year's ritual. I sit down, facing the seven items. At the moment I assume the New Year has started, I kiss the imaginary image of my wife, and open the book of Hafez's poetry to a random page in the hope of finding a clue about my future hidden in the poem. And I cry, quietly.

The next day, the door opens. It's Brother Rasouli. He sits down by the door, watching me compile my list of books, and says: "I've been feeling bad since the day you received your visitor. We've been told that communist women are loose. That family doesn't mean anything to them and that everyone is having an affair with someone else. But the visit confused me. I haven't seen this much love and warmth in a family before."

I don't know what to say. I talk about my love for my wife and our simple life. He picks up the list and asks: "Do you need anything? I am about to leave this place and the Corps altogether."

I say: "A dictionary, if that's possible."

He says: "I'll try."

He stands up. We shake hands and kiss each other. A few days later, when I return from the bathroom, I see a little dictionary on the cell floor. I'll never see Brother Rasouli again, but to this day, I can remember his face.

Chapter 20

Sex in the Torture Chamber

The Ornament of the Righteous *was penned by the renowned Shi'a scholar Muhammad Baqir Majlisi. The book was written in the seventeenth century at a time when the ruling Safavid dynasty in Iran had made Shi'ism the official religion of the country. This popular book offers advice on recommended customs and modes of behaviour, organized by topic. Certain sections of the book deal with sexual matters, which in places read like modern pornography.*

The book was seriously in demand in the prison. Initially, they were pleased that a canonical work of Shi'ism had so many readers in a prison full of communists. Later on, when they realized that the prisoners were only interested in the book's sexual content, they took it away.

This twentieth letter has no direct connection to you personally, Brother Hamid. But it reveals the depths of the culture you believe in. After the revolution, you assumed that by censoring the sexual content of this book,[83] *which is one of the most important reference works for Shi'ism and an essential source of all of the Ayatollahs' writings, society's morals would be protected. Just as you thought that you would kill all thought except for your own Taliban-style way of thinking by killing and torturing the best of Iran's sons and daughters.*

Moshtarek Prison, autumn 1984

Iqbal (an Arabic and Kurdish name meaning good fortune) was only twenty-four when the Islamic Republic clamped down on Iran's

Kurdistan region. Thousands fled to safety, among them Iqbal, who sought refuge in Tehran. He was eventually arrested and for a few days in 1984 became my guest in the solitary confinement cell.

In search of employment and a roof over his head, Iqbal went to a public loans office,[84] run by a religious couple in the south of Tehran. Some men who work in Islamic institutions are addressed by the common title of Haj Aqa and their wives, who are wrapped in black chadors, are referred to as Haj Khanum.

As luck would have it, when Iqbal arrived at the loans office, Haj Khanum was in the director's office. He managed to sweet-talk her into employing him. When Haj Aqa arrived, Haj Khanum explained that the helpless young Kurd should be hired because he had lost all his family. Unlike most Kurds, they were Shia Muslims, and the enemies of Iran had killed them.

Haj Aqa believed the lies that Iqbal had fed to his wife and so Iqbal was hired. He was a hard-working young man, and more importantly, he was seriously committed to fulfilling his religious duties. He never missed his prayers, performing them exactly on time and taking part in all of the religious rites and ceremonies. On Monday nights, he attended prayer ceremonies where radical believers placed the Qur'an on their heads and punched their chests, weeping profusely. He had even been spotted performing the Jafar Tayyar prayer[85] in the middle of the night. On Friday nights he would certainly attend the Kumayl prayers[86] and his Fridays were spent fasting as well as attending the Nudbah[87] prayer ceremony at Tehran's large cemetery. Whenever he had time off work, he either read the *The Book of Eloquence* or *The Ornament of the Righteous*. Iqbal was one of the latter book's devotees, and he used to tell me: "You are stupid. Prayer is not going to help you, no matter how much you pray. You have to study this book so that you can act in line with Shia scholars' instructions from early in the morning when you get up to go to the toilet, until the night when you lie beside your wife."

He would then stand up and walk. He would pace up and down the tiny cell and ask:

"In your view, is it allowed to kiss a woman down there?"

I would laugh and say, "Drop it, Iqbal."

He used to reply, "Fear not."

"Meaning?"

"Meaning that it *is* possible. There are a thousand hadith[88] about this."

Then he would walk up and down, reciting the hadith. When he reached the "fear not" passage, I'd join him and we would read together, laughing out aloud:

They asked what will happen if the man and woman's clothes are removed at the moment of intercourse. He said, fear not, it's allowed. Again, they asked, what if the woman's vagina was kissed? He said, fear not, it's allowed.

It has been related in numerous credible hadith verses that there should be no speaking during the moment of intercourse. But looking at the vagina and kissing it is allowed.

They asked if someone undressed his wife and looked at her, what would happen to them. He said that there is no pleasure greater than this. They asked what if he played with his wife or slave's vagina with his hands and fingers? He said, it's allowed but nothing should be placed inside the woman unless it's part of the human body. They asked is it allowed to have intercourse in water pool and he said, fear not, it's allowed.

They asked explicitly about having intercourse in a bath and he said, it's allowed.

It has been related that if someone has intimately embraced a slave and wanted to sleep with another slave before performing the ritual bath, he should perform the ablution. They asked, is a man allowed to sleep with two slaves? He said no, it's banned. What about sleeping with two free women? He said, that's allowed.

We kept holding sex education classes in our little cell. But making him talk about the rest of his life was not easy, although his life story was worth listening to.

Haj Aqa and Haj Khanum had no children of their own. They fell head over heels in love with this pious young man and decided to get him a wife. First they bought him a little flat and furnished it. Then they started looking for a girl to his taste. Iqbal told Haj Khanum and Haj Aqa: "You are my guardians. If you come across a pious girl, get her for me. I don't care for looks."

But they insisted that Islam allows men and women to see each other prior to marriage and they took him with them on their match-making visits. First there would be lengthy discussions with the girl's family. Then the girl would appear, wrapped up in a white chador. Iqbal rejected them all until it came to Zahra's turn. She was fair like marble. Pretty like the moon.

Iqbal agreed to the marriage without hesitation and in the blink of an eye, he became a groom, entering the wedding chamber with the moon-faced girl. But Moonface turned out to be a pious girl in the truest sense of the word. She wouldn't undress in front of her husband. Iqbal was not allowed to enter the bathroom while she was there because this was a sin. But the main adventure was on Friday nights. She would take a bath[89] and would accompany Iqbal to the Kumayl prayer ceremony. They would perform a lengthy prayer and weep and sob, asking God for forgiveness. When they returned, Moonface would insist that Iqbal should sleep with her. This religious duty has to be performed on Friday nights, except when the woman has her period. It has its own special rituals and prayers and Iqbal would oblige and perform them.

But that was not the end of it. It was not only that the night in question had to be a Friday night, there were numerous conditions relating to the time and place that had to be taken into consideration. Every aspect of such matters is meticulously detailed in *The Ornament of the Righteous:*

> *Do not have intercourse under a fruit tree because if a child is created, he would either become a torturer and killer or will lead the brutal and the unjust.*

Do not have intercourse in sunlight. Pull the curtains or else, if a child is created, the child will always live in a bad state and worry until it dies.

Do not have intercourse in the middle of the call for prayers or else, if a child is created, it would not fear to shed blood.

Do not have intercourse on the rooftop or else, if a child is created, it would create divisions, be deceptive and would want to introduce unlawful innovations.

If you are intending to travel, do not have intercourse on the night prior to travel or else, if a child is created, he would become wasteful and wasteful people are Satan's brothers. And if you are setting off on a journey that takes three days, do not have intercourse or else, if a child is created, he would become a supporter of those who are brutal and unjust.

Have intercourse on Monday nights, for if a child is created, he will be able to recite the Qur'an from memory and would be content with the fate as chosen for him by God.

If you have intercourse on a Thursday night and a child is created, he would become a Shari'a judge or a scholar. And if you have intercourse on a Thursday around noon, and a child is created, Satan will never approach him and God will make him healthy physically and mentally.

If you have intercourse on a Thursday night and a child is created, he'll become a famous sage, and if you have intercourse on Friday night after the Isha'a prayer,[90] there is hope that he will become one of God's chosen ones.

Do not have intercourse in the first hour of the night or else, if a child is created, you cannot be sure that he's not a magician, forsaking the hereafter for the sake of worldly power.

Eventually, the time would come when all the most favourable conditions were met. The excited young man, who had been waiting impatiently for the night's adventures, would be intensely aroused and keen to progress affairs quickly. When Iqbal got to this point in his story, he would hold his stomach with his hand and laugh out loud and then say: "When I entered, Zahra pulled away and protested: 'You forgot to say "In the name of God, the Compassionate, the Merciful".'"

"So I quickly learned that at the moment of entering, I had to say 'In the name of God, the Compassionate, the Merciful' or else my child would be considered an offspring of Satan's. It made me laugh so much that I nearly lost my erection. But I quickly collected myself."

Iqbal had become used to all this, and despite the complications, gave Moonface two children. At the time of his arrest, one of them was nearly a year old, the second was still inside Moonface.

One day, security officials turned up and arrested him at work inside the loan office. During the interrogation, he realized that his younger brother had also been arrested. Iqbal never found out who had grassed on him. His coming to Tehran and his method of hiding had made the interrogators even more curious, putting him under intense pressure to confess. One day, they called him up. He went and returned that night. They had taken him to the family court. The fair Moonface had asked the court to divorce her from this heretic.[91] The judge had obliged. The woman had screamed in the courtroom: "I hate this bastard."

And Iqbal became an unmarried man.

In the daytime, he would walk around reciting sections of *The Ornament of the Righteous* from memory. He used to say: "That book was seriously in demand in the prison. Initially, they were pleased that a canonical work of Shi'ism had so many readers in a prison full of communists. Later on, when they realized that prisoners were only interested in the book's sexual content, they took it away."

Eventually, Iqbal was taken away. I don't know what happened to him. He himself believed that they were about to release him. We embraced each other to say goodbye.

While I was writing this book, it occurred to me to read *The Ornament of the Righteous* again. When I got hold of the post-revolutionary edition of the book, I realized that the relevant section had been censored. Eventually, I found a pre-revolutionary edition in the house of a veteran communist. The book's pages were loose. I found the passages that Iqbal used to recite from memory. I wrote them down and the memory of those days made me laugh.

On the last day of autumn, a guard turns up and says: "Collect all your belongings."

The phrase is filled with possible meanings: transfer to another prison, freedom, execution. I gather up all my belongings, which fit into a small plastic bag. I sit down on the blankets and stare at the walls and the door. My heart is heavy. I am being let out of that solitary confinement cell after exactly 682 days. This could be the longest, or at least one of the longest, solitary confinement sentences ordered by the Islamic Republic. I have become so used to cell number fifteen that the thought of leaving it makes me sad. I discover the truth of the phrase: "One even gets used to one's own grave."

I follow the guard up the stairs. When we reach the second floor, he pulls aside a curtain and sends me inside. I take off my blindfold.

A group of people are waiting there expectantly, wondering who this newcomer will be. They are all part of the Party's leadership and close friends of mine. We embrace each other. We cry and we laugh.

I am now in an ordinary block, number 107. The block has its own bathroom and toilet. It's comfortable, relatively spacious and sunny. The doorway, which opens into a round room, has a curtain instead of an iron door.

All of the men have undergone intensive, prolonged torture. They have all confessed to spying and have accepted the charge of participating in the coup.

We have a TV set and newspapers in the block. After 682 days, my eyes light up at the sight of coloured images and being allowed to touch a newspaper. The Iran-Iraq war is fully underway and the media is full of propaganda.

We perform our prayers. It's a scene from a horrific decade of sheer terror but we are still in its very beginning. We do our ablution collectively. Hussein leads the prayers. We all queue behind him. The block had been jam-packed with various leftist prisoners before my arrival. Most of them were Tudeh Party members who'd been arrested during the second clampdown in 1983. They all used to queue up behind Hussein for prayers. But now, it's only us, the Party's leadership. I am one of the youngest and the least experienced of them. The others have lengthy prison terms behind them from the Shah's time. They had been involved in hijacking planes; they had lived in secret locations and had fought an armed struggle. And now, they are standing, praying to a God they do not believe in. Torture has broken them.

No one says a word. There's no need for talking. Whatever is going through my mind is also going through their minds. Sometimes, when we bow down longer than necessary, I see a mischievous smile appear on Rashid's lips. Back then, we used to be close friends. I guess he's grinning at his own life and at what's happened to us. Later, when we meet up again in freedom, I remind him of that smile and he says: "Yes, I was laughing. It made me laugh to watch how fear had made us lift our arses to bow down to God."

When the prayer finishes, we return to our real selves. Back to what we used to be. None of us is older than forty years of age. There's still mischief in us and sometimes our loud laughter fills the air. We both know and don't know what is awaiting us. No one has been to court yet. We have all lied, confessing to all sorts of things. We've all been accused of being KGB spies but I am the only one who has the honour of being accused of spying for Savak as well as the British Secret Intelligence Service, MI6.

The first news I hear once released from solitary confinement is of Rahman's death. Rahman's departure means that the Party as I knew it, the Party that was Rahman Hatefi, is now finished, and in fact has been gone for years. The news of Rahman's death – Rahman who had influenced my entire political life for better or worse – was the final, missing piece that I needed to construct my new beliefs. I was myself again. I returned to myself. A human being who no longer followed a leader and was no longer a member of any party. But a man who loved justice and believed that love was the source of life.

Chapter 21

Goodbye to Moshtarek Prison, Hello to Evin

Evin Prison was the largest torture centre holding political prisoners in Iran. During the Islamic regime, Tehran's gangsters and hoodlums, who had been appointed as prison guards and executioners, put into practice court orders issued by Haqqani's Taliban-style madrasa. Much later, in the summer of 1988, thousands of political prisoners, men and women, young and old, were hanged from the pipes of the prison's heating system.

Ayatollah Khomeini said, "Prisons should be places of learning." And the Shah's prisons, which had been closed for a while, were rapidly reopened and extended. Moshtarek Prison specialized in left-wing groups. Solitary confinement and sleeping on blankets with our eyes blindfolded were part of our early lessons. Then came the lashing, handcuffs, eating shit and sleeping in coffins. The lessons were taught by the experienced experts of the Revolutionary Guards Corps. When they had done their work we were handed over to the experts of Evin Prison.

My twenty-first letter is a goodbye letter from Moshtarek Prison, Brother Hamid. I have spent around two and a half years in this place. After exactly 869 days, I have been released from your service. As you know very well, I have spent 682 of these days in a solitary confinement cell. I am now leaving for Evin with your blessing, so I can complete my studies at the Islamic Republic's "university".

Evin Prison, summer 1985

In late June 1985, they call us up. We are ready at lightning speed. They make us run and board a minibus, which sets off immediately. We are blindfolded. A while later, they order us to take off our blindfolds and put them into our pockets.

Suddenly we could see the roads of Tehran. Life was carrying on. No one was paying attention to this minibus full of people dressed in blue uniforms and guarded by the Revolutionary Guards Corps. Watching ordinary life, the streets and the people, was intensely pleasant after such a long time spent in a prison cell. We were moving in the direction of the mountains to the north of the city and it was obvious that we were on our way to Evin. When we started to move down the street leading to Evin and reached Peech-e Tobah,[92] they ordered us to put our blindfolds back on.

The original owner of this delightful garden was the aristocratic offspring of a dynastic clan who had served as prime minister during some perilous times. He set up the garden in one of Tehran's most beautiful summer pastures, where the twin villages of Evin and Darakeh are situated. During his lifetime, which he spent facing anger and scorn, he sold the garden to Savak. Were he to come back to life and see the way his garden had been invaded by hoodlums, he would certainly have died of another heart attack.

Assadollah Lajevardi, originally a clothes merchant from Tehran's bazaars, who presided over the first Islamic court and transformed himself into a serious torturer, was the head of Evin Prison. He ran a special training system there, which ended, in 1988, with the shedding of the blood of thousands of prisoners. The prison system is still intact. The judges, who were under the tutelage of Hujjatul Islam Nayeri, the chief justice of the time, completed the picture. The majority of them belonged to Haqqani's circle,[93] in other words, they were Taliban, though Taliban with Iranian identity cards.

The "teaching" at Evin was just like that in Moshtarek, though lessons were also taught to members of religious groups, including Muslims, Jews, Armenians and Baha'is. The experts in charge of our tutelage were thugs from the roughest areas of Tehran. Lajevardi had brought the most violent gangsters in to Evin, and put them in charge of all prison affairs, from cooking to guarding the prison.

The transfer of prisoners carried on until about midnight. I was taken to one of the cells in the "sanitorium", a less regimented section of the prison. This was a very large, L-shaped building that had been unfinished prior to the revolution, but Lajevardi had quickly completed it. The solitary confinement cells were the same shape as their Israeli counterparts and included a toilet and a wash basin. The uncompromising rule in this block was complete silence. The only sound that was permitted to break the silence was the screaming of prisoners being tortured in the interrogation rooms.

The sun shone through the high windows of the cells. If you bent over and someone stood on your back, they could see Melli University (now Beheshti) and the mountains to the north of Tehran through the window. We calculated the time according to the university lecture bells. Evin's horrible food was pushed into the cell through an opening at the bottom of the cell door. We were allowed a five-minute wash once a week.

The corridors are filled with prisoners on the day I am taken for interrogation. A young prisoner who has only just been brought in, is being beaten, blows being rained on him with tremendous force. A young woman prisoner is crying and two little girls are running after each other calling: "Rana …"

"Ziba …"

So I realize Hussein Abi must also be here. How can I find him? I lift my hand and shout out: "Brother, bathroom."

Someone hits me hard on my head: "Shut up."

Then he makes me stand up and takes me with him. I take off my blindfold inside the interrogation room. A heavyset thug, who is so overweight he can hardly get up from his chair, places some questions in front of me. It's the same old questions, though this time they have used letterheaded paper, and hence given it an official appearance. I write down the answers. I deny the accusations and write: "These confessions have been taken from me by force and are legally invalid."

The interrogator reads my writing. He spits and says: "Fuck off, turd."

A few days later, I am settled in. Accompanied by a guard, we walk past the pool and enter the "university". This two storey building used to serve as Savak's administration and relaxation centre. It's located towards the rear of Evin, just at the foot of the mountains. Lajevardi has introduced some changes to the place, transforming it into a block where prisoners who had already been taught "general lessons" in the solitary confinement cells were sent to learn "special lessons". The place of learning has a series of rooms called "closed doors", where sixteen people are kept in a space intended for four. The only activity allowed is two hours per day in the fresh air. Everything else, even pencils or personal hygiene items are strictly banned here.

Around ten days later I am taken to the general block. Prisoners belonging to Mujahedin-e Khalq have been put in charge of the blocks and cells. I am received by Ibrahim. He's a very young man, and the youngest child of a famous Mujahedin-e Khalq family. In line with the rules, he sends me to a quarantine room to wait for the council of prison duty officials to confirm my identity. As soon as I enter the room, which is bare except for a three-tier bunk, someone jumps up and embraces me. It's Foroud, a university friend. The Tudeh Party members follow him. They tell me that I have to gain the officials' trust immediately or else I'll be in trouble – I must attend the Nudbah prayer, which is to be held the same night. I do my ablution and we enter the ceremony. The lights are turned off. Someone recites the prayers in a loud voice. The prisoners hold copies of the Qur'an over their heads and sob. I manage to control myself until the end of the class. When we leave, I tell myself: "I will not do that again. Attending this ceremony was against my promise to myself."

I will no longer attend the class, but I do continue to perform my prayers. The following day, I shave my beard and make my face look like my own again. I trim the tips of my moustache.[94] I am sitting in a corner of the block, watching the others, when Ibrahim enters and seats himself beside me. He asks me a few questions, and he takes my answers to be analysed by the council of prison duty officials. On his return, my place in the block is clarified. I have been stamped "not one of us".

I am taken to room number six, a room for prisoners whose files are still active. Goorzad who was arrested during an armed Mujahedin operation and is curiously aggressive for his young age, is in charge. He has a seriously one-sided view of the world.

In the mornings we have two sessions of "televised classes". Videotapes are played, showing the clerics' endlessly tiresome speeches, all of them are about morals. We are forced to squat on the floor, and listen. I gradually learn to sleep with my eyes wide open.

In the evening, we collectively perform our prayers,[95] with Goorzad as our prayer leader. He lectures us between the two prayers. And every day he talks at length about peeing while standing up, quoting various hadith on this issue. Brother Sharif, the guard in charge of the block, keeps repeating: "It has been handed down clearly in a hadith: If a man pees while standing, the angels' cries will reach the skies."

I am reminded of Iqbal, who used to walk up and down, repeating: "Do not have intercourse with your wife standing up because that's how mules copulate and if a child is created, he'll pee in his bed like a mule."

I ask myself: "Do mules have beds to pee on?" I can't find an answer. I can't help but picture a mule lying on a red bed covered in white sheets and peeing.

We are forced to pray before eating. Goorzad recites the prayer and we repeat his words loudly. We then chant a long list of condemnations, beginning with "Death to the US!" and "Death to the Soviet Union!"

In the evening, a tablecloth is spread on the floor in front of the TV and we are seated on it in time for the news. It is always reported that the Islamic army has been victorious on the frontline in the war against Iraq. We are made to follow Goorzad in this too, lifting our fists and shouting "God is Great" (*"Allah 'u 'Akbar"*) three times. Then they give us dinner, which is always tasteless. We said it was blander than water.

After dinner, Goorzad collects the leftover bread crusts from the tablecloth and distributes them to us. We have to eat our share while he watches. Not throwing away bread crusts, like not peeing while standing, is part of the "special lessons" which are very important and are taught every day by Brother Sharif. He has a degree in his field of expertise: publicly whipping prisoners.

Since I was the last prisoner to join the block, I've been allocated a place close to the door. During the nights when we sleep in the courtyard, my place is next to a small field of mirabilis. The nights are very beautiful in Evin village. A fresh breeze sweeps in from the mountains. The sky appears to be drowning in stars and there's the maddening scent of mirabilis. I get myself under the blanket as soon as I can, and lose myself for hours in the beauty of this paradise at the heart of which humans have created a hell.

We are now allowed visitors every two weeks and they let us write one six-line letter, per month.

One morning, we are walking in the corridor just before the fresh air hour when Ibrahim enters. He's holding a box of sweets in his hand and shouts: "Today, two members of the Mujahedin were sent to the hereafter."

Then he distributes the sweets to us. Later, the others tell me that he had just returned from firing the final shots at his father and mother.

We have a library, which is full of religious books, prayer books and books on morals. The only book worth reading is Victor Hugo's *Les Misérables* and because the book is in high demand, they have created a reading timetable for it. I register my name with the official in charge of the library and am given two hours per week to read the book. That is, until the Mujahedin analyse it and come to the conclusion that it leads readers astray from the correct path, and it is taken away.

Behzad sleeps next to me. We are both scorned by the block's internal powers. He has an astonishing story. He had been fighting in Tehran and Kurdistan, and had blown up a few trucks belonging to the Revolutionary Guards Corps. He's a master of explosions. When they got close to him, he decided to leave Iran. He told me how he managed to get himself to the northwest of Iran in the perilous conditions of 1983, in disguise, before trying to cross the border into Turkmenistan in the Soviet Union. On the night of his escape, he had just finished walking the dangerous route and his hand had touched the metal fence when car lights had been switched on and he had been arrested. He had been tortured and confessed, and now he was awaiting his sentence, which he knew would be hanging.

Every evening, around sunset, we sit by the window in the corridor, which looks out towards Evin Fairground and Hotel Azadi. Behzad sings songs to himself. We can hear the sounds of everyday life from far away, and the shrieks of children on fairground rides break through the sky before reaching us.

I haven't yet been to court but assume that my sentence will be the same as his. I share his sorrow. This young man, who has done some violent things, has such a fragile soul. His hand doesn't shake when launching a rocket, but the sound of a child can make him cry. His wife is somewhere in the same block.

One day, they call him up. When he returns, it becomes clear that they had taken him to see his wife. They had read out the hanging verdict to both of them. Wife and husband had spent a few minutes crying in each other's arms, saying their final farewells.

From that day onwards, Behzad's unruffled calm turns to anger, which intensifies day by day. Fruit is brought into the block once a week. The prison guards sell the fruit to the prisoners, but the powers within the block, the Mujahedin, have banned the individual consumption of fruit, viewing it as a sign of greed. They are the ones who decide how much fruit should go to each room or whether to buy any fruit at all. When they buy a single melon for a room of twelve people, it becomes clear that even scraping the last flesh from the skin is considered greedy and hence, it too is banned.

Behzad is by now indifferent to the instructions issued by the officials of the "prison within the prison" and buys grapes by the kilo. He puts the grapes under the room's air cooler. He forgets them and the grapes go off and fruit flies appear.

Goorzad orders the cellmates to come together and put Behzad on trial on charges of greed.

I try to make Goorzad understand Behzad's emotional state, but he pulls a face, raising his eyebrows, and says: "The Marxists, too, are only thinking about their stomachs and that which is below their stomachs."

And on the day when they finally came for Behzad to hang him, I was the only one to accompany him to the door and to kiss him one last time. Over the years, I have tried to find his name in books and documents covering that time but I haven't found any mention of him so far. But I always remember that young man, who apparently didn't care about anything but war and death, who had fallen into a death trap while only one step away from freedom.

Another day, an old acquaintance arrives in the block. He's a young man, thin and very tall. Mohammad Malmir, a temperamental poet whom I knew from my time at *Kayhan* where I had published his beautiful poems.

He is exactly the same, except that he now has only one eye and is claiming to be god. We have a few people who claim to be prophets, but Malmir has become god and this is new. They say that he was blinded with a broom handle inside the "madhouse", a restricted section allocated specifically to those who claim to be prophets. Sometimes, when the poet fully comes to his senses, he notices me and tells me the story of how he was blinded in one eye: "A man was claiming to be a prophet. I said to him, 'You are lying.' He said, 'Why do you say I am lying?' I said, 'If you were a prophet, you would have been sent by me, as I am god. But I don't like you.' He became angry and poked me in the eye with a broom handle."

The poet/god had a habit of walking about the block, reciting poetry in a loud voice. One day, he climbed onto a little stool and delivered a speech against Kianuri. He spoke beautifully, and the whole block gathered around him. The Mujahedin guys became excited and applauded him. When he reached the climax of his speech, he turned to Ibrahim and said: "And yet, despite all of this, Rajavi deserves to eat Kianuri's shit."

Chaos broke out in the block. Guards appeared and Mohammad Malmir, the mad poet from the southern part of Iran, was also boycotted.

Another day, the poet/god stood up on the stool, again dressed in a long raincoat, one of his eyes dark and expressionless, the other sparkling. He recites an ode to Imam Ali. It is a truly engaging ode. Again everybody gathers around him. The guards also turn up. Brother Sharif watches this wise but mad poet with pleasure and quietly applauds him. He recites and recites and when he finishes, everybody is left feeling astonished and astounded. The poet/god lifts his hand and says: "But …"

And starts throwing around filthy insults addressing them to the same Imam in whose honour he has just recited the ode. Once again the Mujahedin and the guards pounce on him, taking him outside, punching and kicking him as they go.

At the time for the evening prayers, after delivering a speech about peeing, Brother Sharif reports that Mohammad Malmir has been sentenced to hanging for insulting Imam Ali[96] and the sentence is going to be carried out soon.

They summon me early in the morning of 5 August. As usual, they call out all the names together. We walk down. They take us to the court building in a minibus. Then the guard sets off and we follow him. The guard sits me down in a large hall. I have a very long wait. I know that the final moment has arrived. I have decided to tell the court that I have been tortured and made to say all the things that I have said. That I am not a spy. That I am denouncing the Party and accepting the Islamic Republic. That I want to lead a life in line with the Republic's laws.

It takes a long time. A very long time. A thousand years. Just as the muezzin begins his call for the evening prayer, someone arrives and puts his hand on my shoulder. He asks my name. He puts some pieces of paper in my hand and says:

"It's the charge sheet. You have half an hour to read it. We'll call you up tomorrow to come to court."

I ask: "Can I take it with me?"

He says: "No."

"Can I have a pen and paper to take notes?"

"No, no. Face the wall, lift your blindfold and read."

I do as I am told. The charge sheet is three pages long. My eyes go straight to the first article: "The accused has not refrained from any action to overthrow the sacred administration of the Islamic Republic."

I turn the pages quickly and see the rest of the accusations: infiltration of the office of the president, acquisition of intelligence and its transmission to the enemy. British spy. Soviet spy. And everything that I had written under Brother Hamid's torture. Now it's been sent to the court as evidence of my confession. Along with a request that I should be hanged.

The same man takes away the charge sheet and I am returned to the prison.

I tell Foroud what's in my heart and give the Party members a brief summary of the charge sheet. Five minutes later, the whole block knows that the sentence of hanging has been requested for me.

In the evening, as soon as the door opens, I go out into the court-yard. It's a moonlit night. I sit down in a corner, next to the mirabilis, and review my whole life. I am one step away from death. I am frightened. I look at the sky and the moon and I gather together in my mind all the final earthly elements of my life. My only wish is to be able to see my wife one more time. To tell her everything. Could I? I twist and turn in my cold bedding, divorcing myself from life, preparing myself for death and repeating the words I will say to the court a hundred times.

The next day, when we get off the minibus, they take me straight to a room and I hear a voice: "Take off your blindfold."

I take it off and put on my glasses. The image before me comes into focus. Mr Nayeri, who at the time was very young, is leaning on a chair with a thick file in front of him. Behind him, a window with metal bars opens onto a green space, and above the window is a clock showing eight thirty in the morning, 6 August 1985. A middle-aged man from the north of Iran is seated to Mr Nayeri's left. He is both a secretary and a court representative. Describing him as a defence lawyer would be a joke.

I say hello. Mr Nayeri makes a movement with his head and says: "Don't you have anything to say in your defence?"

I say: "Of course. My confessions have all been taken by force."

He shakes his head and says: "Everybody says this. So you, too, had no idea of anything?"

"No."

The court secretary and representative says: "This son of a bitch is a chief spy."

Nayeri asks me: "How did you address Kianuri?"

"Haj Aqa, Father ..."

"You had no idea that you were calling this faithless old man Haj Aqa?"

He then opens the file and leafs through it. I see a large envelope inside the file. Nayeri pulls it out, emptying its contents. It's the pages of the first stage of interrogation, which Brother Hamid had torn into pieces after I had repented so he could throw them away. This is just one example of the tricks of interrogation.

Nayeri puts the papers back on the desk.

"So you are not a spy?"

"No."

As if he had just remembered something, Nayeri calls the guard. He gives him his car keys and says: "Put those sacks of rice on the backseat of my car."

And asks me: "And the other confessions?"

I say: "I have never been an agent for the Soviets or the British."

He says: "That you are a spy is clear from your crimes ..."

And he signals to the guard, who's playing with the car keys, to take me away. Then he closes the file. His last sentence smells of death. I say: "Could you do me a favour, Haj Aqa? If the verdict is execution, could I call my wife?"

"It is not necessary at this time."

On the way back, I am hearing the clock tick in my mind. It started at eight thirty and ended at eight thirty-six. My fate has been decided in six minutes.

The following day is visiting day. Telephone desk number fifteen. When I pick up the phone, I immediately tell my wife: "It's over. Death sentence. I am innocent. I've not been a spy. I haven't been a Savak spy. If they hang me, don't let it destroy your life. But I am finished."

I watch her black chador, which she's been forced to put on for the visit, slip back as she sits down behind the glass screen, on the other side of the desk.

One evening, about a month later, they call me up. It's neither visiting time nor the time to sort out administrative procedures. Foroud and the Party members gather round. They don't say anything but I can see in their eyes that they are thinking of the hanging.

But how come they haven't picked up my belongings?

That's not unprecedented, though. Sometimes people are picked up to be "hit", to use the prison term, and their belongings collected afterwards. I say my farewells to my fellow Party members and walk down the stairs. A very thin young man is already waiting outside. So there are two of us. We board the minibus. As usual, we prisoners have not been told where we are being taken or why. I sit next to the window and pull up my blindfold. On the last night there's no longer any need for this constant tool of torture. The driver doesn't make a fuss about my blindfold. He must know that I am being taken to be hanged. I put on my glasses and stare at the beautiful night. The prison courtyard is glittering in the moonlight. It is truly a reflection of paradise. Water flows in the streams. Birds sing. Flowers bloom. A pleasant breeze is blowing through the open window. It's a beautiful night for dying. Against my will, I review my life. I tell myself: "Maybe they'll let me phone my wife before they hang me."

But what would be the point? We don't have a phone at home. So I must go to my grave, without having heard my wife's voice. My tears are flowing down my cheeks, drop by drop. I am not scared any more. I am totally numb.

The minibus stops. The dreamlike spring night is clear and bright. I can see both the city and the mountains at once. I ask the young man: "Why have they brought you here?"

His voice is shaking: "To hang me."

He too has lifted his blindfold. He's one of the Mujahedin. The bus driver leaves and a little later, there's the sound of shuffling slippers. I remember your words, Brother Hamid: "I would like to shoot the final bullet myself."

But the slippers are not yours. I had no idea at the time that you had been appointed deputy in the Information Ministry's security department, too important an official now to appear at the hanging ceremony in slippers. The slippers belong to a young guard, one of the regime's young thugs who plays football in the prison courtyard and takes the prisoners to the gallows. He doesn't tell us to put on our blindfolds either. He says: "Follow me."

We set off. We turn. We enter a building where someone is throwing herself into my arms. It's my wife. She says: "Fifteen years. They have given you fifteen years."

Then she collapses, sobbing, wrapped up in her chador. I talk to her but she can't hear me; she's just crying. The young man's mother has also embraced her son.

The guard says: "Ten minutes for you."

And then he faces the Mujahed man: "You, twenty minutes."

The young man looks at his watch and starts crying. My wife is also crying bitterly, endlessly. Much later, she told me that she had been waiting outside Evin's walls since five in the morning. When I had told her the news of my death sentence, she had immediately gone to Khamenei's office. She had already sent numerous letters to him without ever receiving an answer. This time she'd written that her husband was going to be hanged under the pretence of infiltration of Khamenei's office and Khamenei certainly knew that this was not true.

The day before our reunion, a letter had arrived at our home from Khamenei's office. My wife had opened the letter and seen a photocopy of the letter that I had sent to Khamenei from prison. She saw that Khamenei had written a single sentence on the back: "In the name of the Almighty, I was already familiar with his views."

Just that. Early the next morning, my wife had arrived outside Evin with the letter, and together with some other individuals she had managed to get an appointment with Ali Razini, who had replaced Asadollah Lajevardi. They had been taken to the Husseinieh in the evening, a Shia institution where religious and cultural events take place, such as prayers and sermons. Ali Razini was seated on a raised dais, receiving the family members of prisoners one by one. When my wife's turn came, she handed him the copy of Khamenei's letter. Razini opened the file, returned the copy and said: "There's no need. The original letter is here. Fifteen years."

With difficulty my wife stopped herself from crying out with joy and stood up to leave. But Razini pointed at her and an elderly woman and said: "Sit down."

They waited until the sun went down. When all the other families had left, Razini called a guard and said: "Take these two people back with you."

And gave him a piece of paper.

My wife panicked. Thugs like him terrify everybody. My wife thought the worst, and assumed that he intended to rape her. She said that as she walked out she was shaking with the fear of rape at the hands of this dirty monster. The guard put them into the minibus and as he stepped out of the bus he told them that they had been given permission for a visit.

I embrace my wife. She keeps crying.

The minibus takes us back to Evin. I am so happy that I can hardly stand on my own two feet. But I don't want anyone to know. I tell the others: "I had a visitor."

I fall into a deep, comfortable sleep.

A few days later, they call me up. I sign the fifteen-year prison term inside the administration office. The term becomes official on signing, and because the four years that have passed since my arrest do not count, my term altogether becomes nineteen years. I can no longer keep my joy to myself. By sheer chance that day sweets have been brought into the prison. I buy some and share them with the others in my block.

Chapter 22

Ghezel Hesar Prison and Stalin's Massacre

Ghezel Hesar is one of the largest prisons in the Middle East. It was built during the Shah's time for regular prisoners. Like US prisons, this one has four towers, one at each of the four corners of its 1500-hectare grounds. During the Shah's time no political prisoners were held here. But after the revolution, two units of the prison were allocated to political prisoners and Haj Davoud Rahmani, a criminal on a par with Asadollah Lajevardi, took charge of them. He tortured Armenian teenagers and young men into their graves and then he disappeared. He is one of the few torturers that no one has a single photograph of.

They are moving us away from Tehran, Brother Hamid, and I thought I would be moving away from you. So far away that your hands couldn't reach me. But I was wrong.

Your hands, the bloodied fingers of your culture, were exerting control everywhere.

This is my twenty-second letter to you, and I am writing it from very far away. Very far away. I don't know why I imagine that one day it will reach you.

Ghezel Hesar Prison, autumn 1985

It was autumn and a line of buses was taking us to another prison, travelling along the main motorway that leads from Tehran up to the north-west of Iran. As we drove, memories of mountains and deserts came flooding back to me. The buses were filled from front to back with prisoners who had been sentenced and were now being taken to Ghezel Hesar Prison to serve their sentences.

It is evening when we alight in front of the steps of unit number three. They divide us into blocks. They send me to cell number eight, I am sharing the cell with three other leftists and eight Mujahedin. The person in charge of the cell is, of course, one of them. In Evin, renegade Mujahedin were put in charge of blocks and cells. Here, the people loyal to the Mujahedin are in charge: the two sides of the same coin.

A meeting is held that evening. It's been arranged to cast votes for and against changing the bedsheets. The person in charge of the cell introduces the issue. Then he collects votes. He asks for the views of every single Mujahed. He bypasses me and the three other leftists who happen to sit beside me, and says: "Approved unanimously."

We leftists do not exist for them. A while later things become clear to me. There are poles that are opposite each other: the oppressive prison guards and the innocent prisoners. Each side desires nothing less than the total annihilation of the other. If an individual fails to obey the prisoners' own rules, he is counted as an enemy who is siding with the guards. If he doesn't conduct himself as the guards wish him to behave, he is considered an enemy of the administration. There is no grey zone between the black and white frontlines. If you tried to move towards the grey zone so that you could be true to yourself, you would be condemned by both sides.

A few days after my arrival, I notice that the leader of the Iranian Trotskyists, Babak Zahraie, is also here. Completely isolated, he is held in the first cell on the right side of the block. The cell is small and has become known as the cell of the "directionless", those with no political affiliations.

I seek him out and we immediately become friends. He's a sweet man, literate and open. We discuss Stalin. He's confident that Stalin killed three million people, I argue that he killed only a few. Eventually, we agree on three hundred thousand people, laugh and shake hands.

That same night, Hussein Abi comes to find me. I used to truly love him. Now, he talks to me in a cautious manner. He says I shouldn't speak to Babak, that he's an enemy of the Party and a CIA spy. I tell him that the rest of the prisoners are also enemies of the Party, but there is no evidence that Babak is a CIA spy. Also, even if he were a spy, what secret do I have that might be useful to him?

Laughing, Hussein says: "Sod off. When you perform your prayers, I know that you're faking it. And now you are hanging out with a CIA spy. Have you completely distanced yourself from us?"

I explained my position: "I have made up my mind. I don't want to belong to any organization. I want to be independent."

Our relationship becomes cold. I realize that after every meeting or conversation I have with Hussein, my relationship with most of the others becomes colder too. But a few of them remain friendly until the last day. Ismael is one of them; a tiny, military man, incredibly kind, he loves grapes. As at Evin, the Mujahedin have set up rules for this block. And, as at Evin, they have decided that eating fruit is a sign of greed. Hence, I am the only one that buys any of the fruit that is offered for sale. In the evening Ismael and I sit in the corridor, to chat and share my grapes.

In the middle of the night, the man in charge of the block wakes me up to take me out of the cell. He hands me over to Samad who resembles an Afghan bricklayer. He speaks quietly, muttering. After a few questions of a general nature, he starts asking about the Freemasons in Iran and their work, and the Intelligence Services' operational methods. Alarm bells start ringing in my head. You have returned, Brother Hamid, dressed in a different set of clothing. I am overwhelmed by an intense feeling of danger.

A few days later, I am called up, and asked to pick up my belongings. I am taken to Evin in a private car and delivered to the sanatorium. An official collects me and makes me stand outside a cell, and angrily tells me to take my clothes off. I take off my clothes. I take off everything apart from my underpants. He shouts: "Take them off!"

I can't believe it. I have only seen scenes like this in films. I begin to take off my underpants a little hesitantly. He abruptly drags them down.

"Bend over, you piece of filth."

A mixture of fear and embarrassment floods over me. I bend slightly.

"More."

With great reluctance I bend over a little more, every instinct screaming at me to refuse. My face is burning in shame.

"Now open up."

I grip the two sides of my buttocks and pull them apart. My heart and my hands are trembling. Suddenly, a hand is thrust into my anus. I cry out involuntarily. The gloved hand is twisting around inside my anus and I am choking with hatred and anger. He takes off his dirty glove and gives it to me: "Throw it into the toilet." Then he pushes me, naked as I am, into one of those infamous Israeli-style cells with a sink and toilet. I want to throw the glove into the toilet, but the toilet is blocked and filled to overflowing with a stinking mess of water and excrement.

I spend the whole night pacing the cell, breathing in the disgusting smell. I drink water from the tap, and am given nothing else. I am terrified that everything is about to start all over again. They come for me in the morning with my clothes, and I end up standing in a long corridor, facing the wall.

I hear a conversation between a man and a woman. I realize that they are husband and wife and have been brought together for a visit. Their voices sound very young. A bit later, I hear a child crying. From the words of the guard, who's brought in the child, I gather that the child has been brought in so his parents can see him. They promise the child, who's now stopped crying and is laughing, that they'll soon be released and will not abandon him. Then, it seems that a guard has appeared and taken away the child. The woman's crying takes over from the child's weeping. Her husband is consoling her that this is only the first visit and that they'll be able to be together with their child another time. Then I hear the guard's voice: "Enough. Say goodbye to each other."

They say their goodbyes and leave.

I hear a guard's voice telling another guard: "They have taken them both," meaning they are to be hanged.

I start trembling from head to toe. This had been the final meeting of a husband and wife with their child and none of them had been aware of it.

I wait for a while before someone comes for me. We set off. We walk down a steep road. We get into a private car parked by the gate. When we leave Evin, the driver says: "Take off your blindfold."

I was seated in the back and there were two people in the front. I guessed from the route we were taking that we were returning to Moshtarek Prison. An hour later, inside Moshtarek Prison again, I put on the blue prison clothes, walk past the courtyard and enter an elongated cell neighbouring the toilets on the left side in block number one. The walls are slippery wet from dirty toilet water.

There is a constant sound of children playing in the corridor. I assume that I'll be seeing you, Brother Hamid. I've really been missing you. But you are not here. A young man of around thirty, smartly dressed, comes into my cell. He shakes my hand. He asks me respectfully to sit down. Apparently, he wants information about Maryam Firooz, a princess from the Qajar dynasty and Kianuri's wife. Her birthday, her family, her personal habits, her love affairs. And I have absolutely no idea about any of this. I have never even spoken to her. I quickly realize that they are interested in trying to discover if she has any relationship with the Freemasons, and if therefore they have influence on the Party. But how can they put me in the same category as Maryam? Where did they get this stupid idea from?

It is clear that your well-dressed successor did not believe anything I said. He repeats what Nayeri said, though in different words: "We've got to have a look at your file."

I stay in the wet cell for a few days, listening to the sound of little girls playing, alone with my own thoughts until they call me up again. The usual routine. I get into a car. A hand pushes my head down. I wait for a long time in that position. There's the sound of little girls being put into the car. The car sets off. After a while a voice says: "Take off your blindfold and lift your head."

I lift my head and put on my glasses. I first see Ferdowsi's statue. Then the two little girls who are seated next to me. Then the pale face of a man with a long beard.

"Hussein Abi!"

We kiss each other on the cheeks.

The guard seated next to the driver asks: "Do you know this lunatic?"

He answers: "We shared a cell."

The guard says: "Shut up. Never mind."

Hussein Abi held my hand, pressing it, while he talked to the children: "When you see Mum, don't start crying, okay? Don't tell her that Grandma has gone to God. Okay Rana? Okay Ziba?"

He has told me before that Rana is just like her mother. I stroke his daughters' heads. He smiles at me.

They drop Hussein Abi and his children off at Evin and take me to Ghezel Hesar. As soon as I enter, I request to be taken to the "directionless" cell. It is obvious that I am still walking on a knife edge. But I am even more determined to keep my independence.

There are three people in the cell. Two very young prisoners who tell me that they are Mujahedin supporters and have been put in charge of the block by their Party. The two men, belonging to the military wing of the Party, have been given short sentences. They have also decided to live their own lives and have requested to be transferred to this cell. The request meets opposition on the part of the block but the grey zone is beginning to take shape.

These days I shave my beard every day and I have trimmed my moustache. I dress carefully. I perform my prayers but spend most of my time either reading or talking to Babak Zahraie. Some Party members come to visit me. One of them is Dariush, who visits often.

When I heard that he had been hanged during the 1988 massacres, I cried for him, sobbing loudly.

There are many organizational rules in the prison block. Rules of hygiene have to be obeyed to the death. Bed sheets and curtains have to be changed frequently. Fruit can now only be eaten once a month. Biting into the rind of a watermelon is a sign of greed. We are not supposed to change our clothes in front of each other when getting ready for the washroom or to see visitors. We are supposed to go behind a curtain. We are forced to sleep in our trousers on hot summer nights. Getting into bed dressed only in underwear is regarded as decadent. The competition between the government and the Mujahedin to prove which one is more orthodox has reached a high point.

Babak Zahraie is the only one who disregards the rules. He sleeps in white sleeping shorts and doesn't care if the blanket slips off. When others complain one day, he walks through the whole block wearing only those same shorts. There is pandemonium, but Babak will not submit.

Babak belonged to a different world. It was like having a leftist New Yorker on one side and revolutionary villagers from Tehran's outskirts on the other. Two unfamiliar worlds that had been brought together in prison for the same reason – opposing the Islamic regime. With every passing day, I felt more and more cut off from the rest of the prisoners.

Eventually I asked to be transferred to the "workers block". There is no sign of the "prison inside the prison" on this block. There is no secret organization managing it. It's not as tidy as my previous blocks, there are no flowers or herbs in the courtyard, but I am no longer a prisoner of multiple regulations. I am allowed to choose my cell. In political blocks even doctors are not allowed to work, but in the workers' block, everybody is busy. You choose an occupation from one of the various physical tasks in the prison. I put on a worker's uniform and join the team in charge of harvesting chilli peppers. Along with the ordinary prisoners, mostly armed robbers, I go off to the huge fields enclosed by Ghezel Hesar's high walls, which have been allocated to farming. There are horses that are said to belong to Haj Davoud.

The air is pleasant. We pick the peppers from beneath the low branches and put them into sacks. I feel well. I feel I am myself again. Just like the teenager I used to be back in the old days, working in a shoe factory in the summer.

A few days later, when we return, laughing and talking and with sacks filled with chilli peppers hanging over our shoulders, I come face to face with the man in charge of the cultural section. A fresh group of prisoners has been brought in and are climbing out of a minibus. He says: "Why have you opted for this sort of thing? You ought to be writing with that hand."

I say to him: "I'd rather work in the mud than write things that I don't believe in."

The following day the cultural section bans me from picking peppers.

Chapter 23

Purgatory in Hell

A new prison was built during the Shah's time to hold political prisoners. It's located not far from Ghezel Hesar Prison. Initially, it was called Gawhar Dasht, after the newly built neighbourhood where it's located. Work on the prison was completed after the revolution. But the name of the prison and the neighbourhood was changed after Mohammad-Ali Rajai, the Islamic Republic's second president, was assassinated. In contrast to Evin Prison, no foreign reporter has ever visited this prison. There is no film footage from inside the prison.

Hello, Brother Hamid. You are no longer an unknown soldier. I talked about you in great detail during an interview with the Voice of America's television channel. They even showed your picture on TV. This time, it's I who have entered your life. You might find yourself forced to leave your work as a security official because of me and start looking at life from a different angle, an angle unrelated to torture or whipping.

Rajai Shahr Prison, autumn 1986

At dawn, we are woken and ordered to get ready quickly, and to pack all our belongings. People had been whispering that parts of Ghezel Hesar's political sections would be dissolved, and now we find ourselves being transferred. Around seven in the morning we board the minibuses that have been lined up in front of the prison block. Then we are made to wait until the evening, after all the blocks have been emptied. The driver of our minibus gets irritated and keeps saying: "They hired us for four hours but we've been made to wait from the morning until now. Do they take us for fools?"

A uniquely witty and eloquent armed robber, who's been given a life sentence, says in response to the driver: "Man, all these guys were called up to answer two questions but ended up eating porridge for five or six years."

Laughter bursts out inside the minibus. By the time we set off, it's dark outside. We keep asking where we are being taken, but the guards are silent.

It doesn't take long for the walls of the Rajai Shahr Prison to come into view. We are told to put on our blindfolds.

The minibus door opens, and the icy air outside makes me shiver. We walk through an open space. Then we enter a corridor. Eventually, we are ordered to take off our blindfolds. I open my eyes and find myself inside a large hall. It's a Husseinieh. The air is intensely cold. I am shivering so violently my teeth chatter. It is some time before a few blankets are thrown on the hall floor. Groups of three prisoners have to share two blankets. One to lie on, and one to cover ourselves with. A bit later, thin slices of bread and cheese are brought in. That's our dinner for tonight.

We eat the bread and cheese, put our blankets on the freezing floor and stretch ourselves out on them. We put our belongings under our heads. The blankets are too short, so our feet stick out at the bottom, and too narrow, so they only properly cover the person in the middle. The two on the outside are freezing. We keep turning, twisting and laughing until the morning. The following day we are sent to the ordinary cells. There is no division of prisoners into political and non-political categories here and no organized body of prisoners in charge of the block allocating us to our cells. Neither is there the sort of internal organization to take charge of "the prison inside the prison".

There are three prisoners in each solitary confinement cell. We put our belongings in a corner and start our new lives.

A few days later, we are taken to the Jihad block.[97] A number of cells are located on the left of the courtyard. Inside one is a cleric from the north of Iran who the men have nicknamed Golden Willy. The cleric has been accused of taking advantage of his position as a Qur'an teacher by sleeping with thirty-five virgins on the pretext of helping them enter paradise by sleeping with a holy man. I watch him from afar, he's always busy meditating and praying. Every week, he's one of the first to go to the meeting hall to see his wife.

To the right of the courtyard there's a very large cell that was obviously built later than the rest. There's a shop and a barber's stand at the entrance to the cell.

The cells are lined with barracks-style beds. Prisoners are allowed to live on their own or to share living costs with a group of others as they wish. There are newspapers in the block and a television set, and prisoners have put their names down for magazines that are brought in regularly, including a magazine about the cinema.

A spacious courtyard is located between the cell and the brick building. In the evenings, prisoners can walk up and down the courtyard, nicknamed "the boulevard". The south of the courtyard lies on steep ground, and the sky, the mountains and the broad horizon are always visible from there. The boulevard is placed between two little gardens filled with flowers, and gently curves to the north. Further along is a volleyball court where prisoners play in the evenings. Mr Mortazavi, the prison head, sometimes joins them.

We take turns to do prison duties such as cleaning. The people in charge of the block are ordinary prisoners. Amir is in charge of our block. He is always busy with jobs like mopping the floors. Later, in the outside world, Amir became a composer of film music. While I watched his first film, I kept remembering him sweating over his mop.

There are no divisions separating political groups. The Mujahedin, a diverse group of leftists and monarchists, all live together. The revolution has thrown together a group of people with very diverse political views, from an ageing Maoist and excellent cook who, to cover the cost of studying in Europe had ended up serving the French ambassador in Spain, to the sergeant who appears to be kissing the Shah's feet in that famous photograph that shows the exile of the last king of Iran.

There is no pressure. Collective prayers are rarely performed. The Husseinieh is only used on special religious occasions, when speeches are delivered and mourning ceremonies held. The Jihad block in the Rajai Shahr Prison is the closest thing to that "place" that had been intended to function as a "university". A place where free speech allows political prisoners opposed to the Islamic Republic to learn the truth of Islam and the fairness of the administration before they are freed again.

This explanation starts and ends with Haj Aqa Sayyed Hussein Mortazavi, known as Haji by all. He's a young cleric loyal to the Ayatollah Montazeri's faction. Clinging to Haji is Brother Sajjad, a man with an angry face, always ready for service and dressed in military uniform. He belongs to the extremist faction. He used to be in charge of the administration at Moshtarek Prison. Back at Moshtarek Prison, we used to only hear the sound of his voice but now, we can also see his face. He knows the leftist convicts very well and makes no secret of his disagreement with Haji's methods. The Haji's soft shoes and Brother Sajjad's tough boots are the two wings of the administration. The two walk together, each awaiting the demise of the other.

Life here is bearable. With Amir's help I manage to find a little desk. From then on, my bed becomes my office. I read and write as much as I can.

To my right is Foroud's bed, he spends most of his time thinking and reading. He is still sentenced to be hanged[98] but from time to time his laughter shakes the prison cell. Right opposite Foroud is Hamid's bed. Hamid's father had been a diplomat during the Shah's time and Hamid had returned to Iran together with his dentist wife to help support the revolution. His father, who had once served as the Iranian ambassador to the Soviet Union, had advised him against it, but he had returned anyway. He has a degree in law. He speaks and writes good English and we teach him to write in Persian. He had been employed at the Central Bank and later, because of his command of legal matters and English, he had been tasked with accompanying the Iranian delegation in charge of signing the Algerian contract for the release of American hostages.

He lived a happy life in Tehran, socializing in diplomatic circles through his father's contacts, unaware that the Islamic association was keeping an eye on him. Eventually, they raided his home on the night of his wife's birthday and arrested him on the charge of espionage. He was imprisoned until the general amnesty which followed the mass killing of political prisoners. Today he lives in America.

Foroud, Hamid and I become a team of three. Our conversations always revolve on literature. One day I come across an old film magazine, which takes me back to my love of cinema. I spent many years writing film reviews and now, this magazine (in a few years I will become the editor-in-chief of its rival) allows me to rediscover the world of the movies. I start thinking about writing a film script. I go to sleep with this thought in my mind.

An unknown fear wakes me that night. I see my wife; it's as if she's just left my side. She's dressed in a white nightgown, floating in the air like an angel. She reaches the window and passes through it. And all the while I worry that one of the many sleeping men will wake and see her in her thin nightgown. I still don't know whether I saw that vision while awake or whether it just felt like I had been awake even though I had actually been asleep. Be that as it may, a name appeared in my mind and a storyline: *Lady of the Lilies*, about a woman who's searching for her husband.

The following day, I start writing. A few months later, during a New Year visit, I secretly gave the film script to my wife. She hid it under her chador and took it out with her. We sold the script for a good price after I was freed, which helped us to begin our lives all over again from scratch.

My days are spent like this. I've already spent five years in prison, but only two of them count as part of my sentence. I have twelve long years ahead of me.

Every so often they allow each family to bring three books for their prisoner. My wife is brilliant, making sure that I get three excellent books. One of them is Mario Vargas-Llosa's first novel. I immediately start translating it. Whenever I get stuck, I ask Hamid for help and together we untie the knot. The translation was published after my release, introducing Vargas-Llosa's *The Time of the Hero* to Iran for the first time.

We also volunteer to sort out the prison library. We are locked into a spacious room full of books where we take it in turns to sort out the books and read. We are left undisturbed until the evening. Each of us smuggles a book out of the library, I choose a collection of Iraj Mirza's poetry. He was a Qajar prince whose poetry pokes fun at religion and spirituality. In the evening, when we are taken back to our cell I devour it – this banned book has a completely different flavour when read stretched out on a prison bed supplied by the Islamic Republic.

The regular, non-political prisoners have their own life and their own associations. They have leave over the weekends. When they return, they bring back fruit and sweets with them. Drugs have made their way into the prison too,[99] and are distributed among the prisoners.

Early one morning we are forced to get up quickly and go to the Husseinieh. We turn up, sleepy and with our faces unwashed. I am always quick to enter and find a place where I can lean against the wall. My legs have seized up as a result of my interrogation and I can no longer sit down cross-legged. Haj Aqa Mortazavi arrives, looking very happy and light-hearted. Brother Sajjad also turns up, sticking close to Mortazavi. Haj Aqa Mortazavi walks up and stands behind the microphone. His first sentence, after "In the name of God, the merciful," is: "I have come to let you know that you'll be freed soon and your places will be taken by the leaders of the international oppression."

There's whispering in the Husseinieh and we are all looking at each other.

What's happened?

Haj Aqa Mortazavi carries on. In summary, the people who are responsible for us being in prison are the heads of the world arrogance, the United States and the Soviet Union in particular. Once Islam's flag is raised, they'll be arrested and will be imprisoned here instead of us. He doesn't offer any further explanation. We return to our cells, sleepy and dizzy. The loudspeakers start playing nationalistic war songs (this was during the Iran-Iraq War) and the presenter talks about the great victory of Muslim soldiers. Eventually it becomes clear that the night before, the Islamic Republic had won an important battle. Haj Aqa Mortazavi's words were his own private interpretation of the world's future. The head of our prison was as dreamy as we were. We saw socialism conquering the world, he saw Islam doing the same.

On New Year's Day, our visiting time is extended, which is more painful than the meeting that takes place with a glass screen separating the visitor from the prisoner. One is allowed to kiss one's loved ones, to smell them, and then forced to return behind locked doors.

Eventually, again with no warning, we are told to pack all our things and be ready. While we are busy packing up our belongings, it becomes clear that we are being transferred to Evin.

They take us into the courtyard and do a thorough body search of each of us. They confiscate most of our belongings. They make us put on our blindfolds and then take us out.

When we take off our blindfolds, we see a number of buses crowding into the prison courtyard, surrounded by Islamic Revolutionary Guards. We get on board and several tough-looking bearded men dressed in black leather lock our wrists to the arms of the bus seats with handcuffs. When the buses are filled, Haj Aqa Mortazavi turns up. He looks into every single bus, getting on and off each one. I see him speaking to someone who appears to be the head of the Islamic Revolutionary Committee. They both get into the bus and we hear Mortazavi's final words: "Unlock the handcuffs. If anything goes wrong, I'll be responsible."

And the men in black grudgingly unlock the handcuffs. The buses set off, surrounded by black Mercedes Benz cars. We leave behind for good the Jihad block with its delightful courtyard. Tehran appears on the horizon. We circle around Azadi Square. We pass through the streets of Shahrak-e Gharb. Life is going on and we are merely passing through it, like strangers, unaware that the bloodiest days are yet to come.

Chapter 24

Genocide in the Islamic Republic

In the course of one month, and on the orders of Ayatollah Khomeini, the judges passed the death sentence on thousands of men and women, Muslims and Jews, Armenians, Baha'is, communists, pregnant women and elderly men. They recreated the horrors of World War II throughout the country, hanging prisoners en masse, picking up people in trucks at night, and burying them in mass graves.

I've seen Evin's machinery of death, and I have written down everything that I saw and heard there.

Hello Brother Hamid, I am writing my twenty-fourth letter to you.

It's past midnight and once again I couldn't sleep because of the tension. I have been jolted out of sleep. We've finally arrived back in Evin, and are approaching the bloodiest days, the days of murder.

Evin Prison, early summer 1988

Once again I am in Evin. Haj Aqa Mortazavi is the new head of the prison, and has completely transformed it. The place I left two years ago is unrecognizable from the one I have arrived in. We have just been allocated to our "university" blocks.

Bahram Danesh, a seasoned officer who's now seventy-eight years of age, is on my block. He moves his head as if it were a pendulum. He has migraine, a splitting headache that tortures him.

Every day he sends a message to a doctor for a tablet. He sits there, constantly moving his head until the pill arrives. I always go to him, hold him under his arms and together we walk up and down the block. He's an aged officer whose life has been spent either in prison or in exile but he is still standing up for his convictions.

We walk together and review our lives. I have always remembered his words: "We are tiny sparrows, twittering on a branch in the middle of a wild jungle full of predators."

Early in the spring I spot a newcomer standing in the corridor looking lost. He's holding a plastic bag in his hand and looks very familiar. I go up to him. No, it can't be him. This man's beard is half white. But yes, it's him alright. I call him: "Hussein Abi!"

He stares at me. He throws himself into my arms. He says: "They have made my children orphans."

And he sobs, endlessly.

"They have hanged Fariba."

"Fariba?"

"My wife. She married me as Fatimeh but her real name was Fariba. They took us for a farewell visit. Fariba was crying. We kept pleading with them. We threw ourselves at the guard's feet. They killed my wife. They took away my children. They tell me: 'Go, get out, as long as you shut up.' But if I went out, I'd shout 'What's happening here?' I'd set fire to myself and my children."

Hussein Abi finds himself lost in a world between total clarity and complete madness. He doesn't speak to anyone except me. He spends hours in front of his prayer rug, shedding tears. He says: "All my life I used to sit at the bottom of the prayer rug, talking to God. But now I am opening my heart to my wife, talking to her."

They come for me on 1 August 1988. I am made to sit down on a bench in front of an office door with a number of other people. I hear Kianuri's voice, he's speaking to someone. It's a while before he comes out of the office and someone else is led in. The person sitting next to me keeps muttering about Kianuri. He's extremely angry. I recognize the voice of the man who was in charge of the Party's publicity section. I kick his leg unobtrusively and whisper my name. He grabs my hand. We ask after each other's well-being. He first asks about his brother, who has left the country. He says: "Watch out. Kia is plotting to make us come to a compromise with these criminals."

At that moment, I am called in. I enter the office. Haj Nasser, the man in charge, says: "Take off your blindfold."

I do as I'm told, put on my glasses and say hello. Haj Nasser responds to my greeting and signals me to sit down on a chair in front of Kianuri's desk. I see Kianuri for the first time since my arrest. I say hello to him as well. He half stands up in acknowledgement. I sit down. He asks after my wife's well-being. Then he explains the Party's situation. He says the Party has made mistakes, which we all should accept, but our position with regard to the Islamic Republic has been correct.

He is pleading with his eyes for me to accept his words. In the past, Kianuri had spoken with determination, he did not plead. So I explain my situation: "I don't want to be involved in politics at all. I'd like to do cultural work independently though in line with the constitution. That is, if they free me."

He seems relieved. He takes a breath and asks Haj Nasser: "Is there anyone else?"

Haj Nasser tells me: "Go outside and wait until a guard comes for you."

While waiting I hear the voice of a young woman who is arguing with another woman. Later, I learn that the woman was Maryam Firooz, Kianuri's wife. Kianuri had spoken to the men and Maryam to the women.

The events of the following days clarify the meaning of Kianuri and Maryam's discussions with the Party members. A few months later, when Kianuri and I become cellmates, he tells me the full story. Mortazavi had appealed for Kianuri's help in trying to save the lives of the Party members. He asked Kianuri to talk to all the Party members, and somehow make them aware that they are in serious danger. At the time, Mortazavi didn't clarify exactly what was happening, but later Haj Nasser told me that Mortazavi had voted against a proposal by a council preparing the ground for mass execution.

It's probably a day or two later when a talk being held in one of Tehran's mosques is broadcast in the block. The speaker keeps shouting: "Kill them. Kill these people. Kill them."

I do not realize that he means us, we who are walking up and down these corridors, lost and anxious. Bahram Danesh is sitting in front of the entrance to the block and, as usual, is moving his head like a pendulum.

This is the last voice from the outside that we hear. The radio stops. The television sets are taken away. They've stopped bringing in newspapers. What's happened?

On 25 July, the Mujahedin-e Khalq had entered Iran via Iraq, launching a new offensive called Forough Javidan (Eternal Light). The Mujahedin leadership had called up thousands of men and women from across the world to quickly come together in Iraq. They were given a few days' military training and had been told that upon their arrival in Iran, the Iranian people would join them and help to bring down the Islamic Republic. The operation lasted three days and the Mujahedin, who had entered Iranian territory, were all killed.

The Islamic Republic was thus given an excuse to organize and launch the biggest mass murder campaign in Iran's history. The order to kill comes from Ayatollah Khomeini and so Iranian prisons are turned into institutions of mass murder.

This is Ayatollah Khomeini's ruling on the massacre:

Since the treacherous Mujahedin do not truly believe in Islam and whatever they are saying is to deceive and create disunion and because their leaders have recanted Islam and also bearing in mind that they have waged war against God in the northwest and south of the country in cooperation with the Iraqi Ba'ath party and also because their spies are working for Saddam against our Muslim nation, and in view of their cooperation with the World Arrogance and their dishonourable damages from the beginning of the Islamic Republic until now, all those prisoners, throughout the country, who persist in their hypocrisy are considered Moharebs[100] and must be sentenced to hanging. This issue will be decided in Tehran by a majority vote of Hujjatul Islam Nayeri, Mr Ishraqi (Tehran's Prosecutor) and a representative of the Ministry of Intelligence. Needless to say, caution is required, and consensus is preferred. As regards provincial prisons, even though a majority vote of Shari'a judges, Revoutionary Court prosecutors, and representatives of the Ministry of Intelligence is needed, showing mercy to those who have waged war against God is simple-mindedness. Islam's decisiveness against God's enemies is one of the overarching principles of the Islamic regime. I hope that by showing revolutionary anger and hatred towards God's enemies, you will be able to attain God's consent. The gentlemen who have been put in charge of this task should not doubt or hesitate. They should seek to strive hard against the unbelievers and hypocrites.[101] To doubt the legal rulings of Islam amounts to dismissing the pure and immaculate blood of the martyrs. May peace be upon you.

Following this, Evin Prison's legal representative told the family of one of the prisoners: "Everyone's fate is going to be settled soon."

First the prisoners are reassigned to different blocks in the prisons, and contact between the blocks is cut off. Political prisoners are no longer allowed to move freely between the blocks and the kitchen to carry the large pots of tea. Ordinary prisoners are put in charge of this task.

Next they start to round up and take away the Mujahedin prisoners. Two of them, a pair of very young brothers, are on our block. One of them has been sentenced to ten years; the other has been sentenced to hang. Like a pair of swans, they always sit in a corner, heads on one another's shoulders. They come for the one with the death sentence first. I will never forget the brothers' farewell, that silence that was only broken by their sobs. Then they come for the one who has been sentenced to ten years. We can all sense that something is about to happen, but so far no one knows what, and there is no way we can find out.

Then it is the turn of the man who's in charge of making the dinner arrangements. He was a Mujahed, with a very big belly, very young, very mischievous. He liked preparing dinner. He would throw down the tablecloth with a flourish and say: "Tonight we are serving a stew. A unique occasion, not a night like any other night." I have forgotten his name, but I'll never forget his sweet smile and his light-hearted words.

And then they begin to round up the leftists. The first one to be called up from our hall is Hussein Abi. He puts on his blindfold and leaves. I wait and wait, he doesn't come back. The evening arrives, it becomes night. I am unable to sleep. What's happening? Why hasn't he come back? My mind is busy with these thoughts but just as my eyes become tired, Hussein Abi crawls into his bed.

I ask him: "Where have you been?"

He says: "Shush. They are killing. Watch out."

I say: "What do you mean?"

"The court …"

His teeth chatter as he talks. They had asked him: Do you believe in your party? He had answered that his party were Fatimeh, Rana and Ziba. He was in love with them. They had asked him: Are you a Muslim? He had answered that yes he was, but not the way they were Muslims. They had told him that they meant whether he said his prayers. He had replied that he had been praying since he was a child, but not their kind of prayer. The court judges had whispered to each other. Then they had signalled to Haj Mojtaba Halwai, the deputy prison security chief and the man in charge of carrying out the executions. Haj Mojtaba had told him by the door: "You'll be quiet and not say a word to anyone or else I will stick your tongue into your arse."

Hussein Abi tells me all this and then turns his back to me. The next morning, Hussein Abi is behind me as we queue for the bathrooms, ready to perform our ablution for the morning prayers. He quietly tells me the rest of the story. We have not even reached the bathroom when they come for him and take him away.

There's no news for a few days. We walk up and down the corridors like caged chickens waiting for a brutal hand to pull us out of the cage. We talk about everything except the thing we should talk about. Our eyes are fixed on the door and our ears alert for sounds.

There is a gang of thieves in charge of bringing round tea and food to the prisoners, who are patients of Dr Fariborz Baghai, who is in a cell upstairs. This excellent gynaecologist, who used to be the deputy head of a large hospital in Frankfurt, had come back to Iran to help the revolution and ended up in jail for twelve years. The thieves warned the doctor what was happening, and what sort of questions were being asked in court, and that after the Mujahedin, they had started to round up the leftists. Dr Baghai made sure that everyone on the block also heard about this, passing on the information through the same group of ordinary prisoners and hence, clarifying the situation for us.

The next one to be called up is Rahim Araqi. He had been a prisoner during the Shah's time. One of Iran's best architects, we used to call him Rahim the Bear due to the fat he was carrying on his body. Rahim kisses us on our cheeks and says: "Keep an eye on my children if you happen to live through this."

He loved his daughter, Nazli, who had developed into a tall and slender woman who loved her father dearly. I kept imagining the Gentle Bear standing in front of a firing squad. I was not yet aware that they had started hanging people.

These thoughts make me anxious. I keep pacing up and down,

and looking at his empty bed. His book of architecture, which he managed to get hold of with great difficulty, still lying open on his blanket.

Rahim doesn't return. The following day they fold up his blanket and collect his belongings. I saw him again years later in the outside world, when he explained the miracle of his rescue, but I have not been able to get in touch with him to ask his permission to tell his story here.

I am walking up and down the corridor, deep in thought, when Bahram Danesh grabs hold of my arm: "Are you scared of being seen with me?"

I laugh. I give him a kiss on his cheek and together we start walking again. He tells me for the umpteenth time the story of his escape following the defeat of the Khorasani troops' uprising. How he had crossed the arid desert and then thrown himself into a river and got himself to the Soviet Union.

It's as if he knows that his turn has arrived today. They come for him. He kisses me on my cheeks and says: "I am not coming back. One sparrow less is not going to affect the world."

And that old man, his body bent by lengthy episodes of torture with a head that is always about to explode from a migraine, went away. I always recall his words: "We are tiny sparrows, twittering on a branch in the middle of a wild jungle full of predators."

The twittering of a sparrow called Bahram will echo in my mind as long as I live, and I see in my mind's eye the head of an ancient-looking man, moving like a pendulum in a clock, tick-tock.

They keep coming for people.

My turn arrives. They come for me on 1 August 1988. I look around, but I can't see a familiar face to say goodbye to. I put the letter I have written for my wife on top of my belongings and leave the cell. The minibus that picks me up is full. I try to look from underneath my blindfold but I don't know anyone in the bus. I feel numb. As if I have died even before being killed.

They make us get out of the bus and take us to the interrogation office. I join a long blindfolded queue, facing the wall. The death calls come at short intervals. We are approaching the doorway to hell. When I reach the door, I can hear a voice on the other side. It's Mehrdad Farjad. After spending many years in Europe, he had returned to Iran to serve the revolution. He is yelling. It seems as if someone is trying to shut him up by placing a hand over his mouth. The voice is muffled and quietens. Suddenly Mehrdad cries out again. His voice is silenced once and for all. I found out later that they had cut off his tongue and taken him to the gallows with his mouth streaming with blood.

Someone grabs me and drags me upright. It's Haj Mojtaba. He opens the door and pushes me inside. "Take off your blindfold."

I recognize the voice of Haj Nasser, the man in charge of the interrogation office, and one of the prosecutors. He calls out my name and asks: "Do you believe in the Tudeh Party?"

I answer: "I hate politics and the Tudeh Party."

Nayeri, the court judge, glances down at the paper on his desk. I suspect he's about to say: "But your file is still open ..."

But he asks: "Do you pray?"

His voice sounds tired. He has already handed down the hanging sentence for thousands of people. I answer: "Yes, Haj Aqa."

"Do you believe in the Islamic Republic?"

"I believed in it before my arrest and I still believe in it now."

Haj Nasser says in a mocking voice: "I bet, like the rest of them, you also claim to have personally served the Islamic Republic."

I say: "I don't know about the others. But my intention was to help the anti-imperialist Islamic Republic."

Nayeri whispers something into Haj Nasser's ear. The whispering seems to take ages. Haj Nasser answers him. Then Nayeri writes something down on a piece of paper and hands it over to Haj Mojtaba. He takes the paper. He tells me: "Put on your blindfold."

I put on my blindfold. Haj Mojtaba takes me out. I feel as if ashes have been thrown over me. I walk down a corridor. A door opens and I find myself in an open space. I take off my blindfold. I am in the sanatorium. Three old men from Moshtarek Prison are standing in front of me, talking. Two of them are over the age of eighty, one of them is even older. We greet each other and kiss each other's cheeks. The three have already been to the court. They are being called for, one at a time. They assume they are about to be freed, but in fact they are on their way to the gallows.

I don't know how much time passes before they come back for me. Once again I enter the block with my eyes blindfolded. A door opens in the corridor and I find myself inside a small solitary confinement cell. I am ready to collapse. I stretch myself out on the floor. Just like during the long days of interrogation and torture, I have gone numb. For only the second time in my life, a light has started to shine in my heart. I tell myself: "God does exist." I remember Khamenei's words back in the cell at Moshtarek Prison: "In your heart of hearts you are a believer, even though you are not aware of it." After a while the door opens. Someone says: "Put on your blindfold."

I put it on. Whoever this is, he enters the cell. He sits down and starts asking questions. The questions are all about my file. I answer him, but I can hear your voice in my head, Brother Hamid: "When the sentence is passed, I would like to shoot the final bullet myself."

The questions finally reach the point I have been waiting for. The part of the file that is still open: England. The questions are all indirect. I answer all of them. Eventually, he asks: "Do you pray?"

"Yes, and I've just missed my prayers. I couldn't go to the bathroom for my ablution."

This is a deliberate tactic on my part. I am holding death at bay by performing my prayers. The divine light that shone in my heart that day actually has nothing to do with prayers.

The man, whoever he might be, takes me to the bathroom. I sense his eyes on me. I give a solid performance of ablution. He takes me back to my cell. He offers me a prayer stone. I ask which way is Mecca. He turns me towards Mecca. He locks the door behind him. I take off the blindfold. I start praying. I imagine he's watching me through the door opening. Then I become tired and collapse. I drank as much water as I could in the bathroom, but I am very hungry. I am glad that my stomach is empty. I have heard that one tends to shit oneself before being hanged. I'd hate that to happen. I picture my corpse hanging and my mouth being pushed into a pile of my own shit. It's making me feel sick. Then I seem to fall into a black hole. I don't know whether it's sleep, or waiting, or the last moments of life before death. The sound of a door opening brings me back to my senses. Again they take me and make me stand at the back of a queue. Again, a thousand years pass before I enter the court. This time there's no Haj Nasser. A tall young man has replaced him. They say he was Evin's Intelligence Director at some point.

The same questions. I give the same answers. Nayeri asks: "Did you have a leadership position in the Party?"

I say: "I have never been in a leadership position. I was just an ordinary member."

Even then I had no idea that what they meant by leading member was someone who was in the pay of the Party. I later discover that the Party had two layers of leadership. Leadership number one and leadership number two, and I had been part of number two. Later, Kianuri explained to me that Haj Nasser had insisted that I had been in the first group and Kianuri had repeatedly denied this and explained that I belonged to the second category. And much later still it dawned on me that the numbers one and two had represented the distance between life and death. Ayatollah Khomeini's death verdict for the Mujahedin has been published. But it is said that one of his unpublished rulings called for the mass murder of all Marxists on the basis of his belief that the leadership of the leftist groups were all supporters of the infidels and hence should be hanged. Decisions about the members of the second layer were left to the courts.

Nayeri is saying: "In that case, give us the declaration of faith."

I am assuming that I am about to be hanged. So I say: "I bear witness that there is no God but Allah … I bear witness …"

Nayeri signals to Haj Mojtaba. He comes to me, and grabs me by the arm.

"Put on your blindfold."

He hasn't gripped my arm tightly and his voice doesn't sound aggressive. I allow myself to hope. Could this mean that I will not be hanged?

I put on my blindfold. Haj Mojtaba takes me outside. He puts my hand on someone's shoulder. This is yet another queue. Is this queue heading to the gallows or towards life?

Chapter 25

Gallows and Mass Murder

The people who were hanged during that bloody summer of 1988 were taken to Khavaran in trucks at night, off-loaded in the abandoned cemetery, and then earth was thrown over them.

I can still hear your voice, Brother Hamid: "I would like to shoot the final bullet myself."

This is my twenty-fifth letter. Looking back at that infernal day, I am running and sense that you are right behind me. You lift your six-shooter, and pull the trigger. You are ready to fire the final bullet that would sort me out.

Evin, September 1988

The queue is finally moving. It's hot. Hot. Hot. They set us off at a run. There are lots of us. Where are we going? We are running blind-folded. I fall to the ground and pick myself up. One of my slippers has fallen off somewhere. I'm at the end of the line.

"Keep running, you piece of filth."

Someone hits me on my head. I run. Once again I have been turned into a dog.

Woof, woof. I am a spy. Woof, woof. Islam is victorious. The left and the right are both destroyed.

I take off the other slipper. The soles of my feet are hot. With my next step, the ground disappears beneath me. I slip. It's a flight of stairs. We all slip and fall on top of each other down the stairs. It's as if there's no end to these stairs. There are people laughing out aloud.

"Get up, you filthy bastards."

I get up. My blindfold has come off. But no one tells me to put it on again.

We are in a large basement. Half dark. There are pipes everywhere. And there are people hanging from them.

"We have hung them up to dry."

And again they make us run. We run and bump into each other. Then they make us sit down. There are row upon row of people hanging from the pipes. Some guards with wheelbarrows arrive. They take the people down one by one and dump them into the wheelbarrows.

When the wheelbarrows are full they are wheeled away. A hand hangs out of one of them and trails along the floor. A pair of glasses is smashed underfoot. A wheelbarrow tilts and its contents fall out.

"Roll up your sleeves."

Wearing short-sleeved shirts is considered a crime. It's a trademark of prostitution. It angers God. It shakes the divine throne.

"You have to roll up your sleeves ..."

A guard is holding a bucket in front of us. Inside there are marker pens.

"Write your name and the name of your group on your wrist."

Everybody is busy writing. Names are being written across Iran. They have been writing for a month now. First the religious ones. Then the communists. Then Jews, Armenians and Baha'is. Kurds, Turks and Baluch. Teenagers and old men. Mothers and sisters. Girls and boys. They are all writing their names. In Rajai Shahr's death camp. In death camps throughout Iran. In Evin. When the names have been written, the people are taken to be hanged, row after row. They are picked up at night in wheelbarrows and thrown into trucks. The trucks take them to the mass graves. They bury the Muslims in mass graves. The rest, the infidels, are taken to an abandoned Baha'i cemetery to the east of Tehran. They've nicknamed the cemetery Damnation End. They throw our corpses to the ground and a digger piles earth over us.

The guards playfully push each other around. They laugh out loud and pluck the best flowers of Iran's gardens from the metal trees.

The more people you hang, the quicker you get to heaven.

They are sending us to hell. Snakes and dragons. Wells filled with shit.

But they themselves are going to heaven. A delightful garden is waiting for them. Beautiful girls. Seven houris every night until they are tired out. Slaves. Seventy of them every night. We will burn while they enjoy themselves. We will be burning until the end of the world and they will be enjoying themselves with houris and slaves. They'll be drinking milk and eating honey from heaven's rivers.

They come to collect the people ahead of me in the queue. They are rolling in large tables on castors. They make the people stand on the tables. They have eaten off these tables and now they are using them for hanging. A bunch of fat guards get up on the tables. They wrap the ropes around the necks of the condemned, quickly, skilfully.

"God is Great. Khomeini's our leader."

The guards murmur their response collectively and pull the tables out from under the prisoners' feet. The prisoners are hanging. They are turning. Human fruit hanging from metal trees as far as the eye can see. They bring in the second round. They are all girls. Wrapped in black chadors. Onto the tables. The dance of death on metal trees.

A guard comes in, and leads me out of the room. We go through another door. I hear the sound of a car door opening.

"Get in."

I see Kianuri in the back of the car. I roll down my sleeve and automatically look at my scarred wrist. I am shaking like a leaf even though it's hot.

The driver is a dark-skinned man with a strong build. He's looking at us in the car's rear-view mirror and asks Kianuri in a thick accent: "Listen, do you still believe in the Soviet Union?"

Kianuri says: "Yes."

The driver asks: "What about America?"

Kianuri answers: "America is our people's main enemy."

With his huge fist the driver punches Kianuri and pushes him down: "Shut up, monster."

Then the driver gets out of the car and spits. Even so, Kianuri says: "The thugs are running the show."

The guard in charge of our transfer arrives. We drive through Evin's large gate, up the Peech-e Tobah (Repentance Turn), and onto the motorway. When the motorway ends, the guard tells us to bend down and he throws a blanket over our heads. I grab hold of Kianuri's hand in the dark. It feels cold and lifeless. Maybe like me, he had assumed that he was going to be hanged. Through the car's movements I try to figure out where we are going but I fail. Eventually the car stops and there's the sound of a large gate opening. We are entering Moshtarek Prison again. I am back at Moshtarek Prison for the seventh time.

A lot has changed here since last time. Complete silence dominates the place. They separate us and hand me the same blue prison uniform, but this time my number is on the shirt pocket. It is far too long to be memorized. We follow the usual route, the triangular courtyard, the stairs, Under the Eight. This time we are taken upstairs. The block's numbers have three digits now, and the cell numbers have been added to them. I am in cell number 6537. In the same old block number six. The guard doesn't open the doors. He just tells you your number. A famous poet had once written about this:

Once upon a time, I used to be a father and a brother, but,
Today I am number six, just that.

At mealtimes they knock on the door and unlock it. The food is left outside the door. When you have collected the food, they relock the door.

I am left alone for forty-eight hours. I get myself ready for prayers. I am waiting for the sound of slippers and for you to arrive at any moment. Your threat is ringing in my ear: "I would like to shoot the final bullet myself."

And I remember the words of the cultural events official at Ghezel Hesar: "It's not like the Shah's time when you could leave, feeling like heroes. We'll destroy your reputation."

The sound of slippers comes eventually. But it's not you, it's the shepherd guard. He doesn't show any sign of recognition, but he presses my hand warmly. We walk down the stairs, pass through a triangular courtyard, to the left, we walk up the stairs. When we reach the first floor, a shiver goes down my spine, but we carry on walking up the stairs. Then he says: "Take off your blindfold."

Once again I find myself in a large hall, filled with sunshine. Two young men, dressed in smart grey suits, are walking up and down and talking to each other in whispers. I say hello. They respond. They come towards me and shake my hand. There's not a single chair in the large hall. They ask me what I am up to. I answer them.

One of them asks a random question and then, suddenly, he asks: "Why did you lie about the garden?"

I answer: "I didn't know anything about it. Brother Hamid put me under pressure, forced me ... That night I told Brother Shamkhani that it was a lie."

The second man says: "You lied so much that you managed to hide the truth."

The other man laughs: "Did you really arrange meetings with the British ambassador at Naderi Cafe?"

I say: "But you must be aware that I have never been that sort of person, and have been lying all along."

They walk away from me. They go to the window and whisper. Then one of them says: "Go to the staircase and wait until they come to fetch you."

The following day they come for me again. The guard takes me to a room on the second floor. I am seated behind a desk, with my blindfold on. I see a file lying on the desk. A hand opens the file and a voice, which sounds young but not aggressive, again brings up all the questions related to the file. Then he asks questions related to religion. Eventually he asks: "Who's your role model?"

I say: "Imam Khomeini."

He says: "Take off your blindfold."

I take it off. I see a young man whose appearance and way of speaking is similar to that of those other two men. They must all be working for the Ministry of Intelligence. He says: "Have you been working?"

I say: "I used to work in the fields at Ghezel Hesar."

He asks: "What about Evin?"

I say: "I can't work in a factory. My arm was damaged during my interrogation."

"Why aren't you doing any cultural work?"

I say: "No one has asked me to."

He says: "Here the people themselves have to ask for work. Especially people like you whose heads are already on the chopping block."

Then he closes the file and calls the guard over. All the way back to my cell, I hear his voice in my ears: "Already on the chopping block; already on the chopping block ..."

They come for me the following evening.

When I board the minibus, I find myself seated next to Kianuri again. It's around ten at night when we arrive. The driver has to hand over some other prisoners and asks us to wait.

I take off my blindfold, slowly, quietly. There's no one around. Kianuri and I are standing around in Evin on this cold night, waiting. I put on my glasses. I see the city in the distance. Life is going on. I see the road that leads away from Evin to the mountains via Darakeh. I can't help thinking that that is the route our companions have always taken to join those who are free. A cold wind is blowing. For the first time, I think of escaping from the prison. I imagine walking down the hill, jumping over the wall and running until I reach a house. I am yearning for freedom. But I have never been a hero, never had the courage for that sort of thing.

The driver eventually returns and hands us over at the prison gate. Kianuri and I are put into a solitary confinement cell. Once again I find myself sharing a cell with a leader. Years ago I shared a cell with a kind and smiling man who has now become the supreme leader of the Islamic Republic, of whom it is said there is not much kindness left. And this time I am with the powerful leader of the Tudeh Party, a man who has reverted to being a helpless child. This seventy something child is incapable of sleeping. We talk for many hours, and Kianuri speaks from the heart in a way I have never heard him speak before.

I too am feeling very strange, and find myself telling my life story to the Party leader. The same story that I told Khamenei but this time the story of Khamenei's time in prison has been added to my story.

Then it's his turn to tell me about his childhood. He tells me about the first time he joined the street protests, at the age of sixteen. He tells me of the painful love that came before he met Maryam and of his love for Maryam. Of his hatred of living in exile before the revolution. Of the little garden they kept in Germany, when life appeared meaningful only when he went into the garden with Maryam.

It was in the sanatorium that I saw you for the third time, Brother Hamid. One day, a crowd appears at the door. You are with Saeed

Emami[102] and Haj Nasser, and behind you there's a large crowd of people dressed in civilian and military clothing.

Saeed Emami asks Kianuri: "Don't you want to become a Muslim?"

Kianuri gives his usual response: "I've been a communist all my life and I am going to remain one."

Emami says: "Tabari used to be like that."

Kianuri answers: "I am not a liar, like Tabari. He is used to hedging his bets."

Saeed Emami glances at Haj Nasser, who as usual has his hands in his pockets, scratching himself down there. Then he asks: "What is your opinion of the Soviet Union? It's going downhill right now."

Kianuri, leaning on his weaker leg, says: "That's an American Imperialist conspiracy. If the Soviet Union is going downhill, then you'll be next in line."

Saeed Emami laughs mockingly, and the delegation accompanying him joins in, and they leave.

It's December 1988. As usual, Kianuri wakes up very early in the morning. We go to the courtyard for some exercise. He's lost weight and is very thin and gaunt. He's always had a limp, but since the torture he was subjected to during his interrogations, he can barely lift his left hand. He resembles a dried up, barren tree trunk, the leaves and fruits of which – a hundred years of leftist movement in Iran – have fallen, leaving its bare branches shivering in the wind. He sits down and gets up with great difficulty. And each time, he calls up the name of one of those hanged.

He's very emotional, especially when we get ready for the weekly visiting time. Early in the morning, after exercise and breakfast, like an excited teenager he presses his clothes with his shrivelled hands. He shaves carefully. He uses a pleasant eau de cologne and before the clock has even struck nine o'clock, he starts walking up and down the corridor. Then he fetches the newspaper and cuts out photographs of children and puts them in a photo album. It's as if each and every single child is his very own child. He loves them. Every week, he takes the album to show it to Maryam. He always keeps a present for her. A flower plucked from the garden, a bit of cheese that his step-daughter, Afsaneh, has brought him.

Finally, they call us. Kianuri sets off, like a young boy in love, limping up the stairs. He talks to his step-daughters on the telephone and he's allowed to see his wife in person for five minutes. I often see Maryam on my way up to the visitors' room, with her long, wavy white hair under the black chador that she is forced to wear for her visit to the prison. She's in her eighties but she still turns up, standing tall and straight and losing herself in Kianuri's arms. When we return to our cell after the visits, we both talk about the sweetness of the meetings and the bitterness of separation in the whispered accounts of our past and our stories.

One day, Kianuri tells me: "Back in the old days, when we were young, we went to the famous museum in St Petersburg. By the stairs, located in a prominent part of the gallery, was a large painting of Muzzaffaruddin Shah. He had given his portrait as a gift to the Russian tsar. The museum guide had just started to explain the painting when Maryam said: 'There's no need for any explanation. My ancestry goes back to the king who's pictured.'"

Another day, he was talking about Afsaneh, his step-daughter. She was trying to get a visitor's appointment when the hated Haj Karbalaie, the official in charge of the visitors' room, asked her: "Just who is this prisoner to you, that you are going to all this trouble to bring him cheese and medicine?"

Afsaneh had answered: "He's the grandson of Sheikh Fazlollah Noori. And you, who are you?"

Kianuri spends most of his time learning English. He's got hold of an easy-to-read novel and I help him. He has an extraordinary talent for learning languages and is picking up English very quickly.

He has a particular attachment to the news. When the TV or radio is available, he listens to the morning, evening and late night news. We have no radio or TV in block number 205. At exactly two in the afternoon, he walks down the stairs, limping and with much difficulty. He presses his ear against the door, trying to listen to the news on the radio belonging to the block's guard.

One day, Kianuri comes running back from his trip downstairs to listen to the news. He kicks my side, waking me up from sleep, and says: "Get up! They are going to release us!"

He had heard the news of an amnesty for the remaining political prisoners.

On the first of January, they move us all up to the top floor. The leftists who have survived are all there. There are just nine or ten people. Most of the original five thousand[103] have fallen victim to the Islamic Republic's violent purges.

We are given a TV set and are allowed to write letters. Once a week we receive visitors. We take turns to read the only newspaper available on the block. Usually, when my turn comes, I open the newspaper without much interest, but one day the headline on the front page pierces my heart, like an arrow: "Mossad agent arrested in Tehran".

Below the heading there's a photograph of a woman, dressed in a white chador. The report says: "Official sources who want to remain anonymous have announced that they have arrested a Mossad spy. The woman, whose name is Sonia Zimmermann ..."

I have still not come back to my senses, when the guard comes for me and says: "Thank your lucky stars. You are going to the interrogation office."

We walk through heavy snow. I'm only wearing slippers and my feet immediately freeze, but my head is hot from the sun. The scent of spring is in the air. Mint plants are sprouting through the snow.

As usual I am forced to wait for a while. Then I enter a room and a voice tells me to sit down. In front of me, I see a man wearing a wintry jumper with a pleasant pattern on it. I hear a voice, asking those same eternal questions. It's as if it's some sort of hobby for them to ask me again and again what I have been up to, when I was arrested, and how long my sentence is. I answer all the questions. Then suddenly, out of the blue: "Right. Let's imagine we let you out. What would you do?"

It's one of those moments when I am myself again and nothing, not even the threat of dying, could stop me. I ask: "Shall I tell the truth or lie?"

He says: "Tell us the lie first."

I say: "I'll join the Hezbollah. I'll never miss a prayer. I'll attend the Nudbah prayer. I'll hold the Qur'an."

The voice says: "Now, tell us the truth."

I say: "I have nothing left in this world apart from my wife, literature and beer. These are the only things of importance to me since I regained my independence in prison."

The man stands up. He comes behind me and pats me on my shoulder: "You are the only one who has not lied to us. Just make sure not to drink too much British beer …"

Later, when I look back on this episode and think about this sentence, I ask myself: "You idiot, what was that about?"

And the phrase, British beer, goes round and round in my head and goes back to the part of the file that had remained active.

Chapter 26

Iran of Today:
The Reign of Thugs

This is my twenty-sixth and last letter, Brother Hamid. We've reached the final chapter, which itself is the beginning of another chapter. It's been two years since I started writing this, spending my nights and days with you. And now the time has come to say goodbye. I don't know why something inside me tells me that we will meet again someday, somewhere. But where? I don't know.

Tehran's streets, 11 February 1989

They have chosen the anniversary of the revolution for our release. There had been approximately five thousand political prisoners in Iran, though some accounts put the number nearer to seven thousand. Of those, only around four to five hundred of us survived. We have lied in court and have been spared death. Now they are freeing us, with much pomp and ceremony. The survivors have all been brought to Evin. We are put onto buses and when the large gate opens, the cameras flash. It's a sunny day.

The buses stop in front of the United Nations' office in Tehran and we are ordered to get out. We stand in a line, surrounded by photographers and the Revolutionary Guards Corps dressed in civilian clothing. The prisoners try to look away or cover their faces with their hands to avoid being photographed. Some of them pull down their woollen hats to cover their faces. The officials in charge, dressed

in civilian clothing, run up and down the queue, swearing and sometimes hitting us to make us turn our faces towards the photographers'
lenses.

A speech is delivered in front of the United Nations office. We get
back on the buses and this time we set off in the direction of the
Rudaki Hall. Rudaki is the name of the first Iranian poet. They could
not handle the name of this hall, which used to serve as an opera
house during the Shah's time, and have now changed it. I have many
memories of this place; the first time I held the hand of my future
wife was in that hall. She's now waiting for me, like the rest of the
families.

We are taken into the hall. I take a seat in the back row. One or
two people give speeches. Then it's Kianuri's turn. He walks up to
the microphone, limping, his back bent. The prisoners applaud him.
He pulls out a text he has already prepared. He coughs a bit. I don't
know what is going through his mind, but he puts the paper back
into his pocket and says:

> Our Party has achieved a great deal, and has made many mistakes. I
> take full responsibility for the mistakes. I have been the main deci-
> sion-maker in the Party and have single-handedly made decisions
> about some issues. I am offering you all my apologies. I apologize to
> all those members of the Party who have been killed …

And suddenly he starts crying, loudly:

> None of my colleagues is to blame. None of you are to blame.

And the sound of his crying permeates the hall. I've seen the Swan
Lake ballet on this stage and Beethoven's Seventh Symphony and
Vivaldi's Four Seasons. And now, I am watching Nurrudin Kianuri.

And the show still goes on.

We get back in the buses and are driven to the front of the parliament building. The parliament, which looks like the one in Paris,

used to be a senate before the revolution. From the bus windows we see all our families, their arms filled with bouquets of flowers, waiting to greet us. When the buses arrive, they start a commotion from behind the barriers that are holding them back.

The survivors of this decade of intense horror, those who have escaped death, at last return to the arms of their mothers, fathers, wives, husbands and children. When we get out of the buses, children squeeze themselves through the bars and run past the guards, and disappear in their fathers' arms.

They make us sit down on the asphalt in front of the marble steps leading to the parliament. My mind goes back to fifty years ago, and the house of my childhood. In my mind, they've killed the fish in the pool and destroyed the pots of geraniums. The stairs to the ancient cellar are covered in mud. No one is sleeping on the roof any more. The house of freedom has been occupied by clerics. Sitting on beds and smoking hookah have been banned. My eyes search for Abgie. The scent of jasmine and chubak shrub is in the air. A woman wrapped up in a white chador is brought out and made to stand in front of the stairs. Led by a cleric, a group of women dressed in thick black chadors turn up and clear a path. My mother is not there to call my name from behind the bars. But my father is behind the bars, crying and swearing. The cleric moves to the front. I think he's Aqa Seyyed, who's become Parliamentary Chief. What a fat belly he now has. The chador-wrapped women are running after him. They pick out someone from the middle of the crowd, take him, and place him next to the woman in the white chador. It's Babak Zahraei. I think he's the son of a poet who had studied abroad and then had returned to Iran.

I am reminded of Afaq Khanum, my mother's Baha'i aunt. Some leaders of the Baha'i community had also been imprisoned in Evin. They were waiting for their turn to be hanged. One of them knew Afaq Khanum. He told me that her husband had been killed in the early days of the revolution and she and her children had become homeless.

Aqa Seyyed reaches the steps. Kianuri is made to stand up in respect. The grandson of Sheikh Fazlollah Noori, now in his seventies, bent and holding his side with his hand, is facing a follower of his own grandfather. Aqa Seyyed speaks in praise of liberty. He says Iran is one of the freest countries in the world. The followers of all religions and sects are free to practice their faith.

You could see the whole of Iran's contemporary history summarized in that scene on that sunny afternoon. We stand up and return to the buses. The buses set off in the direction of Azadi (Liberty) Square.[104] We were coming to the end of the show. They had made sure that the main roads were lined with crowds. The buses took us via side streets and then they made us disembark. We were still standing in a line, surrounded by prison directors and officials. We were still waiting for them to let us go.

Haj Mojtaba seeks me out and tells me to talk to the prison director. My heart sinks. On the way, I ask myself a thousand questions. Then I reach him. The prison director says: "You need to come to the prison tomorrow, at six in the evening. Haj Aqa wants to see you."

A shiver goes up my spine. Haj Aqa is the head of Evin's Intelligence Office. I ask him in a shaky voice: "But have I not been released?"

He says: "Of course you have been freed. But Haj Aqa has some unfinished business with you."

The timing of this smells of you, Brother Hamid. So far, no one has confirmed that my file has been closed. I hear your voice, which is coming from the depths of the torture chamber: "I would like to shoot the final bullet myself."

And it mingles with the mockery of the cultural events' official: "It's not like the Shah's time when you could leave prison as heroes. You'll leave either dead or with your reputation in ruins."

I try one last time: "My family is waiting for me, they are anxious."

Haj Mojtaba talks into a walkie-talkie and says: "Alright. Go ahead. But be at Evin tomorrow at six."

I feel like I have grown wings. I run in the direction of the place where the families are gathered. In the middle of the Islamic Republic's tenth anniversary, the freed prisoners are losing themselves in the arms of their families, shedding tears of happiness.

I cannot see my wife anywhere. I turn around, looking. I'm standing in the shade in Azadi Square. Someone inside me is saying: "You have been in prison for six years but now you are free. Be happy!"

Someone else is responding: "You are not free. You have left freedom behind forever inside the prison blocks, the torture chambers, and with the voices of the companions who walked to the gallows ..."

The sound of my wife's voice, which is the sound of happiness and freedom, rises above all the noise and commotion. I turn in her direction; she's moving towards me, like a swan with open wings. For a moment, we lose ourselves in each other's embrace.

Oh the warmth of love. The scent of life.

We walk, then run, and get into our car, a car we had bought back in the days when life was like a dream. My wife is driving through familiar streets. Tehran, my city. Its streets have now begun to resemble the streets in Pakistan. Its cinemas are either burned down or in ruins. Its women have disappeared under the obligatory hijab. Its guards are all bearded.

My wife is giving me a piece of good news: "I've baked a pizza for you."

And I give her the first bad news: "I have to go back at six tomorrow."

And the barely gained freedom disappears again. It turns bitter. My wife asks: "But why? Haven't you been released?"

I have no answer. We drive down the steep road. The house is still green. A house where exceptionally talented Iranians used to live on every single storey. But after the revolution they disappeared, one by one. The smell of burning fills the stairway. I say: "Hey, you've burned my lunch again?"

We run up the stairs. After six long years, I open the door to my house. With its familiar sounds and smells. I embrace my mother-in-law and my wife disappears into the kitchen. Minutes later, I am seated at the dinner table, having washed my hands and face with apple scented soap. The pizza is totally burned. I look at my wife. Her lips are smiling but her eyes are full of tears.

At six o'clock the next day I get out of the car in front of Evin Prison. I hold my wife's hand until the very last moment. She asks: "Will you come back?"

I have absolutely no idea whether I'll be coming back. I shake my head. I give the guard my name. I throw one last glance at my wife. I go in through the small pedestrian gate. Once again I put on the blindfold and the guard takes me to the ministry block, making me sit down on a bench. It's as if the large building has been deserted. There's not even the sound of footsteps. I stand up and start pacing. I sit down again. I picture my wife, who's waiting for me outside. I think I hear the sound of shuffling slippers and focus, listening. No. There's no one around. A few times I call out: "Brother! Brother!"

My voice echoes and twists in the emptiness of the corridor but there's no sound. I hear Hussein Abi's early morning whispers and see myself, hanging from the pipes, my thick tongue sticking out, my glasses on the floor.

In the ensuing silence I once again review my whole life. It's as if I'm watching a rapidly moving film that's being projected onto my blindfold. Childhood and youth. A country that I had not known at all. Becoming a young man and an understanding that came through the words of a green-eyed man, and then blossomed into full truth. A dream that appeared real. We were young men and women who walked on mountainous roads, who could see that tomorrow lay only one step ahead. Socialism was going to be victorious. Capitalism would be buried, just as Lenin had predicted, humanity would be freed, and people would be equal. We lived for this dream and we went through torture chambers for this dream and some of us died on the gallows for this dream. Inside me, there's always been a rebel, trying to get away from the confinements of these thoughts. I was a poet and writer, a man perpetually in love. The beautiful eyes of a woman could send a shiver down my spine and her smile could make my heart soar.

After all the torture, the pretence of repentance, and the fake prayers, I had not lost my faith, even a tiny bit. But performing prayers had shown me that those who were religious also lived for a dream, just like the infidel. Our dream was supposed to come true on earth, theirs in paradise, which was in a different world. But I came to realize that the world was bigger, more complex and more ruthless than this dream. These thoughts, step by step, took me away from ideology, and back to poetry and literature. Rahman's death, which meant the end of the source that had fed my thinking, gave me the courage to think freely and for myself for the first time in my life. The story of Eden Pastora's life had a serious impact in changing my way of thinking. He was a former revolutionary, a man known as Commander Zero. He had played a leading role in the revolution in Nicaragua and not long after the revolution, a difference of opinion had emerged between him and his comrades. The great commander had rounded up his men and had taken them to a jungle on the border of the country to bring the war to an end. The CIA had established contact with him and had offered him financial support. He had gone through a period of intense reflection and had eventually made an important decision. He released his men. He threw himself into life in the border region, together with his wife and children. For me, he was a role model, an example of a man who had turned his back on politics, and escaped the claws of the terrifying forces of reality.

Later on, the collapse of the Soviet Union, a country I had visited at the height of its power, took with it the last fragments of my beliefs. I had freed myself from myself. And now I was waiting for a meeting that would either end with me, a man who had nothing left in his life but love, beer and literature, being returned to prison, or to Evin's gate being opened wide and freedom.

A hand touches my shoulder: "What are you doing here at this time of the night?"

I don't know why I reply: "What time is it, brother?"

"Eleven at night. You didn't tell me what you are doing here."

"I've been told that Brother Zamani wants to talk to me."

"Wait here."

He leaves and it takes maybe a thousand years for him to come back.

"Get up, come on."

He grabs hold of my arm and takes me with him. We turn a corner. A door opens. I sense that the room is spacious.

"Are you okay, Mr Asadi?"

I can hardly recognize my own voice: "Thank you."

"You are going to go back home, right?"

"I was going home when they told me that you …"

"Yes. I have just one more question for you."

He puts an object into my hand.

"Lift your blindfold slightly, you know how."

I pull up the blindfold just enough to look down. It's the photograph of a woman dressed in a white chador. Brother Zamani is talking, but it's your voice, Brother Hamid, that is ringing in my ears: "Who is this woman?"

Endnotes

1 The term "Under the Eight" is used in all Iranian prisons to refer to the entrance to the detention centre where the guards stand watch. The term started to be used in the Shah's era. At the time, the guards were military men whose rank looked similar to the letter eight in Farsi numerals, which is the shape of a triangle.

2 The term Party in this book refers to the Iranian Communist Party or Tudeh Party, which was supported by the former Soviet Union. The Party's full name is *Hezb-e Tudeh-e Iran* or the Party of the Iranian Masses. Established in 1941, it is Iran's oldest organized union of communists. At the time, World War II was still raging and the allied forces, who had used Iran as "a bridge to victory" to defeat Hitler in the former Soviet Union, had not yet left Iran. Reza Shah Pahlavi, the first ruler of the Pahlavi dynasty (1925–79), had been exiled and his son, Muhammad Reza, a young king, was on the throne and Iran was facing a decade of freedom – or chaos. In that period, a group of educated Iranians abroad, especially in Germany, who were greatly influenced by the Bolshevik revolution, set up the foundations of a pro-Soviet political party. The Party rapidly gained strength and transformed itself into a very powerful organization. Its intention was to establish a socialist government in Iran and it aligned itself in support of the former Soviet Union and against the so-called imperialist governments, particularly the United States and Britain.

The Tudeh Party had considerable influence in its early years, and played an important role during Mohammad Mosaddeq's campaign to nationalize the Anglo-Iranian Oil Company, but it was brutally suppressed following the Anglo-American coup of 1953 against Mosaddeq, which resulted in power being handed to the Shah. A group of the Party's secret military wing were executed, its leaders fled to communist countries, and its influence waned. The Party actively supported the Islamic revolution, aligning itself with Ayatollah Khomeini's anti-Western and anti-capitalist sentiments, and his declared intention of overthrowing the Shah's regime, which was undemocratic and supported by the US. After the victory of the Islamic revolution in 1979, the Party's leaders, consisting mainly of aging individuals, immediately returned to Iran, resurrecting the Party, and pursued a policy supportive of the Islamic government. Although the Party never opposed the Islamic Republic, in 1983 the gradual suppression of political groups reached the Tudeh Party, and its cadres and members of the Central Committee were arrested on the third anniversary of the revolution. The Party's leaders later appeared on the Islamic Republic's television channel and confessed to spying for the Soviet Union. Many years later, when the Party's first secretary, Nurruddin Kianuri, was released from prison and placed under house arrest, he wrote in a number of letters that the confessions were all false and had been extracted under horrific torture. Kianuri is also the grandson of Sheikh Fazlollah Noori, the spiritual father of the current Islamic government. The majority of Party cadres and people close to its leadership were executed during the Islamic holocaust, the account of which is given in this book. See also note 100.

3 Ablution, in original Farsi *wuzu*, is an Islamic-Arabic term that translates as *rooshanaayee* or light. Ablution involves a ritualistic washing of the hands, face and front of the feet. A prayer performed without ablution is considered invalid. Shia believers also perform ablution in preparation for reading the Qur'an. At the start of the war with Iraq, it became commonplace for fighters to perform ablution in preparation for entering a minefield or engaging in combat. It signified that they were preparing for a holy task and entering paradise. Prison interrogators equally performed ablution in preparation for the interrogation process.

4 Fatimeh is the name of a woman who in Shia Islam is considered a saint equal to the Virgin Mary. She was the daughter of Muhmmad,

the prophet of Islam. At the age of nine, she became wife to Ali, the third Muslim caliph and the first Shia Imam. Her sons, Hassan and Hussain, are the second and third Shia Imams and are the pillars of the Shia faith. Hassan, who entered into an agreement over a conflict with the caliph of the time, exemplifies peace for the sake of protecting shi'ism. His brother Hussain, who rebelled against the caliph, could only persuade seventy-two individuals to follow him. They all died in the desert in Karbala. In the Shia faith, Hussain embodies the struggle against oppression. Upon Hussain's martyrdom, the title Sayyed Al-Shohada (Lord of the Martyrs) was given to him. Shia believers mourn his death every year in the first ten days of the month of Muharram, which was the month in which his battle with the caliph took place.

5 Foot whipping, or bastinado, is a common form of corporal punishment, involving beating the bare soles of the feet with a cane, rod or whip. Due to the congregation of nerve endings in the soles of the feet, and the many small bones and tendons, it is extremely painful, and the wounds take a long time to heal.

6 Karbala, which is in present-day Iraq, is the location of Imam Hussain's martyrdom, the third Shia Imam, whose tomb is also in Karbala. During the Iran-Iraq war, Ayatollah Khomeini used to say: "The path to Quds goes through Karbal," meaning that his troops should first conquer Iraq and then move on to Jerusalem in order to "liberate" Israel into the sea. These words of Khomeini were incorporated into war songs called "Nuha" and were played on the radio and television throughout the war with Iraq. Prison interrogators also made use of these songs as musical accompaniment to the torture process.

7 *The Cat* is the name of a novel written by the author of this book and published in 2007 in Farsi. It focuses on the story of the stoning of a famous Iranian actress during Muhammad Khatami's presidency.

8 During the 1970s, hundreds of political dissidents were held, and often tortured, at Moshtarek Prison by the Anti-Sabotage Joint Committee, a branch of Savak, the Shah's secret police. Renamed Tawhid after the Islamic Revolution, it continued to serve as a notorious prison until 2004, when as a propaganda measure it was

transformed into Ebrat Museum, where public guided tours now remind the visitors about the brutality of the Shah's regime.

9 *Kayhan* was founded in 1943, and became one of the largest circulation newspapers in Iran with a circulation in the region of one million prior to the 1979 revolution, publishing separate editions in Iran and London. During the 70s, many of the employees were members of the Tudeh Party, including the deputy editor-in-chief and several key staff. Its assets were seized after the 1979 revolution, and it is now published under the direct supervision of the office of the supreme leader. It is regarded as the most conservative newspaper in Iran, and today has a circulation of about 70,000. *Kayhan* also publishes special foreign editions, including the English-language *Kayhan International*. *Kayhan London* is an independent weekly newspaper, that was edited for many years by the original editor of *Kayhan*.

10 An Iranian lawyer and human rights activist and the 2003 Nobel Peace Laureate.

11 Abgie is a colloquial term, meaning sister in Farsi. In Farsi script, Abgie differs in only one letter from Angie, the shortened version of Angela. The two words sound very similar in Farsi.

12 Chubak, or *Acanthe phylum bracteatum*, is a type of shrub, from the family of coryophyllaceae, which is used as a medicinal plant for its diuretic and anti-inflammatory effects.

13 Ferdowsi, whose birthplace was in western Khorasan, was the world's greatest warrior, his weapon being his poetry. In the early centuries of Iran's conquest at the hands of sword-bearing Arabs, Ferdowsi wrote an epic, *The Book of Kings*, which is comparable to Homer's *Odyssey*. The epic was one of the factors that prevented Iranians from taking on an Arab identity, and Iran remained one of the few Muslim countries that retained its own language and culture. Khayyam, a philosopher, scientist and poet, spread the Epicurian worldview through his quatrains. He stood up against the official religion, which advocated abstinence from worldly pleasures, and instead praised such pleasures as wine-drinking and love-making. Hafez was born after these two poets. He is one of the most popular poets in Iran, and his collection of poems is to be found in almost every Iranian household, next to a

copy of the Qur'an. My mother was dying during the 2500-year cele-
bration of the Iranian monarchy in 1971, lying in a bed in a large state-
run hospital. She quoted these verses from Hafez just before dying,
"Leave the tavern Hafez, you are too old." She was only forty-seven.

14 Iran's Constitutional Revolution in 1905, which was the first of this
type of revolution in the developing world, was organized by a group
of Iranians who had studied abroad, and was modelled on the French
revolution. When the revolution was about to fail, Sattar Khan, who
was in Tabriz, the capital of Azerbaijan Province, carried on fighting
in the only street that was still controlled by the revolutionaries and so
spurred on the people and secured the revolution's success. Following
victory, Sattar Khan was wounded at the hands of a Russian soldier
and died. In 1925, another oppressive monarchical dynasty came to
power, of which Reza Shah Pahlavi was the head. He founded modern Iran on the basis of an authoritarian government that combined
modernization and secularization with strict censorship and state
propaganda. Visits to Sattar Khan's tomb, which is located just outside
Tehran, were banned after the Islamic revolution.

15 The Qur'an is the holy book of Islam.

16 Muhammad Mossadeq was prime minister of Iran from 1951 to 1953,
when he was brought down in a coup d'etat on 19 August 1953
organized and carried our by the United States' CIA, and spent the
rest of his life under house arrest.

17 Haj is a title bestowed on those who have undertaken the haj, or pil-
grimage, to Mecca. Religious men are sometimes referred to as Haj
Aqa in Iran.

18 Muhammad is the name of the Prophet-Founder of Islam.

19 Ali is the name of Muhammad's son-in-law, and the first Shia Imam.
A large percentage of Iranian men are called either Muhammad or Ali.

20 *The Book of Eloquence*, or *Nahj al-Balaghah*, is the most famous
compilation of Imam Ali's sermons, letters and sayings, and for Shia
Muslims is ranked in importance only after the Qur'an and the
Prophet's sayings (hadith).

21 During the Shah's regime, Iran had two anthems, a national anthem
and a royal anthem. The latter was in praise of the king and had more

or less replaced the national anthem. The royal anthem would be played in cinemas just before the start of the film, and viewers would stand up to show respect while it was played.

22 Savak stands for *Sazeman-e Ettela'at va Amniyat-e Keshvar* (National Intelligence and Security Organization) and was the internal security and Intelligence Service in Iran from 1957–79. Formed in 1957 under the guidance of the United States' CIA officers and later instructors from Mossad, the Israeli Intelligence Service, Savak developed into an effective secret agency with as many as 5,000 full-time agents at its peak. Tasked with placing political opponents under surveillance and repressing dissident movements, it had the power to censor the media, screen applicants for government jobs and – using all means necessary including torture – to hunt down (and sometimes assassinate) dissidents. Savak gained a deserved reputation for brutality: with unlimited powers of arrest and detention, it ran its own detention centres such as Evin Prison in Tehran, and interrogation techniques included a wide range of torture techniques. The torture of choice was the bastinado, beating the soles of the feet, but in addition they resorted to sleep deprivation, extensive solitary confinement, standing in one place for hours on end, nail extractions, electrical shocks with cattle prods, cigarette burns, near-drownings; the humiliation of being raped, urinated on, and forced to stand naked, and mock executions. It has been accused of the torture and murder of thousands of political opponents in its twenty-two-year history. Savak was shut down shortly before the 1979 revolution, and the majority of its central staff and agents were hunted down and executed. It was quickly replaced by the much larger Savama (*Sazman-e Ettela'at va Amniat-e Melli-e Iran*), also known as the Ministry of Intelligence and National Security of Iran, which continued to employ many of the mid-level Savak staff. After its disbandment, a museum was opened in Ebrat Prison, Tehran to display and document the atrocities of Savak.

23 "Full or Empty" is a very simple game in which the players are divided into two groups. Each group has a leader who gives a small item to a member of the group, and the other group has to figure out who is hiding the item.

24 Sheikh Mehdi Karroubi, who belongs to the leftist wing of the religious party, first led the Martyrs' Foundation and then became Chairman of Parliament. Following Muhammad Khatami's victory, he joined the reformist front and established a semi-conservative party called The National Trust. In 2009 he ran for the presidency in a controversial election, the result of which was widely disputed. He went on to become one of the most prominent figures in the Green Movement, a populist opposition movement in Iran.

25 Houris are exceptionally beautiful women and slaves are teenage boys, both of which have been promised to pious Muslims as a reward in the afterlife.

26 Established in 1963, *Hezb-e Motalefeh-ye Eslami* is the oldest-running conservative religio-political group in Iran. Known as the Islamic Coalition Society, the group played a major role in providing Khomeini and his religious supporters with important financial and military support in the years leading up to the 1979 revolution. The group, which changed its name to the Islamic Coalition Party in 2004, has exerted a huge influence over the political and economic sectors in post-revolutionary Iran. While it advocates a statist government in the political sphere, Motalefeh backs controlled liberalization of the economy. Despite serious disagreements over economic strategies between Motalefeh and the government of Ahmadinejad, they remain close allies.

27 Naderi Cafe is a very famous cafe located right behind the southern wall of the British Embassy in Tehran. For fifty years the cafe has been the meeting place of the Iranian intelligentsia.

28 A controversial Italian journalist and war correspondent whose memoir, *A Man*, was written to her late lover, Alexandros Panagoulis, the Greek anarchist who attempted to assassinate junta leader Georgios Papadopoulous in 1967.

29 A well-known Iranian poet who was forced into exile because of his beliefs, and died in Vienna in 1996. Some of his more revolutionary poems served as anthems for political parties.

30 Arranged marriages in this context were marriages of convenience that men and women from different political parties entered into in

order to provide each other cover allowing them to carry on with their political activities.

31 A member of the Organization of Iranian People's Fedayeen, the largest socialist party in Iran, which opposes the Islamic regime.

32 "*Bismillah*" means "In the name of God". All surahs (chapters) in the Qur'an apart from one begin with this phrase. People who have strong religious beliefs begin every action with Bismillah, including before a man enters a woman during intercourse. According to one of the hadith, it is essential to recite the phrase, "In the name of God" before penetration; otherwise, if a child is born, it will be the offspring of the devil.

33 Saqi was the name of a notorious torturer during the Pahlavi regime. An aggressive man, who held the rank of a guard, Saqi hated the prisoners who surrendered and loved those who put up resistance even under torture.

34 The National Front is one of the oldest political organizations in Iran. Muhammad Mossadeq was its leader. Shahpour Bakhtiar, one of the oldest members of the National Front, left Iran for Paris shortly after the revolution where he led the National Movement for Iranian Resistance, but he was assassinated by the Iranian regime in 1991.

35 Behazin is the *nom de plume* of Mahmud Etemad Zadeh, a famous Iranian writer and translator. As a young man, he had served in the navy and lost a hand. Subsequently, he turned to literary and political work. After the Islamic revolution, he became a member of the Tudeh Party's Central Committee. He was arrested and spent twelve years in prison and many more under house arrest. He died in 2006. He was one of the founders of the Iranian Writer's Association and for many years he served as its director.

36 On 1 February 1979, Ayatollah Khomeini returned to Tehran from exile in France on a chartered Air France Boeing 747. Every year the period from 1 February, when Khomeini arrived in Iran, to 11 February, the official date of the founding of the Islamic Republic of Iran, is celebrated as the "Decade of Fajr". Designated the "Islamic Revolution's Victory Day", 11 February is a national holiday in Iran, with state-sponsored demonstrations around the country.

37 Early in the revolution, Imam Khomeini would call security officials "the unknown soldiers of the hidden Imam" and so ascribed to them the status of saints. The hidden Imam is the twelfth Imam and Shias believe that he will emerge at some point in time.

38 The Revolutionary Council of the Islamic Revolution of Iran was a group of clerics and political figures selected by Ayatollah Khomeini that was set up secretly in Iran during the last days of the Shah's regime to manage the revolution, and to legislate for the Interim Government of Iran.

39 Ayatollah Yusuf Sane'i is a high-ranking cleric of the Islamic Republic, and Ayatollah Khomeini paid a great deal of attention to him. He is now a supporter of the reformist front.

40 Adas polow is a very popular Iranian dish. The simpler form is made of rice and lentils. Dates, raisins and meat, typically cubes of lamb, can be added to the rice.

41 Established in mid-1979 by a few prominent clergymen, *Hezb-e Jomhouri-ye Eslami*, the Islamic Republican Party, was known for its unfaltering loyalty to Khomeini and its hostility to liberalism. Thanks to its close ties with the Revolutionary Guards Corps, it managed to crush all rival political parties before Khomeini ordered it to disband in 1987 as the internal conflicts within the IRP intensified. Of note, the most serious of these conflicts is said to have been between the then President Ali Khamenei and Prime Minister Mir-Hossein Mousavi, the very same figures who represent the establishment and opposition in Iran today.

42 In Farsi, *Jomhouri-e Eslami*, the official newspaper of the Islamic Republic.

43 Rastakhiz is the name of a party set up by the Shah's government during its final years and at the request of the Shah himself. There was also an eponymous newspaper called *Rastakhiz*.

44 The Nojeh Coup or Uprising on 11 July, 1980 was an attempt by officers loyal to the Shah to overthrow the newly established Islamic Republic of Iran, and the government of Abolhassan Banisadr and Ayatollah Khomeini. It was staged by officers and servicemen from the air force, army and the Secret Service under the leadership of the

former imperial prime minister, Shapour Bakhtiar, who had been operating from Baghdad following the Islamic revolution. It was decisively crushed, and 300 officers involved in the plot were executed. The majority of the officers were serving at the Nojeh airbase, hence the name of the coup.

45 Captain Bahram Afzali was the commander of the Islamic Republic's navy and a member of the Tudeh Party's secret organization. He was hanged in 1983 on the charge of being a Tudeh Party member.

46 Shortly after the revolution Ayatollah Khomeini's government launched a fierce campaign against The People's Mujahedin of Iran, an Islamic socialist organization that supported the overthrow of the Shah.

47 The Fedayeen-e Khalq was the most popular leftist political organization in Iran, and later on united itself with the Tudeh Party.

48 Toopkhaneh Square in Tehran is the oldest square in Iran and is located around 200 metres from Moshtarak Prison.

49 Literally, the Party of God. In the Iranian context, Hezbollah is a common term used by pro-Khomeini revolutionaries to refer to supporters of the Islamic revolution. According to this terminology, people either belong to the Party of God or to the party of Satan.

50 Hafizullah Amin (1929–79) was the second president of the Democratic Republic of Afghanistan. Educated at the universities of Kabul and Columbia, NY, Amin became a teacher before entering politics. He joined the Communist People's Democratic Party of Afghanistan and became a prominent member of the Khalq (aka People) faction. He went on to become joint deputy prime minister (with Babrak Karmal), and as the Khalq faction gained ascendancy, Karmal was exiled to Europe and Amin became prime minister. In September 1979, Amin took President Nur Mohammad Taraki prisoner and assumed the presidency. His rule was notable for its brutality, costing the lives of some 15,000–40,000 Afghans, and lasted only 104 days, before he was in turn the object of a violent coup, and Babrak Karmal took over the presidency. On 27 December 1979, the Soviets invaded Afghanistan, members of the KGB and Spetsnaz GRU stormed the Presidential Palace and assassinated Amin, and Babrak Karmal assumed the presidency with Soviet support.

51 Babrak Karmal (1929–96) was the third president of the Democratic Republic of Afghanistan. A Kabul University graduate in law, Karmal was a founding member and the secretary of the Communist People's Democratic Party of Afghanistan, and when the party split into the Khalq and Parcham factions, he became the leader of the more moderate Parcham (Flag) faction. He went on to serve as a member of the National Assembly of Afghanistan, and deputy prime minister before he was installed by the Soviets as Afghanistan's president in 1979. His lack of international support and failure to fulfil his ambitious programme of reform resulted in civil war, which finally convinced the Soviets to force him to step down from office in 1986. In the remaining years of his life, he divided his time between Afghanistan and Moscow, where he died.

52 Mohammad Najibullah (1947–96) was the fourth and last president of the Democratic Republic of Afghanistan. A Kabul University graduate in medicine, Najibullah held various political offices as member of the Central Committee of the Parcham faction of the Communist People's Democratic Party of Afghanistan, member of the ruling Revolutionary Council, the Afghan ambassador to Iran, and the head of the secret police (KHAD) before replacing Babrak Karmal as president of Afghanistan in 1986. While in office, he introduced some constitutional reforms, including a multiparty political system and freedom of expression, but the 1987 Soviet withdrawal led to an escalation of the civil war in Afghanistan, which finally forced him to resign in 1992 to make way for a neutral interim government. Najibullah sought sanctuary in the UN compound in Kabul, where he lived for four years. Following the fall of Kabul to the Taliban in 1996, he was captured, brutally tortured and killed, and his body hung from a traffic light. Najibullah's supporters refer to him as a "martyr", while his opponents call him the "Butcher of Kabul" for the alleged murder of thousands of Afghans during his time as director-general of the State Information Service (KHAD).

53 Ayatollah Montazeri was very close to Ayatollah Khomeini and of a similar religious rank. He had been secretly chosen to become the next leader. When Khomeini was about to die from advanced cancer,

radicals in the government removed Montazari from power with the help of Khomeini's son, Ahmad Khomeini, under the pretext of his opposition to the killing of political prisoners. Montazari, one of the oldest leaders of the Islamic Republic and a high-ranking theologian, was forced to spend the rest of his days under house arrest. He died in 2009, still protesting against the tyranny of the Islamic Republic.

54 Habibullah Foroughian was a member of the Tudeh Party's Central Committee. He was in charge of preparations for secretly getting the Tudeh Party leaders out of Iran via Afghanistan.

55 Communist parties that supported the Soviet Union called themselves fraternal parties.

56 Manuchehr Behzadi is one of 1,000 people identified by name in a UN Human Rights Commission's Special Representative's Report, "Names and particulars of persons allegedly executed by the Islamic Republic of Iran during the period July–December 1988", published on 26 January, 1989.

57 So nicknamed because Ayatollah Jawade Amolee, who taught ethics, gave very lengthy talks, speaking very slowly, sending his audience to sleep.

58 The first two are names of ancient kings of Persia, and the third one is the pen name of Ali Esfandiari, the founder of modern Persian poetry, rather than Islamic names with religious significance, such as Muhammad or Ali.

59 Islamic fundamentalists believe that communists and infidels are polluted and this pollution can be physically transmitted. However, if the body is dry, the transmission of pollution is not possible.

60 In Shia Islam, repentance is part of the theoretical framework, and no matter how many sins a person might have committed, the doors of repentance are open to them and they can return to God, asking for forgiveness. Interrogators would use various methods to force prisoners to repent and then they would either accept or reject the repentance as if they were God. To prove the authenticity of their repentance, prisoners were forced to do various things: to spy on others, lash others, and often they would fire the last shot or the *coup de*

grâce, killing their former companions or even family members, to prove their repentance.

61 Cucumber yoghurt is a Persian appetiser, often served while drinking alcohol.

62 *The Ornament of the Righteous,* or *Hilyat al-Muttaqi* is a very popular book by Mulla Muhammad Baqir Majlisi (1628–1699), who became the most influential Shia scholar of his time. During his life, the ruling Safavid dynasty had transformed Shi'ism, making it Iran's official religion, and this book is regarded as one of the most important reference books for Shia Muslims. It is a collection of traditions or hadith that are attributed, sometimes dubiously, to the Prophet Muhammad and Shia Imams, grouped by topic. The hadith offer advice on recommended customs and modes of behaviour, and can determine every aspect of a Shia believer's life.

63 The prayer rug is a square or rectangular-shaped woven carpet, usually decorated with verses from the Qur'an. The Shias place the rug on the floor in preparation for prayers and put a prayer stone, a rectangular object, on top of the rug. When Shias pray, they kneel on the prayer rug and place their forehead on the prayer stone, uttering the required verses.

64 A prayer stone is usually made out of unbaked clay, to represent the humility of the owner, preferably taken from the vicinity of Mecca or one of the shrines to the Imams and martyrs of Shi'ism, foremost among which are the shrine of Imam Hussain at Karbala, Iraq and the shrine of Imam Riza in Mashhad, Iran. The prayer stone is placed on the prayer rug so that the forehead rests on it when one prays, thus conferring blessings on the worshipper. When the prayer is finished, they kiss the prayer stone, place it in the middle of the rug, and fold the rug with care and respect.

65 The creed is in Arabic and saying it amounts to conversion to Shia Islam. The Shia creed consists of the standard Muslim creed plus this verse: I bear witness that Ali is the friend of God.

66 Sheikh Fazlollah Noori was a prominent Shia Muslim cleric in Iran during the late nineteenth and early twentieth century, who fought against the Iranian constitutional revolution and was executed for

treason. Today he is revered as a martyr (*shahid*) in the fight against democracy by Islamic conservatives in Iran.

67 In line with ancient Iranian traditions, which originated 2500 years ago, on New Year's Eve, which is the last day of winter and the first day of spring in the northern hemisphere, a table is set up and seven items, all beginning with the Farsi letter "seen", or "s", are placed on it. The items usually include a large, red apple, which is placed in a crystal bowl filled with water and then put in front of a mirror. Iranians believe that when the New Year arrives, the apple turns in the water. Similarly, a small goldfish is placed inside a separate crystal container filled with water. When Islam arrived in Iran, a copy of the Qur'an and a copy of Hafez's poetry collection were added to the items. Iranians who are religious recite the Qur'an on New Year's Eve, the rest read from Hafez's poetry.

68 In earlier times, a cannon shot would be fired to announce the New Year and then traditional music would be played, using ancient instruments like the Saaz and Naqaara.

69 Kavah Golestan was a famous Iranian photojournalist who died after stepping on a mine while working for the BBC in Iraq in 2003.

70 These are aristocratic Persian names uncommon among practicing Muslims.

71 One of the titles of the twelfth Imam, sometimes referred to as the hidden Imam, whose return is eagerly awaited by Shia Muslims.

72 This phrase, "I ate shit", has a double meaning, both the literal meaning and also, "I repent". Here it is used in both its senses.

73 Ali Shamkhani was born in southern Iran and is of Arab descent. He was one of the founding members of the Revolutionary Guards Corps and later became commander of the navy. He was defence minister under Muhammad Khatemi.

74 The abbreviated form of Mashadi, designating someone who has visited the shrine of the eighth Imam, Imam Reza in Mashhad, northeast Iran.

75 Abdul Basit is an Arab famous for his Qur'an recitations.

76 A fatwa is an order issued by the most important ayatollahs, which is considered binding by their followers. In the case of this fatwa, bread

is regarded as sacred, and throwing it away is therefore viewed as a sin. Instead, it should be given to other living creatures such as birds.

77 Soon after their arrest, the Tudeh Party's first secretary, Kianuri, along with all the important members of the Central Committee, appeared on television and confessed that the Party had been spying for the Soviet Union. The leaders were over sixty years of age and had undergone intense torture. The majority of them were hanged during the 1988 mass killings.

78 A 1926 Soviet film by Vsevolod Pudovkin. Based on a novel of the same title by Maxim Gorky, the movie portrays a woman's turbulent life during the Russian revolution of 1905.

79 Bahram Beyzaie's critically acclaimed first feature film, made in 1971, depicts the life struggles of an intellectual and honest teacher in pre-revolutionary Iran. In post-revolutionary Iran, Beyzaie has been under huge pressure due to his religious affiliation.

80 Imam Reza is the eighth Imam of the Shia Muslims, and his shrine is visited by 15 to 20 million pilgrims every year. It is a vast complex, including a university, museum, library, seminaries, vast prayer halls, and a cemetery.

81 In colloquial Persian, the "Blues" refers to Esteghlal Football Club fans, while the "Reds" stands for Persepolis Football Club supporters. The Tehran derby between these two popular football clubs and archrivals is the biggest football match in Asia.

82 The Peykar (Struggle) Organization was formed in 1979 from a Mujahedin splinter group. It advocated the total separation of the religious establishment from the state. In 1982, several Peykar leaders were arrested, and the organization was disbanded.

83 After the revolution, the Islamic Republic censored the chapter dealing with sexual questions.

84 The loans office is a type of Islamic private bank set up by an Islamic organization with a focus on small investments.

85 The Jafar Tayyar prayer consists of a lengthy form of prayer that the very religious perform after the night prayers. It sometimes extends throughout the night.

86 According to instruction books published by the Islamic Republic,

the Kumayl prayer was taught by Imam Ali to Kumayl, one of his close companions, hence its name. According to Muhammad Baqir Majlisi, the author of *The Ornament of the Righteous*, the prayer should be performed at night in the middle of the Sha'ban month, or every Thursday night, to protect one from the evils of the enemy and to seek forgiveness for one's sins.

87 A Shia cultural and religious tradition is to cry and grieve for the coming of the twelfth Imam, who is believed to be in occultation. *Nudbah* means to mourn and cry for the dead and to praise them.

88 Hadith are the sayings of the Prophet Muhammad (and, in Shia Islam, also from the Shia Imams) that have been handed down orally before being collected and written down by several Muslim scholars. They are regarded as important tools for understanding the Qur'an and questions of Islamic law.

89 Taking a bath here refers to the religious, ritualistic bathing procedure that precedes and follows intercourse and is accompanied by a specific set of prayers.

90 This is the last of the five daily prayers Muslims perform from dawn till dusk.

91 The word used in the original manuscript is *monafeq*, meaning a two-faced, conniving person. Following the Islamic revolution, *monafeq* was used to refer to members of Mujahedin-e Khalq.

92 Peech-e Tobah, or Repentance Turn, is the name of the road that leads down to Evin Prison. It is very steep and has a sharp bend. Lajevardi, the cold-hearted butcher of Evin, boasted that every time prisoners reached the bend, the fear they felt made them repent immediately.

93 Haqqani's circle is composed of hardline clergymen based in the holy city of Qom and led by Ayatollah Mohammad-Taqi Mesbah-Yazdi, a prominent theologian who is believed to exert a huge influence over President Ahmadinejad. The group derives its name from the Haqqani Seminary, established in 1964, whose graduates occupy key political and security positions in Iran today. Haqqani alumni are known for their radical political activism grounded in a messianic belief in the imminent return of the Mahdi, the twelfth Imam in Shi'ism.

94 According to Shia religious instruction, if a man is sporting a moustache, he must cut it short to prevent the moustache from getting wet when drinking liquids.

95 Collective prayers are performed together in unison, and one of the people in the group leads the prayer. Shias believe that those who pray collectively will receive greater rewards than those who pray individually.

96 The punishment for insulting Imam Ali sometimes includes hanging.

97 Jihad is an Arabic term meaning voluntary, holy struggle or war, including both physical war and the internal spiritual war to improve oneself. The block was named with the second definition in mind.

98 A death sentence is one of the cruellest sentences issued in Iran. The prisoner sentenced to execution can be hanged or shot at any time, whenever it's deemed necessary. Consequently, the prisoner would often spend years, never knowing when the sentence would be carried out. Some individuals have spent up to twelve years in this situation.

99 Drugs would sometimes be carefully wrapped in multiple plastic sheets, swallowed and brought into prison undetected.

100 Moharebeh is an Islamic offence that means "waging war against God". Those convicted of being Moharebs face execution under Iran's Shari'a legal code.

101 Qur'an: 9: 73.

102 Saeed Emami, also known as Saeed Eslami, was the Islamic Republic's most terrifying security official. He returned from the US after the Islamic revolution, and became Deputy Minister of Intelligence, in which role he organized the mass murder of the intelligentsia, the so-called Serial Murders. He was imprisoned during Muhammad Khatemi's leadership and was mysteriously killed while in prison.

103 One thousand individuals were identified by name in a UN Human Rights Commission's Special Representative's Report, "Names and Particulars of Persons Allegedly Executed by the Islamic Republic of Iran during the period July–December 1988", published on 26 January, 1989. The report specifies that although 1,000 names are mentioned, "in all probability" there were several thousand victims.

"Most of the alleged victims were members of the Mujahedin. However, members of the Tudeh Party, People's Fedayeen Organization, Rahe Kargar, and Komala Organization, and eleven mullahs were also said to be among the alleged victims."

104 Azadi Square, or Liberty Square, is the name of a very large square in the west of Tehran. In the middle of the square, a beautiful tower was erected in 1971, combining both Sassanid and Islamic architectural styles, in commemoration of the 2,500th anniversary of the Persian Empire. Initially, the tower and the square were called the Martyrs' Tower and Square but after the revolution, the square was renamed Liberty Square.